THE YOUNG AND RESTLESS LIFE OF WILLIAM J. BELL

Creator of *The Young and the Restless* and *The Bold and the Beautiful*

MICHAEL MALONEY
WITH LEE PHILLIP BELL
FOREWORD BY DAVID HASSELHOFF

Cover design by Pete Garceau
Internal images provided by CBS Photo Archive; courtesy of Elanie Lee; provided by NBCU Photo Bank; courtesy of Sandra Johnson; provided by WBBM-TV

Published by Sourcebooks, Inc.
P.O. Box 4410, Naperville, Illinois 60567-4410
(630) 961-3900
Fax: (630) 961-2168
www.sourcebooks.com

Library of Congress Cataloging-in-Publication Data

Maloney, Michael
The young and restless life of William J. Bell : creator of The young and the restless and The bold and the beautiful / by Michael Maloney with Lee Phillip Bell ; foreword by David Hasselhoff.
p. cm.
Includes bibliographical references.
1. Bell, William J., 1927-2005. 2. Television producers and directors—United States—Biography. 3. Television writers—United States—Biography. 4. Television soap operas—United States. I. Bell, Lee Phillip. II. Title.
PN1992.4.B385M35 2012
791.4502'8'092—dc23
[B]

2012004200

Printed and bound in the United States of America.
BG 10 9 8 7 6 5 4 3 2 1

To Bill and Lee

"[F]or things to happen, you've got to make them happen."

—William J. Bell, 1979

CONTENTS

FOREWORD

Whenever I think of Bill Bell, I think of him in his navy blue blazer with his perfectly cropped hair, casting a radiant smile like one that you'd see on Santa Claus on Christmas morning.

He took a chance on me when he cast me on *The Young and the Restless* in 1975. He told me that I was fairly "green" as an actor, but that there wasn't a bad angle on me. I was replacing William Grey Espy in the role of Dr. William Foster Jr., aka Snapper. Espy had been very popular in the part, and I thought I was going to be fired when I couldn't get it together and get over my nerves.

I said to the stage manager the first day I walked onto the set, "Where's the director?" I had no idea there was even a control booth. It took me a couple of years to turn it all around. Eventually I did, thanks to Bill, who never gave up on me, and also to Jeanne Cooper, who plays Katherine Chancellor. She took me under her wing and gave me acting lessons.

Thanks to Bill, my experience on *Y&R* molded me from a terrified, insecure geeky guy to a confident, positive force in the soap-opera world. Being on *Y&R* also helped shape my work ethic. The most important thing I remember about Bill was that he believed in me. He was always positive about my growth as an actor.

I grew up in LaGrange, Illinois, not far from where Bill and his wife, Lee Phillip Bell, lived. Lee was an amazing presence in Chicago. She was the Oprah Winfrey of that era of television. I remember the first time I met Bill and Lee. They invited my parents and me to their home in Lake Geneva, Wisconsin, and they were both so gracious. We all went out on Bill's boat and toured the lake, talked about the show, and had dinner. Bill was a positive guy with an amazing sense of class. His belief in me gave me the confidence to continue my acting.

Meeting Bill and Lee's children when they were very young was a wonderful experience. I still see Bill and Lee's daughter, Lauralee, at the gym. The last time I saw their son Brad, he was driving about 110 miles an hour down the Pacific Coast Highway in a charity race for the CHP (California Highway Patrol) 11-99 Foundation. I'd left *Y&R* years earlier, but I said to him, "I still want on the show!" He yelled back, "Anytime! The door is always open!"

I was on *Y&R* in 1980 when I called Bill and told him that producers wanted to cast me in *Semi-Tough*, a TV series on ABC with Markie Post that was based on the feature film from a few years earlier with Burt Reynolds and Jill Clayburgh. I told Bill that this was my dream and I really wanted to do it. I said I could do *Y&R* and the nighttime show at the same time. Bill said, "Yes, absolutely." He was the reason that I was able to do both shows. He and executive producer John Conboy could have exercised an option in my contract, but they didn't want to stand in my way.

We had the kind of relationship that's hard to come by in Hollywood.

Semi-Tough only ran for four episodes. I came back like a puppy dog with my tail between my legs, but Bill never made me feel like anything but a valued member of his *Y&R* family.

Being on *Y&R* was always a fun time. One of my best recollections was Snapper doing a very provocative demonstration of the Heimlich maneuver with his wife, Chris, played by the very attractive Trish Stewart. It seemed like Snapper and Chris were always in bed together. I used to say, "When the ratings are low, all the clothes go!" But the ratings never were low. *Y&R* was always at the top. I know it's remained on top of the world for thirty-nine years now, which is unbelievably amazing and a tribute to Bill Bell.

After I left *Y&R*, I landed the series *Knight Rider*. Then, I was cast on *Baywatch* and became executive producer in 1991. Critics said the show was about women in bikinis on the beach, but the real reason viewers came back each week was because of the relationship that my character, Mitch Buchannon, had with his son, Hobie, played by Jeremy Jackson. The relationship that Snapper had on *Y&R* with his son, Chuckie, whom he gave a kidney to, was a precursor of Mitch and Hobie.

I tried to put the same storytelling values that I learned from Bill into every *Baywatch* script. I made sure the stories had heart, humor, and action. On *Baywatch*, we had romance, not sex; action, not violence; and if anyone ever drowned, it happened off camera. I learned a lot about character development from being on *Y&R* and from Bill. I loved his tenacity and his fierce loyalty.

Bill invited me to host *Y&R*'s twentieth anniversary party in March, 1993, at the Four Seasons Hotel in Beverly Hills. I was honored. That was an amazing evening. Seeing Bill and Lee and their children and everyone from the show that night reminded me of my time at *Y&R* and the discipline I'd learned there. You can lose that when you go to primetime and surround yourself with enablers. You always need someone there to tell you the truth. Bill taught me that the truth was my friend. And he was always there to tell me the truth in a positive way.

Bill radiated a light that was so positive. I never saw him angry. Bill was a gentleman. He knew what he wanted, and he did everything with class.

It's an honor to be included in this biography.

Sincerely,
David Hasselhoff

David Hasselhoff played Dr. William "Snapper" Foster Jr. on The Young and the Restless *from 1975–82 and again in 2010.*

PREFACE

The millions of fans who watch Bill's shows know him as a wonderful and talented writer who created characters including Victor Newman, Katherine Chancellor, Nikki Newman, and Ridge and Brooke Forrester. Bill loved writing for them and for so many others.

I know him as an even more miraculous husband and father. I feel so grateful to him for the wonderful times we had together and for our children and grandchildren.

I wanted this book to be written so that our grandchildren Liam and Sabrina; Chasen, Caroline, Charlotte, and Oliver; and Christian and Samantha will know the contributions that their grandfather and their parents made to television and to daytime dramas.

Because Bill would fight for something when he knew it was important for his show, I also hope that this book can serve as an example to anyone who wants to start their own show on television or, as so many are doing today, on the Internet.

Bill was a tremendous provider for his family and for all of his employees. He loved writing dramatic serials. He wrote two different shows almost every day for most of his career. It kept him very busy so it was good that I had something to keep me busy, too!

He made many difficult decisions as a producer and writer, but he knew how to make them look like they weren't a big deal. Bill didn't worry about the little things in life. He worried about his family and he worried about his scripts.

Bill loved what he did so much that he never liked to be away from the show for long. When you love what you do, and Bill truly did love what he did, you never have to take a vacation. We did take trips to China, Japan, Italy, and Egypt, but they were always quick ones. Bill would never really leave work behind. He'd bring his typewriter with us when we traveled.

He always asked for my opinions about the show, but he truly began taking my input when we started *The Young and the Restless.* We talked about it for a long time before the show went on the air—about how it would be different from other shows he'd written and about the types of stories he wanted to tell. Bill wanted to bring more music to daytime and he did.

I'll never forget when Bill got the deal to do *Y&R*. "Let's go to the Polo Lounge and figure out the show," he said. We wrote out all the characters on cocktail napkins. Then Bill typed up the show's "bible" and gave it to John Mitchell at Screen Gems, and then we were on our way.

We moved to California in 1986 so Bill could be closer to *Y&R* and so we could start *The Bold and the Beautiful.* Bill would do the same things in Los Angeles that he did in Chicago. He got up early and went to bed late. He'd always stop working to watch the shows each day right when his audiences watched. He cared about what the viewers saw. I have a picture of Bill that was taken at our summer home in Lake Geneva. He's talking to producer Ed Scott at *Y&R*, and Bill's just screaming! That was taken right after a show had aired.

Bill let his feelings be known about what he liked and what he didn't like, and then it was over. He'd move on to the next script and the next show.

I left WBBM-TV in Chicago when we came to Los Angeles, but that was all right. This was going to be another step in our lives. We were all very busy once we got there. We met with actors for *B&B*. I remember the first day that Ronn Moss came to the studio. He was very quiet and very nice. Katherine Kelly Lang is marvelous, and of course, we knew we wanted to work again with Susan Flannery and John McCook, who had played parts for Bill on *Days of our Lives* and *The Young and the Restless*.

After Bill retired, we were able to travel more. Bill always kept in touch with Kay Alden, who took over as head writer at *Y&R*. He'd go down to the studio and watch the shows being taped. He knew everyone there and he spent time talking to people on the sets. He had a good time doing that.

I chose Michael to write this book because Bill knew him and liked him. He always read and liked what Michael wrote about the shows.

Different people will remember Bill in different ways. To me, he was wonderful, just great. He was a husband, a father, a son, a writer, a creator, and an executive.

He was everything.

Lee Phillip Bell

INTRODUCTION

I've had the incredibly exciting experience of creating stories and characters with whom countless of millions of you in the audience have become involved. Characters you've welcomed into your home each day…Stories of families and relationships, romance and conflict, with people you love to love or love to hate, characters who have captivated you for whatever reason.

—Bill Bell in his Lifetime Achievement Award
acceptance speech at the 1992 Daytime
Emmy Awards in New York City

One day in the late 1980s, one of Bill Bell's young stars was having a particularly bad time taping scenes for a front-burner, emotion-packed storyline on *The Young and the Restless.*

In a temporary burst of frustration, the actor slammed his script down on the studio floor at CBS Television City in Hollywood proclaiming, "I could type better s— with my d—."

The thespian was unaware that Bill, the show's creator, head writer, and senior executive producer, was working with his writers in his office two floors above and had witnessed the outburst on an in-house monitor.

Producers and head writers at other shows have fired actors on the spot for far less egregious acts. Bill was certainly not a man to be trifled with, but he was known for being able to see the bigger picture. He always made his decisions based on what was best for his show, not his ego. Knowing that it wouldn't serve his story or his audience well if he recast or killed off this pivotal player (who remains a big fan favorite and was doing an otherwise admirable job in bringing Bill's stories to life), Bill refrained from pink-slipping the star.

Still, he couldn't let the moment pass without sending his foul-mouthed actor a pointed message. Bill called down to the control booth and left word for the agitated player: "Tell him I have an IBM Selectric typewriter. He can come up anytime and give it a try."

Then it was back to work for everyone. The actor regained his composure and completed his scenes. Bill went back to his meeting and turned out another episode of daily drama. He'd been doing that for more than thirty-five years, having studied under Irna Phillips, who has been called the Queen of Soaps.

Irna was a broadcasting pioneer who created several radio dramas that Bill listened to as a child while growing up in Elmwood Park, Illinois. Later, she successfully ushered *The Guiding Light* into the television era. Then she went on to create or cocreate *As the World Turns*, *Another World*, and *Days of our Lives*. Irna taught Bill certain principles about soap operas that he adhered to for his entire career.

Bill created diverse and dynamic characters, yet audiences found these larger-than-life personas relatable. He believed in the sanctity of never revealing what was going to happen until viewers saw it on the air. If fans wanted to learn a baby's paternity, see if the ailing heroine lived or died, or find out whether or not the star-crossed lovers' wedding was finally going to happen, they had to tune in both today and tomorrow. And they couldn't wait until tomorrow.

Bill's stories were actor-proof. He could cast classically trained thespians or inexperienced newcomers, and viewers would embrace his characters with equal devotion. Acting technique would come in time. Bill's story, however, was in place from day one.

Bill wrote many fictional romances and love stories. Some, like Victor and Nikki on *Y&R* or Ridge and Brooke on *B&B*, were epic, but they all paled in comparison to his real-life marriage of more than fifty years with Lee Phillip.

Lee, a pioneer in the days of live TV in Chicago and host of *The Lee Phillip Show*, met Bill at her television studio. They shared an elevator ride one morning, and the rest was history. They fell in love, worked hard, and cocreated two soap operas (*The Young and the Restless* and *The Bold and the Beautiful*) and three children: William (Bill), Bradley, and Lauralee. All three have successfully followed their parents in the world of soap operas, each in a different role. Bill is president of the family's production and distribution companies. Bradley serves as head writer and executive producer of *B&B*. Lauralee, taking a cue from her mother's on-camera career, acted on *Y&R* as model-turned-lawyer Cricket Blair Williams, a role she continues to reprise.

The Bells moved to Los Angeles in 1986, setting up shop at CBS Television City in Hollywood and a residence in Beverly Hills. For Lee, going west meant bidding adieu to her career in front of the camera in the Windy City. She made the move to a new city and a new career, as coexecutive producer of *B&B*, the same way she does everything else—with quiet grace.

Scores of people (actors, writers, crew members) were able to buy homes and send their children to college thanks to the consistent work that Bill's passion for storytelling provided.

Like other great leaders, Bill hired smart people to work with him.

He let them do what they did best while he orchestrated the lives, loves, machinations, and maladies of his characters.

His career, like the destinies of those characters, unfolded slowly and matured over time. Bill went from being Irna's student to becoming the head writer of *Days of our Lives* in 1966, saving it from cancellation. In 1973, he and Lee launched *Y&R*, which revolutionized the serial form. In 1987, they brought *B&B* to life so their children could experience what it was like to launch a new series and be fully involved in a family business.

Long before *Donahue* and *Oprah* premiered, Lee tackled many social issues on her Chicago-based talk show, and she later advised Bill on how best to incorporate them into his storylines. Ironically, he never addressed on air the one (Alzheimer's) that struck closest to home, though his son Bradley would do so five years after Bill's untimely death.

Over his five-decade career in dramatic serials, Bill wrote thousands and thousands of hours of compelling story.

This is his.

Chapter 1

BACKSTORY

What happened in the past to characters greatly affects them in the future.

—Bill Bell in his proposal for *The Young and the Restless*, 1972

William Joseph (Bill) Bell kept an autograph book on the desk in his study at his home in Beverly Hills. It doesn't, however, contain the names of the stars he made as creator and head writer of dramatic serials. Rather, the book holds signatures and well-wishes from his eighth-grade classmates and teachers at St. Celestine School in Elmwood Park, Illinois, a Chicago suburb.

Bill had his sights set on becoming a doctor, but the born storyteller in him recorded his memories from the night of his graduation from grade school. "This was the first time I ever danced," he wrote of being at his school's commencement banquet. "After dinner we went to Daisy Dairy and then to Henrici's. After that, [I] walked home."

Bill also recorded his school's colors (blue and gold), his favorite teacher (Sister Jean Patricia), his favorite friend (Bill Reilly), and his favorite subject (arithmetic). One fellow pupil, Ralph Martin, wrote, "Dear Bill, I wish you a lot of luck as a doctor. P.S. I hope you are a good one."

"Dear Bill, When you get big, I hope you won't have to dig. Good Luck," wrote classmate Casper Caravello.

In addition to a career in medicine, Bill, a devout Catholic, entertained the idea of becoming a priest. He sought advice on which direction his career path should take from his mother, Gertrude.

"Bill always went to her for suggestions," says Mary Gertrude Bell Neuenschwander, Bill's sister. "Our father, who was an accountant, was a kind man and a very hard worker, but Bill listened more to our mother. I was closer to her and I think Bill was, too. Our mother told us to follow our hearts and to do what we wanted. She was marvelous."

As a serial writer, Bill named characters after family and friends, but Mary can't recall that he ever dedicated one to their mother. "For Bill, there was only one Trudy," she says.

Gertrude and William Jennings Bell raised their children in a two-story home located thirty-five miles northwest of Chicago. "We grew up in a nice-sized home," Mary recalls. "We were on a lake, and there was a ranch. It was neat."

As most of us were, Bill was introduced to soap operas by his mother. He listened with her to serial dramas, including *Our Gal Sunday*, *The Romance of Helen Trent*, and *Life Can Be Beautiful* on the radio.

"I'd come home from school, and Mom would have soup and a sandwich waiting for me," Bill was quoted as saying in *Worlds without End: The Art and History of the Soap Opera*. "Mom was a great fan of the serials, always listened, and before long, I was hooked, too."

One program in particular caught Bill's ear because the announcer read the name of the show's creator along with the title of the drama: "*The Guiding Light*, created by Irna Phillips."

Bill lost touch with radio soaps after he began attending St. Mel

High School and his schedule shifted, but he never forgot Irna's name or lost his interest in serialized drama.

As a writer, Bill brought greater characterization and depth to the fictional personas that he created than had been seen previously on daytime dramas. One of the greatest examples is Victor Newman of *The Young and the Restless*. Viewers grew to feel sympathy for Victor after learning that as a little boy, Victor (born Christian Miller) had been left in an orphanage by his destitute mother. Forced to fend for himself, Christian endured, changed his name to Victor Newman, and created a financial empire so he could never be hurt again, becoming literally a "new man" in the process.

Bill's son Bradley, head writer and executive producer of *The Bold and the Beautiful*, followed in his father's footsteps by shedding light on the controlling Stephanie Forrester. Viewers understood the domineering matriarch a great deal more after learning that Steph had been physically abused by her father while her mother, Ann, looked the other way.

Fortunately, Bill's own childhood was very different from Victor's and Stephanie's. His parents divorced, but not until Bill was well into adulthood. He wasn't driven to achieve because of something that was lacking in his own life, but rather from an innate desire to entertain and educate. Bill was very grateful for the love and advantages that his parents gave him. He knew he'd received so much in life, particularly his mother's love.

"Our mother was awesome," says Mary. "She took in foster children. I came along and she fell in love with me. She nurtured me, gave me security, and did the same for Bill."

Bill's tremendous work ethic developed early in life. He recounted his childhood jobs at a birthday celebration that was held for him on the *Y&R* set in 2001.

"When I was six, I cut grass and shoveled snow for family and neighbors," Bill recalled. Subsequent gigs included being an altar boy at St. Celestine and delivering newspapers. "Since there was very little radio and no television, I would need to bike down the street yelling out, 'Extra! Extra!' People would emerge from their homes, their hands extended with two pennies for each paper."

At the age of thirteen, Bill worked as a stock boy for the A&P food market after school and on weekends. Later, he reset bowling pins at a local bowling alley and also retrieved golf balls from the local range. "The jocks would wager on who could come closest to hitting the kid," Bill said.

Next, Bill worked as an orderly at St. Anne's Hospital in Chicago. "I did the bedpan routine—50 cents an hour, which then was good money." In 1944, Bill got into publishing. He was made the coeditor of *High Shopper*, a publication slanted to teens. Then he worked for the Railway Express Agency moving freight before joining the Navy.

Bill was made a U.S. Navy Pharmacist's Mate, Third Class, and worked in Naval hospitals for nineteen months in Oakland, San Francisco, and San Diego, California, before moving on to one in Farragut, Idaho.

Bill got into broadcasting after applying for a job as a writer for *The Gold Coast Show* at WBBM Radio in Chicago. "Mr. Mort Hall, the boss, told me to write a sample script," Bill said. "The next day I came back with two scripts and got the job." Bill remained there for three years before moving into advertising.

He used his hard-earned money to purchase a television set for his family. "It was a big sucker," Bill recalled in a 1998 interview with journalist Alan Carter for the Academy of Television Arts & Sciences. "The screen was small. You could buy a magnifying glass to put in front of it, which made it ten inches. God forbid, if you'd lean your head to the right or to the left, you'd get a distortion, but it was thrilling! You'd watch anything because it was coming into your home."

"Bill himself would be poor material for a daytime character," entertainment writer Clifford Terry wrote in the *Chicago Tribune* in 1973. "After all, how tormented can someone be whose favorite word is 'nifty'?"

Terry made this assessment about Bill by observing his even-keeled and kind nature. He noted that Bill didn't hold traditional positions like his on-screen characters did, such as attorney Mickey Horton on *Days* or newspaper publisher Stuart Brooks on *Y&R*. But Bill had yet to create many of his iconic career-defining characters.

"There's a little of me in most of the male characters I've created," Bill told veteran soap-opera journalist Dorothy Vine. "There's some of me in John Abbott, Jack Abbott, Eric Forrester, and even in Victor Newman. I create characters to tell a story, and when you do that, you have to start with some of yourself so you can understand and motivate them."

Bill's younger self can also be found in two family-oriented and ambitious brothers whom he created for *Y&R*, Snapper and Greg Foster. These lower-class siblings became a doctor and a lawyer.

"I knew that I wanted a poor family in the overall plan [for the show]," Bill said. "I hoped [Snapper and Greg] might be an inspiration to other young men—self-educated, family-oriented, both about to embark on careers in professions [and] who succeeded because they had the attitude that 'for things to happen, you've got to make them happen.'"

Bill Bell was a man who made things happen.

Chapter 2

MAD MEN

Bill Bell would have fit in perfectly on the TV series Mad Men. *He didn't have that dark edge that Don Draper has, but he always had that smile.*

—Thomas Phillips, Irna Phillips's son

Bill Bell worked in the world of advertising before he became a soap-opera writer. That's where he met Jerry Birn, who became his best friend. Together, they sold a lot of ads and shared a lot of laughs.

"It was inevitable," Jerry said of his lifelong union with Bill. "We became good, close friends. We palled around together. We worked hard, played hard, and laughed hard."

Jerry wasn't always sure it would pan out that way. In fact, he was concerned about his future at McCann Erickson, one of Chicago's top advertising firms, after Bill was hired. Bill's hotshot reputation as a writer of comedy sketches and ad copy at WBBM-TV preceded him. Having someone come on board could mean that someone else would soon be walking the plank! However, Jerry's first impressions of Bill were that he was a warm and confident man. And, Jerry thought, if the reactions from the secretaries were any indication, rather handsome, too.

"It was clear I was going to be the second best-looking guy in the department," Jerry said, chuckling.

Jerry's boss asked him to take Bill out to lunch on his first day. Bill recommended Riccardo's, which was located on North Rush Street below the Wrigley Building.

"You can get a great lunch for a buck," Bill enthused. The two men got to know each other over a meal, swapping stories about their lives and first jobs. Jerry had worked as a movie usher. Bill revealed that he'd lied about his age to enlist in the Navy during World War II.

The conversation hit a bump after Bill inadvertently revealed that he was making more money than Jerry was.

"I ordered a drink," Jerry recalled.

Fibbing about his age to join the military wasn't the only tale Bill wanted to spin. He shared his dream of wanting to write TV dramas. Jerry wasn't too impressed, never dreaming he'd someday join Bill's writing team at *Y&R*. "Hell, most of us never watched soap operas," Jerry said, laughing. "I sure didn't, but here was this young guy from WBBM. He was going to be a soap-opera writer!"

First, though, there were advertising campaigns to create. Bill was put on the firm's most important account, Standard Oil. He sought Jerry's advice after executives at the fuel company edited Bill's copy, shredding it, he felt, of any creativity.

"Their suggestions were sophomoric, amateurish, and hopeless," Jerry said. But he advised Bill to incorporate them anyway. Jerry added that Bill had another option: tell the inept oil execs the truth.

"I felt bad," Jerry said about planting the idea in Bill's head. "He was going to get canned for sure if he followed my advice."

Bill told the Standard Oil executives that they needed to go with his original concept. "He did it with such conviction, vigor, and honesty [that] they were floored," Jerry remembered. "He told them they could fire him, but he wasn't about to put his name on the crap they scratched over his work. Then he walked out."

Bill would later take a similar stance with network executives at NBC who tried to tinker with his storylines.

After his discussion with the oil execs, Bill waited for his bosses at the agency to fire him. "It never happened," Jerry marveled. "The head of our office got a letter from the advertising director at Standard Oil applauding Bill. They wanted him kept on the account and also hoped that Bill Bell represented the kind of honesty and integrity at the rest of the agency."

Bill and Jerry were blown away. Jerry recalled that Bill had just one question: "Do you think I might get a raise?"

When they weren't coming up with advertising campaigns, Bill and Jerry hung out at a local watering hole, the Bowl and Bottle. Jerry played wingman to Bill, who had his share of lady admirers. "If you followed him around, you could pick up his rejects, which were far better than my first choices," Jerry said, smiling.

The bar became a second office for Bill and Jerry, especially after they landed the Spanish green olive account. What better way to become familiar with the product than by sampling it in Martinis? "I may have started Bill on Martinis at that point, but I never saw him drunk," Jerry said.

Over drinks, Bill and Jerry came up with the slogan, "The olive with the taillight," after noticing that the olives had pimentos in them. That gave Jerry the idea that McCann Erickson should pursue a taillight account, too. "The agency passed," he said.

One reason Bill and Jerry hit it off so well was because they shared a similar sense of humor. They worked hard but knew it was vital to laugh, too. "It was important for creative people to be bright, clever, show some flair, and also have one-liners ready," Jerry said.

Slaving over a food-account campaign, Bill and Jerry faced an uphill battle in trying to win over one of the clients, a female executive. "This was in the day when women in business felt underappreciated and underpaid," Jerry said. "She had one question for us after our presentation, and it was a beauty! She wanted to know how much experience we had in food accounts."

The two men stumbled to make themselves sound more experienced than they were.

"Well, how much experience do you have?"

Taking a beat, Bill and Jerry then deadpanned in unison: "We eat."

They got a laugh but not the account.

Writing soap operas wasn't Bill's only ambition. He also wanted to write at least one memorable ad that contained a jingle. He got his chance when the Milnot Company, a manufacturer of canned evaporated milk, sought the services of McCann Erickson. Bill came up with the following:

Milnot
Will not
Cost a lot

Bill presented the professionally recorded tune to the client, only to discover that Milnot had just implemented a price increase.

Milnot
Will now
Cost a lot

"Back to the Bowl and Bottle for research," Jerry recalled.

Bill and Jerry switched from Martinis to beer when they tackled the Gettelman Brewing Company account in Milwaukee. Jerry watched the color drain from Bill's face when the beer execs suggested that he and Bill sample their product—at an 8 a.m. meeting. Bill bravely raised his glass and made a toast. Jerry followed suit. Then Bill let loose with a comment on the ale.

"Burp!"

And that was just the prologue. Soon Bill bolted for the men's room, much to the amusement of the beer people. The clients cried out: "Hit the bowl, Bill!"

Jerry tried to drown out the sounds of Bill's heaving and the toilet flushing by playing a jingle on the tape recorder they'd brought along for the presentation.

"It wasn't the beer?" an exec asked a pale Bill upon his return.

"Of course not," Bill lied. And to prove it, he took another swig. Jerry closed his eyes. Bill managed to refrain from losing it again—until they hit the parking lot.

Bill wondered if he'd managed to convince them. "Only if they were deaf, dumb, and blind," Jerry said, chuckling.

The two established a new policy—no more morning meetings unless they were trying to land an orange-juice account.

Television changed the advertising world. Suddenly, clients were able to promote their products in a whole new way. Standard Oil began running TV ads during Chicago Bears game broadcasts. Bill and Jerry got to work with legendary announcer Jack Brickhouse during home games from Soldier Field. Brickhouse, along with Lee's columnist pal Irv Kupcinet, called games on WGN-AM radio. Jack read the sports plays, but Jerry remembers getting the "weather" on one occasion, too, courtesy of Brickhouse's salivary glands!

"Bill found out that when Jack turned away from the microphone, it was to clear his throat and spit." One time, when Jerry was handing some copy to Brickhouse, it was windy enough that Jerry ended up taking one right in the eye!

Perks came with the gig, including post-game parties at the Quarterback Club. Jerry once made the faux pas of asking Bears coach George Halas after his team had lost why they hadn't gone around the end instead of trying to run the ball up the middle.

Halas took Jerry's advice about as well as Bill would an actor saying to him, "What you should really do with my character is..."

Jerry gave Bill a TV credit after assigning him the task of coaching a model who'd been hired for a Standard Oil commercial but couldn't remember his lines.

Bill learned early in his TV career that talent can often be hired for looks and personality, and hopefully, solid performances will follow. He employed that policy in casting attractive actors for his serials.

There were many perils to working in live TV. Bill took a cameraman out on the road to capture footage of motorists who couldn't get their cars to start during the cold Chicago winter due to vapor lock. (Vapor lock occurred when liquid fuel changed to gas, preventing a car's engine from working.)

"Thousands of drivers were getting stuck along the side of the road," Jerry recalled of the pre-fuel injector days of automobiles. "It was a damn good idea that Bill had."

When Bill and his cameraman failed to return with film in time for an evening broadcast, people feared they'd been in an accident. Producers awkwardly filled the ten minutes of airtime that Bill had promised them. After the show ended, Bill rushed in, explaining that he'd been stuck out in the suburbs due to—what else—vapor lock!

Competing media had gotten wind of the snafu and had a field day.

Standard Oil was mocked, but Bill came up with a surprise twist, as he would later with his storylines.

"It was the cameraman's car," Bill claimed. And he'd put gas from Standard Oil's competitor in his tank! Not only was Bill's client off the hook, but the competition was hung out to dry.

"Bill had gone from bum to hero," Jerry recalled. "I always wondered if the photographer had truly filled his car up with the competition. Then I chided myself for thinking that. Bill was straightforward. He wouldn't do anything like that. Would he?"

Bill was a traditionalist. He later rejected the computer age, preferring to stick with his trusted typewriter, but he did try to move from using traditional advertising storyboards to employing live models for presentations. Jack Tinker, a top-ranking writer at McCann Erickson, shot the idea down.

"Bill started to get up and debate, but I managed to grab him before he ended his career," Jerry said.

Next, the two men took on another brewery. Jerry recalled that this new client was so imposing that he could have been an inspiration or even a prototype for villains that Bill later created, such as *Y&R* mobster Joseph Anthony. While Bill's fictional Mafioso had piranha in his office, the beer client had a parrot. The bird took a liking to Bill (hey, who didn't?), but that didn't stop the exec from firing the agency anyway. He later gave the company a second shot, provided that they send Bill and Jerry, aka "the kids," to do the presentation. The two ad men went to his office and made a solid pitch.

"Well, my young friends, I'll tell you how I feel about all this," the client said, as he proceeded to recall a glorious Saturday evening and a party he was attending. "Beautiful music was playing; people were dancing. The sky was clear and filled with stars." Then, the client's tone grew cold and calculating. "But my young friends, I don't feel like dancing!" The "mad men" made a mad dash for the door. When they returned to the agency, Jerry let Bill, a born storyteller, recap their encounter.

"It wasn't long before laughter roared through the conference room," Jerry said. The client teasing them, combined with the affectionate parrot that took a liking to Bill, made for a colorful and entertaining tale.

Jerry and Bill were the Butch Cassidy and Sundance Kid of the advertising world. Things changed, however, when Bill met his own Etta Place, television personality Lee Phillip.

"I'd seen Bill in a lot of circumstances, but never like this," Jerry recalled of Bill after he began dating Lee. "He was captivated."

Jerry jokingly referred to Bill choosing to spend more time with Lee and less with him as their "divorce."

"We became a '9 to 5' couple. Then, it was 'Lee time.'"

Around this time, Bill started reaching out to serial creator Irna Phillips, hoping he could land a position with her. "Bill was knocking on clients' doors with one hand and on Irna's with the other," Jerry said.

Soon, Bill confided in Jerry that he wanted to propose to Lee. Jerry suggested employing the tradition of getting down on one knee and asking her. "Bill told me that I had no imagination. He walked out on me in total disrespect."

The next day, Bill joyfully shared with his pal that he'd asked Lee and she had accepted.

"How'd you do it?" Jerry asked.

"I got down on one knee and proposed," Bill deadpanned.

After a celebratory dance around Jerry's office, Bill asked his best friend to be his best man. Jerry gladly said yes and began to plan Bill's bachelor party.

The send-off from Bill's single life went swimmingly. However, Bill took his friend aside during the festivities and asked him where the whores were.

A stunned Jerry told Bill that since Bill's father and future father-in-law were present, he didn't think that it would be appropriate to have any "entertainment."

"Bill looked at me for a while," Jerry recalled. "Then he said it was the first time I'd ever shown any judgment and I'd 'passed the whore test.'"

Bill and Jerry saw less of each other after Bill got married. Jerry eventually moved on to an advertising job in New York while Bill landed his life-altering opportunity with Irna. The two men stayed in touch primarily through holiday notes. "He had the best Christmas line ever written on his and Lee's cards—'The Bells Are Ringing!'" Jerry said.

The years passed. Jerry took an early retirement from advertising in the mid-1980s, later calling the move "the dumbest thing I ever did."

Then Lee called him to say that Bill and their son Bill Jr., were working on a primetime television pilot called *Mad Avenue* set in the world of advertising. Lee thought Jerry would make a great consultant on the project.

Thanks to Etta, Butch and Sundance rode again.

The pilot aired as part of the *CBS Summer Playhouse* series on August 23, 1988. It starred soap veteran Harley Jane Kozak (*Guiding Light*, *Santa Barbara*) and James Sikking (*Hill Street Blues*). The forgettable plot was scored with annoying techno music from the '80s.

"Bill didn't have time to write it, and the network selected a studio and gave them total creative control over it," Jerry lamented. "The final script, which made Bill and me throw up, was put on film. [The series] wasn't picked up."

Jerry, however, had become a student of dramatic serials after reconnecting with Bill. He began flooding his pal with story ideas for *Y&R*. Next, Jerry relocated to L.A. and Bill gave him an office right next to his at CBS.

"It was like we hadn't missed a beat," Jerry warmly recalled. "And it had been thirty years."

What Bill had done in those three intervening decades was to redefine the world of soap operas.

Chapter 3

WHEN BILL MET LEE

We just adopted a baby!

—Bill to Lee during their first date

Excuse me, I have to leave.

—Lee

Bill was always punctual so Jerry knew that something was up when his friend showed up tardy at McCann Erickson after lunch one day.

Something was. The stars had finally aligned for Bill to make his first date with Lee. He'd known her casually for approximately six months through their work together at WBBM-TV. Bill wrote copy for a program that followed one of Lee's many live broadcasts, but he hadn't quite found the right opportunity to ask her out. That changed one morning when they found themselves riding the same elevator from the TV station's lobby. Bill had made a date with his future wife by the time they'd reached the fifth floor.

When Bill told Jerry about their encounter, Jerry chuckled that he would have made a date with Lee by the third floor. "But Bill wasn't joking," Jerry said. "He couldn't stop talking about her. He was in love."

"Bill came home one day and sat my mother down," recalls Mary, Bill's sister. "Lee was on a fifteen-minute program doing the weather, and Bill said to our mother, 'That's the girl I'm going to marry.'"

Although Bill and Lee made their careers in TV, their college majors should have pointed them down different paths. Lee majored in bacteriology at Northwestern University. Bill had studied pre-medicine at the University of Michigan and DePaul University.

As a soap-opera head writer, Bill concocted all kinds of obstacles to keep his lovers apart. Ironically, he almost torpedoed his own romance with Lee thanks to his simple misuse of a pronoun.

Bill's parents had recently adopted four-year-old Mary, and Bill shared the news enthusiastically with Lee over coffee: "We just adopted a baby!"

Naturally, Lee assumed "we" meant that Bill and his *wife* had taken a child into their home. "Bill said, 'Mary's just darling,'" Lee recalls with a laugh. "I said, 'Well, that's...nice.'" Next, Lee did what any proper young lady would do upon discovering that her date was otherwise committed.

"I left, got a cab, and went home," Lee says. "I told my roommates what had happened." Fortunately, one of her pals had friends in advertising and did some investigating. She called Lee the next day and told her that Bill was single.

"Well, then how did he adopt a baby?" Lee naturally wondered, later learning that Bill's parents were the ones who had adopted Mary.

Bill called Lee after their abbreviated date to find out why things had ended so quickly. "I told him I wasn't feeling well," Lee covered. "Then we went on to date for a year and a half. We got engaged and then we got married. After we started dating exclusively, I told him the real reason I'd left. He thought it was pretty funny."

Bill wasn't married, but Lee did have a rival for his affections. To Mary, Bill was the big brother who gave her a pearl necklace the day she came to live with the Bells. She wasn't ready to share him with anyone.

"I wasn't a happy camper at that point," Mary recalls. "I wanted Billy all to myself, just like all little girls who have crushes on their big brothers do. Billy was always the one who cheered me up. He knew what to do if I was feeling down."

Lee has that gift, as well. Sensing Mary's feelings of loss, Lee gave her future sister-in-law a doll. "The doll's name was Lee," Mary warmly recollects. "She was beautiful, had blond hair and pearl earrings, and looked just like Lee."

The gift was classic Lee, a subtle yet thoughtful gesture that allowed Mary to grow comfortable around Bill's intended. "Lee always knows how to make everybody feel important," says Margot Wain, director of daytime programming for CBS Entertainment, who began her career at Chicago's WBBM-TV.

Soon Mary grew to love her brother's fiancée just as she did the doll. "Lee's a listener," Mary says. "Not many people listen. They act like they do, but their minds are usually somewhere else."

Russ Phillip, Lee's younger brother, was a teenager when Bill and Lee got together, but he could relate to Mary's emotions.

"Lee and I had an older brother named J.R., and he tended to dominate me," Russ says. "I'd go to Lee for advice and strength. She was always there to provide it for me, as she is today. When I was growing up, she helped me get my priorities in order, encouraging me to pursue my education and to also have a good time. My sister is very easygoing with people. She gets them to open their hearts and they start to talk about themselves."

Russ hit it off with Bill immediately. "I loved him from the first time I saw him," Russ says, recalling his sister having other suitors, including a doctor and a musician. "But Bill had a charisma that didn't stop. My parents loved him. He and Lee were magic together."

Bill and Lee wed on October 23, 1954, at the Riverside Presbyterian Church in Riverside, Illinois. Reverend J. Merion Kadyk performed the ceremony. Lee's gown was made of eggshell slipper satin, bordered with lace and re-embroidered with seed pearls and iridescent beads. Her bouquet, from Phillip's Flowers, of course, was made of white orchids surrounded by stephanotis. Russ was a groomsman and Mary happily served as flower girl as three hundred family members and friends gathered to celebrate the wedding of William Joseph Bell and Loreley (Lee) June Phillip. The reception was held at the Riverside Country Club.

"Our wedding day, as most wedding days are, was organized confusion," Lee recalled in a column for the publication *Chicago's American* in the mid-1960s. "Last minute alterations on my wedding dress, a hairdo that wouldn't stay in place, Bill's tuxedo tails that didn't fit, and plane tickets that for two hours were hopelessly lost.

"But somehow by the time the wedding march began at six that night, everything fell into place and it was truly a lovely wedding. My bouquet went to the maid of honor, who was married a few months later. We left the reception promptly at eleven and hurried to the airport, followed by scores of friends, only to learn our flight would be delayed by three hours."

Lee was the celebrity in the family long before Bill became an icon in the soap-opera world. In fact, at social functions that they'd attend for Lee's career, Bill would often be introduced as "Mr. Phillip."

"Fortunately, I have a very understanding husband," Lee told the *Chicago Daily Tribune* in 1958.

"That works both ways," Bill said. "It's the wife's attitude that can either make or break the marriage."

Both were too secure and also engrossed in their careers to care what other people thought of their less-than-traditional work roles. Bill would chuckle when people would think he was "Mr. Phillip" or Bob Bell, the Chicago-area performer known to children as TV's Bozo the Clown.

"Bill would say, 'We have this confusion,'" Russ recalls. "'My wife is well-known. I am not. I'm only a writer. People introduce me as "Mr. Phillip" or "Bob Bell." He's Bozo. I might *be* a bozo, but I'm not Bob Bell.'"

Bill and Lee's first apartment was a modest studio on North Lake Shore Drive. They each earned a good living, but they were well aware of the mercurial nature of positions in media and show business so they chose not to live beyond their means. Their Murphy bed, which came out of the wall, took up most of their living space.

"I remember looking around their apartment and finally said, 'Lee, where's the bedroom?'" Russ says. "She chuckled and said, 'We don't have one!' I was amazed that they could live in an apartment that a single person would have trouble living in, but they were extremely happy."

Their small residence didn't keep Bill and Lee from entertaining. Bill's fellow workers from the advertising agency were frequent guests at the studio apartment. Parties started soon after work and ran past midnight. Coats were stacked on chairs. Bill and Lee bought a chicken large enough to feed everyone, but it was so big that their rotisserie oven could barely turn it over.

Cigar smoke filled the room, but it was the number of invitees that caused the crowd to spill out into the hallway. Neighbors didn't mind the commotion because they were always welcome to join in the fun. Bill served his famous horseradish-and-ketchup dip.

"People would dip the shrimp, eat it, and then take a big drink of scotch," recalls Lee, laughing. "I never tasted it, but I thought it must be terrible!"

With help from Lee's parents, Bill and Lee went in on a small farm near Lake Geneva, Wisconsin. After a long week of devising ad campaigns or later slaving over rewrites for Irna Phillips, Bill and Lee went to the country where they could take in the fresh air and open spaces.

"He loved it!" Lee recalls. "Bill would work with the chickens and the pigs and the cows. He'd pitch hay. He was always doing something physical, building a garage or taking cases of eggs (Miss Lee's Eggs) into the city to sell them."

Tom Langan, a former producer at *Y&R*, wasn't surprised to learn that his mentor had experienced life on a farm. "The farm represents the basics of life," says Langan, who also served as coexecutive producer and head writer of *Days of our Lives*. "When you live on a farm, you're watching nature and the supreme animal in relation to the subordinate animals. You see the hierarchy in a natural way. You learn about predators. If you look at Bill's characters, you'll see that they mirror the animal kingdom in many situations."

Bill took few vacations in life, but as a devout baseball fan he allowed himself the annual treat of going to the Chicago Cubs' opening day at Wrigley Field. Lee's connection with the Wrigley family (she sat on the company's board) got her husband a choice front-row seat.

By the early '60s, Bill and Lee had become even more established in their careers. As WBBM-TV's top broadcast personality, Lee was the toast of Chicago, performing multiple live broadcasts daily. Bill had become invaluable to Irna Phillips. They could afford to move, so they took a one-bedroom apartment in the same complex as their studio. "Lee and Bill thought they'd gone to heaven because of all the extra room," Russ recalls with a smile.

All that was missing from the couple's idyllic life together were children. "I said to Bill that we ought to think about adopting," Lee says. They visited several agencies and began the process of becoming adoptive parents just as Bill's father and mother had done with Mary.

Then Lee learned she was pregnant with their son, William James (Bill), who was born on July 7, 1962. Bradley Phillip came next on June 29, 1964. Bill and Lee's daughter, Lauralee Kristen, was born on December 22, 1968.

Chapter 4

IRNA

She was the most difficult person I ever met who was in this business.

—Paul Rauch, Emmy-winning executive producer,
Another World, *One Life to Live*, *Santa Barbara*,
Guiding Light, and *The Young and the Restless*

Rita Marshall, the no-nonsense soap-opera producer of fictional *Southwest General* in the film *Tootsie* (played with precision by actress Doris Belack), was modeled after Gloria Monty, the iconic and iron-willed producer who helmed *General Hospital* in its heyday. However, the part of the stern celluloid executive could have just as easily been patterned after Irna Phillips, the legendary creator and head writer of several serialized dramas.

A former school teacher, Irna successfully ushered her radio soaps into the television era, generating millions of dollars of revenue for the networks in the process.

Bill and Lee's first apartment was within a short walking distance of Irna's residence on North Astor Street in Chicago. Bill had made a few attempts to get an interview with her but had met with little success. He moved his idea of working in serials to the backburner and went on to take the advertising world by a storm. Following advice that he'd later give to aspiring soap-opera writers, however, he simply did not give up. After marrying Lee, which thrust him into Chicago's social scene, and meeting Irna's niece, who worked in advertising, Bill was able to secure a one-on-one meeting with Irna in the mid-1950s.

"She was a brilliant lady," Bill said. "I wish there were more like her."

In her unpublished autobiography, Irna recalled meeting Bill. "Louise [Phillips] asked me if I'd see a young man who was very interested in writing serials," Irna wrote. "Louise was working as a media buyer for an advertising agency, and the young man, Bill Bell, had been an account executive for the same agency. Bill had some writing experience. He left the advertising game to write a book which was never published." (Yet, unlike Irna, Bill completed his book. A bound copy of *The Rat Race*, a novel set in the advertising world, sits on a shelf in Bill's library.) With a partner, he had also written a large number of comedy skits. However, he had no serial-writing experience.

"I didn't feel I had the time to teach anyone, but I agreed to see Bill. I had forgotten I had met him and his partner a few years before when they submitted several audition scripts for *The Brighter Day*. Bill and his partner were essentially comedy writers, and their scripts were not suitable for *The Brighter Day*."

Irna was reluctant to hire Bill for another reason. She felt that for a serial writer to be successful, he or she needed to be mentally unbalanced because the field is so demanding.

Irna told Bill: "You're not crazy enough!"

Still, she admired Bill's persistence. "At our third meeting, Bill said he was willing to work for nothing if I would teach him to write dramatic serials. I've never believed in letting people work for nothing. I had experienced that several times in my career. I told Bill [that] if he was really serious, I would start him at seventy-five dollars a week, which he gratefully accepted.

"Bill came to my home each morning and listened and observed while I dictated scripts for *The Guiding Light*. He became familiar with my long-term outlines and characterizations, my 'square' system of outlines, and many other techniques of the craft."

Bill recalled being greeted by Irna's assistant, Rose Cooperman, and then hearing Irna come down the hallway.

"It was almost like building an aura of suspense," Bill said. "Suddenly, she emerged. I was looking up. Then I was looking down," referencing Irna's diminutive stature.

Bill listened more than he spoke during their interview. Not surprisingly, Irna took a liking to him and gave Bill his first assignment—write an episode of *GL*. "[He] proved to be a very apt pupil and contributed many good ideas," Irna recalled. "He made rapid progress, much of which I attributed to our daily contact. But he was also highly competitive and ambitious."

Irna preferred to work with her protégés in person. "In this way," she felt, "there would be a constant free flow of ideas and criticism. I had worked long distance with Aggie [Agnes Nixon] for quite a while, but both of us began to feel the strain. Because Bill was coming along so well, I thought I'd like to try him on the half-hour format [with *As the World Turns*. But I wouldn't do it without Aggie's consent. I asked her if she would be more comfortable writing *The Guiding Light*, which was a fifteen-minute show. She welcomed the opportunity."

Irna recalled Bill going through a learning curve as he adjusted to *ATWT*'s thirty-minute format. "Many of his scripts were weak and needed rewriting. He would argue with me but always managed to control his temper. I knew he had great pride, but he tended to be overconfident about his work. I was a hard taskmaster, but I knew my craft and I knew how to teach it.

"I had a great deal of faith in Bill's work. He had sound arguments, good ideas, and an excellent source of story motivation. However, he was not strong as a dialogue writer. With these points in mind, I altered my approach in working with him. Instead of dictating outlines, for the most part we would discuss the script for the day. Bill was first rate in these verbal exchanges. Once we had agreed upon the script, I dictated it to Rose. Sometimes I would dictate only the outline and Bill would write the scripts. As his work improved, I steadily increased his salary. He and I worked together for ten years, and at the end of that time he was earning a thousand dollars a week."

Irna was a powerhouse. She ruled her shows with an iron fist and demanded that everyone around her be as passionate and driven as she was about soap operas. Bill shared her passion, which led to their successful relationship. However, actors, producers, directors, and other personnel lived in fear of Irna firing them on what would appear to be a whim.

"She was very regal and tough," Bill recalled. "She was sometimes exceedingly charming, but almost always very focused on what her show was all about. Who was doing their job well. Who wasn't."

"When Irna came to the studio, your job was on the line," says Don Hastings, who played Dr. Bob Hughes on *ATWT* from 1960 until the show's finale in 2010. "If you had a few bad shows, you might be replaced."

If Irna felt a performer had packed on a few pounds, she'd write dialogue into the show that had the character acknowledging the weight gain. The lines would repeat in future scripts until the actor slimmed down. She called performers by their character names, a policy that Bill adopted, because, to them, that's who the actors were.

Irna went to see one of her *ATWT* stars, Rosemary Prinz, who played the popular Penny Hughes, in a stage production of *Two for the*

Seesaw in Chicago. After the performance, Irna went backstage and huffed to Prinz: "Penny would *never* appear in a show like this!"

Prinz, whose character Penny had become a widow, recalled appearing on Lee's talk show with her dog, a schnauzer named Murray. After seeing himself on a monitor, Murray started yapping, which elicited a few laughs from Lee and her guest. "We were having all this fun," Prinz recalled to journalist Lynda Hirsch. "I did not have my foot out the studio door when Irna called. She was furious. 'You have destroyed the character of Penny. She is a recent widow.' Irna only wanted me to grieve."

Irna couldn't always dictate how her stars behaved off camera, but on screen she expected her scripts to be performed as written. After watching *ATWT* in her apartment with Bill, she'd call the production office in New York City with notes on the day's broadcast.

"Hello, Irna! *As the World Turns*!" the receptionist would cheerfully answer the telephone. But if Irna hadn't liked that day's show, she'd bark, "Not today it didn't!"

The receptionist got a reprieve when the show wrapped for the day. Bill, however, wasn't as fortunate. After leaving Irna's apartment at the end of the day (with the assignment of turning in a script the following morning), Bill often received additional calls from Irna throughout the evening. She'd rant about her assorted maladies in addition to giving more storyline notes.

Bill had opportunities to return to advertising, but he knew he'd landed a once-in-a-lifetime opportunity with Irna. Her off-hour calls, while intrusive, were a small price to pay in exchange for learning from a gifted storyteller and the most influential force in dramatic serials for television.

An admitted hypochondriac, Irna likely used her position as Bill's boss and mentor to create a friendship with him. If anyone was in a position to blur the lines, perhaps fooling herself in the process, it was Irna. As the creative force behind *ATWT*, daytime's top-rated television program, Irna had immense power. She knew if she said, "Jump!" many would respond by saying, "How high?"

Bill and Lee would have weekend getaways planned to their Lake Geneva home, but a call from Irna often changed everything. It wasn't uncommon for Irna to contact Bill on a Saturday morning and summon him to her apartment for rewriting duty.

Bill may have been tempted to tell Irna he wasn't going to be available twenty-four hours a day, seven days a week, but he never did. "You wouldn't say that to Irna—ever," Lee says. "She'd come first."

"Irna literally meddled in Bill's marriage," says Sherman Magidson, one of Irna's (and later, one of Bill's) writers, who was also a highly successful Chicago trial attorney. "I don't mean romantically or sexually, but she'd meddle in the sense of trying to take his attention away from Lee and give it to her."

Paul Rauch recalls Irna summoning him and fellow executive Bob Short from New York to her apartment when he was a supervising producer for Procter & Gamble productions. They were sent for two days before Christmas, not for a story meeting but to simply look at her Christmas tree. When they arrived, Bill was still there, of course, writing.

"She insisted," Rauch recalls. "Once we admired her tree, we were free to leave."

Bill never openly judged Irna's eccentricities or complained about her. In fact, he understood her.

"Irna was tough," Bill said. "And you know why? She was a little lady of ninety pounds in a man's world. If she didn't eat guys alive and castrate them, she wasn't going to survive."

"I don't think it had anything to do with her being a woman," says Fred Silverman, the legendary TV programming executive, who was in charge of CBS Daytime in the '60s. "She was just a difficult person. It was in her genes. I was one of the few people she got along with, actually. She and Bill had different dispositions. If there was ever somebody who was a nice guy, I'd say it was Bill Bell."

Lee had a good relationship with Irna, too. "She was very nice to me. And I liked her—except that she'd keep calling Bill all the time. But I didn't care. I knew this was important to Bill. Irna was nice. And I was busy. Bill learned a lot from her."

Lee recalls sitting at various tables with Bill and Irna at one of Irna's favorite restaurants—all on the same evening. "We'd sit at one for a while, and then Irna would say she felt a draft," Lee said, laughing. "Irna would call the maitre d' over, and we'd switch to another table. One night, we sat at three different places!"

Irna worked with a large calendar to keep track of her characters and storylines, planning the lives, dreams, and schemes of Lisa and the Hughes, Lowell, and Stewart families on *ATWT*. Her outlines were so detailed that they seldom required a great deal of input from her dialogue writers.

Bill learned from Irna that a final script that strayed too far from the head writer's outline could be potentially worthless if it required revisions that there simply wasn't time to make.

Over time, Bill took a more active role with *ATWT*. "I was with Irna almost every day," Bill said. "I became, at the very least, a cocontributor with her."

Executives from P&G met periodically with Irna and Bill to discuss plotlines, but given *ATWT*'s success, the gatherings were more social get-togethers than story conferences.

"Irna wouldn't get approval from anyone," Rauch recalls. "Bill learned to be the same way. You don't argue with someone getting the numbers Irna was."

Occasionally, Irna would travel from Chicago by train (she hated to fly) to P&G's headquarters in Cincinnati for story conferences.

During one visit, executives insisted upon knowing when *ATWT*'s Jeff and Penny were going to be married. Irna refused to say when or even if it would happen. The neckties persisted, demanding to know when the ceremony would take place!

"I'm not telling," the diminutive tyrant firmly replied. She then stood up and marched out of the conference room.

Irna and Bill rarely killed off characters, but when they did, viewers who had made deep emotional investments in them were understandably devastated. Characters didn't make trips back from that great soap opera in the sky with the frequency they do today. So fans were shocked and saddened when Jeff, Penny's beloved husband (yes, Irna finally married them), met a tragic end in a fatal car accident on August 23, 1962. The term "supercouple" hadn't been invented yet, but that's what Jeff and Penny were.

"We felt we could advance our story best if [Jeff] were no longer on the show," Bill said. "We don't kill our people often, but when we do, it opens the door for more story."

Irna and Bill were watching *ATWT* on Friday, November 22, 1963, when CBS anchor Walter Cronkite broke in with the news that President John F. Kennedy had been shot while riding in a motorcade in Dallas.

"I was stunned, obviously," Bill said. "Irna wanted to work, but I just walked out." His instinct was to be with Lee and their son Bill, who was less than two years old, so he went home.

Regular programming was pre-empted for the next four days while America mourned JFK. Viewers watched reports on the president's assassination, his killer being shot by Jack Ruby, and the funeral procession.

Irna and Bill had their characters on *ATWT* make reference to the national tragedy when the show returned to the airwaves the following week. "We wanted to make things a little more understandable," Bill said.

It's been said that people "arrive" in show business when their sex lives become fodder for idle chatter. For Bill, that happened when whispers began that he and Irna were having an affair. Bill would accompany Irna and Rose on trips to New York to check on *ATWT*'s production. The three would share either a hotel suite or rooms on separate floors during these sojourns.

Once, after checking in, Bill went to the hotel's bar to watch the World Series. When a controlling Irna couldn't contact Bill in his room, she panicked and telephoned Lee back in Chicago, demanding to know where he was. Irna's next move was to alert the New York City police department! Bill was quite surprised to find officers waiting for him when he returned to his room after the game concluded.

Gossips speculated that Bill, happily married to Lee, romanced the lonely writer to gain entry into the world of soap-opera storytelling.

He addressed the rumors directly in a 1998 interview for the Academy of Television Arts & Sciences. "The mandate was to make the interview about Bill's career and how *Y&R* was created," recalls journalist Alan Carter, who was surprised when Bill addressed the matter.

"Irna and I did everything together," Bill said in discussing their relationship, hastening to add with a chuckle, "Well, in terms of scripts. I don't want any more rumors to get started on that one!"

Bill put the speculation about his relationship with Irna being anything other than business and friendship to rest with one word: "Never."

Irna had power, and the actresses that Bill wrote for had beauty. "Bill lived in a world of beautiful women," says Sherman Magidson.

"But he realized that his wife was the most beautiful of them all because she also had a head on her shoulders. That was important to him."

Bill did play a role in Irna's personal life by becoming a substitute father to her two adopted children, Katherine and Thomas.

"My mother was always concerned about providing me with a male influence," recalls Thomas. "I remember joining Bill at a fairly posh athletic club along Lake Shore Drive just about every Saturday. I was aware of the role he was playing because my mother had used other males in the same way, but Bill never did it in a way that indicated he was doing it begrudgingly."

A romantic tie between his mother and Bill strikes Thomas as unlikely. "I have no memory that would incline me to say that there was something that went on there," he says. "There were suggestions, however, that my mother had relationships with lawyers and doctors she used as consultants. There was even a legend she went out with Al Capone!"

~

ATWT's success led to more opportunities for Irna and Bill. They cocreated *Another World*, which debuted on May 4, 1964, for NBC's daytime lineup. The show's bible, dated August 26, 1963, is titled simply "*Another World*" and ran a mere twenty-four pages.

"In a community not too far from Oakdale, a community near the university—one that is certainly not what we usually think of as suburbia but not completely cosmopolitan either—live two families," Irna and Bill wrote.

They compared *AW* patriarch Jim Matthews to *ATWT*'s Chris Hughes and Jim's wife, Mary, to Chris's wife, Nancy. "As far as *Another World* is concerned, we believe that in some way we all create 'another world' for ourselves. If we didn't, facing reality twenty-four hours a day would be too much. But as for another world for women, we feel that the viewer, who we hope will come to know all the people to whom you've been introduced, will recognize in this story that a home and a family should be solidified and not attacked."

They also developed a primetime spinoff for *ATWT*'s Lisa, played by Eileen Fulton. Fulton recalls Irna playfully chastising her on *The David Frost Show* in 1972 for "never delivering a script the way it was written." Still, Irna could not deny the actress's appeal. Lisa's antics, which included hiring a maid to do the housework while Lisa went out on the town to spend Bob's hard-earned money, were tame by today's standards, but audiences found her antics delightful fun. The nighttime show, originally called *The Woman Lisa*, was retitled *Our Private World*, and aired on Wednesday and Friday evenings from May to September in 1965.

Bill found the two-episode-a-week format too limiting. It was the first series he'd written that didn't unfold in the real-time realm of Monday through Friday. He preferred the daily format.

"You can tell richer stories," Bill said of daytime serials. "You can pace them and build a more loyal audience."

Creating *AW* also provided valuable lessons. "It was a whole new level of learning," Bill said of starting up an original daytime series. *AW*, which Rose Cooperman titled and which chronicled the lives of the Matthews family. Bill later realized that launching the series with a funeral was too depressing. He and Irna soon left *AW* and James Lipton took over as head writer. Next, Agnes Nixon assumed head writing duties. Her Alice/Steve/Rachel triangle put the show on the map.

"Aggie did a fabulous job with that show," praised Bill.

Bill learned many things from Irna, including the importance of protecting his writers. *ATWT* cast member Don Hastings was privy to what went on in the writers' room, courtesy of his own brief writing stint with Irna. He recalls: "If someone from P&G or CBS didn't like a script and said, 'Who wrote this?' Irna would say, '*I* write all the scripts! If you don't like it, it's my fault because *I'm* the one who said this is something that should be broadcast!'"

After a decade with Irna, Bill was ready for a new challenge. One arrived when Betty Corday, wife of the late Ted Corday, a former *ATWT* director and cocreator of *Days of our Lives*, contacted Bill about taking over head writing duties at *Days of our Lives*.

The NBC serial, which featured the beloved Horton clan, had been struggling in the ratings and was headed for cancellation. The peacock network had launched both *Days* and *Morning Star*, a short-lived serial also cocreated by Ted Corday. *Morning Star* didn't last, but *Days* was still hanging in there.

"It was the moment of truth," recalled Bill, who talked Betty's offer over with Lee before accepting it. He realized he could either stay with Irna or venture out on his own. The fact that *Days* hadn't found its creative footing yet actually made the opportunity even more attractive.

Bill accepted Betty's invitation and informed Irna that he was leaving her employ. Irna wasn't happy with Bill's choice. Unlike the countless reunions that his star-crossed lovers experienced, Bill never returned to his mentor. The two lost touch after Bill turned his full attention to saving *Days* while Irna, after also leaving *ATWT*, collaborated with her daughter, Katherine, in developing the short-lived soap *A World Apart*.

Irna felt that Bill was motivated to strike out on his own because of Lee's great success as a TV personality. "For quite some time Lee earned considerably more than [Bill]. I believe this was the source of much of his competitive and ambitious drive," Irna wrote in her autobiography. "It is my opinion this sense of competition sometimes clouded Bill's judgment and made it very difficult for him to accept my criticism."

Magidson disagrees. "If there was motivation to do what others had not done, I think Bill's father served that purpose. Bill wasn't motivated to 'catch up' to Lee. They had a wonderful relationship. Were there obstacles and kinks? Yes. Was it bad? No. They loved each other."

Later, Irna returned briefly to write *ATWT*. The ratings slipped and the formerly untouchable but always indomitable Irna was relieved of her writing duties.

On December 23, 1973, Irna Phillips died of natural causes at the age of seventy-two in her apartment in Chicago's Gold Coast area. Her obituary in the *Chicago Tribune* said she requested a private burial service and that her family would not issue a public notice of her death.

Agnes Nixon learned of her mentor's passing when she called her home on Christmas Eve. Phillips' maid, Alice, eventually revealed to Nixon that Phillips had died, almost afraid that her former boss would rise from the grave and scold her for going against her wishes. Irna's desire to slip away quietly spoke to a great loneliness that she felt throughout her life. Speaking of her enviable career, Irna told *Time* magazine in 1940, "I'd give it all up if a man came along."

Irna received posthumous Daytime Emmy Award nominations as cocreator of *Days*, but she did not live long enough to receive many accolades. She is commemorated on a signpost outside her North Astor Street residence. The memorial, funded by the Chicago Tribune Foundation and the Chicago Cultural Center Foundation, credits her as the "mother of soap opera."

Bill understood that Irna felt hurt by his decision to leave, but Thomas feels his mother may have actually encouraged Bill to go out on his own.

"My mother was the kind of person who felt, 'I taught you every goddamn thing I can. You're ready to go!'" Like a mother bird gently nudging her robin out of the nest? "No," Thomas says, laughing. "More like a dad who'd say, 'Get the f— out of here!'"

Irna cared greatly for Bill and admired his talent. "I had a great deal of faith in Bill's work," she wrote in her autobiography. "I was extremely fond of him. He was a very good friend to me and my children."

Bill didn't leave Irna without giving the move a great deal of thought. He also never failed to honor the contributions she made to his career. "None of us do anything of consequence alone," Bill said in 1992 when accepting the Lifetime Achievement Emmy.

"Like Aggie Nixon, I, too, had that legend of all legends, Irna Phillips, who invested a lot of herself in me."

Bill, in fact, viewed going to *Days* in 1966 in a positive light. He was, after all, leaving Irna's employ to save a show that she, along with Ted Corday, had created.

And save it he did.

Chapter 5

THE LEE PHILLIP BELL SHOW

The most fabulous lady I ever met.

—Bill Bell, 1998

Lee Phillip is proof that a nice person doesn't have to finish last.

—Mary Daniels, *Chicago Tribune*, 1976

In 1953, producers from a local program on WBKB-TV in Chicago wanted a floral expert to appear on air and show viewers how to arrange flowers. Naturally, they went to the best in town—Phillip's Flowers & Gifts, which was founded in 1923 by Lee's parents. It continues to be a family-run business and is one of the area's premier floral companies.

Lee and her brother J.R. appeared in the segment. Station manager Sterling "Red" Quinlan witnessed how the camera captured Lee's natural grace and charm. He was also impressed with Lee's ability to arrange flowers backwards so that the camera could properly capture the floral demonstration. Quinlan invited Lee to stay.

"I thought it would last a few weeks," Lee says of her broadcasting career. But she quickly became a full-time fixture at the station. Lee was one of the few on-air personalities who survived the transition when CBS acquired WBKB, renaming it WBBM-TV. H. Leslie Atlas became the new top honcho.

"Les was really the guy who discovered Lee," says Al Schwartz, who worked at WBBM-TV as Lee's stage manager and producer. Later, Schwartz moved to Los Angeles and became a producer for Dick Clark Productions before moving on to Associated Television International. Both production companies have produced the Daytime Emmy Award shows.

Lee would report to the studio at 7:30 each morning and would perform her last broadcast as late as 10:15 in the evening. (Local programs were, like the soaps themselves, fifteen minutes in length.) In between, Lee would perform a variety of duties, from reading the news to appearing in commercials alongside future ABC newsman Frank Reynolds.

"I was used to working seven days a week," Lee says. "They were all live shows."

She had Saturday evenings off, but then it was back to the studio on Sunday mornings to do *The Friendship Show* with local children.

There's an adage about it being unwise to ever work with children or pets in show business, especially on live TV, but Lee invited children and also a few animals, including a chimpanzee and a parrot, from the local zoo to appear on a *Friendship Show* live broadcast.

"The guy who brought the animals down trusted the chimpanzee a little too much," Schwartz grimly recalls. "While the show was on the air, and with all the kids watching in the studio and at home, the chimp grabbed the parakeet and bit its head right off."

Pandemonium erupted instantly. Understandably, children went into hysterics. Crying youngsters started to vomit. Schwartz yelled for the director to cut to a commercial. In the middle of the maelstrom, levelheaded Lee was calming her traumatized studio audience.

"Lee got everyone back on set. The prop guy removed the parakeet carcass and brought on another animal," Schwartz recalls.

Parakeets naturally thought twice about appearing on Lee's show, but nobody else did. Celebrities, politicians, and people from everyday life sat in the chair opposite Lee. During her broadcasting career, which spanned four decades, Lee interviewed four U.S. Presidents, movie and TV stars (John Wayne, Lucille Ball), and fellow Chicagoans. She recorded segments in France, Greece, and other locales.

The names of her shows changed over the years—*Shopping With Miss Lee*, *The Lee Phillip Show*, *Meet Miss Lee*, *Noonbreak*, and *Lee Phillip's Chicago*—but at the heart of each program was, of course, Lee. She greeted every guest with sincerity, enthusiasm, expertise, and warmth. Some of Lee's broadcasts have been preserved by the Museum of Broadcast Communications in Chicago and can be viewed online (at www.museum.tv).

"The purpose of this show is to serve our viewers, leave them with something that applies to their lives," Lee said in a 1976 *Chicago Tribune* article. "Our show is to serve and entertain at the same time."

"Lee's an extension of the audience," Schwartz explains. "She has that ability to be one of 'us,' but also be up there talking to one of 'them.'"

"I've known Lee for a long time," said Preston Bradley, a spiritual leader whom Lee and Bill named their second son after. "She's one of the loveliest persons I've ever met, one of the finest women I've ever known. She is just fundamentally an honest person. She has a sense of rectitude altogether too uncommon."

"I've seen her work through two pregnancies and the flu," said Judy Muntz, Lee's longtime producer at WBBM-TV, in the 1976 *Chicago Tribune* article. "She somehow finds energy, [even] if she's sick or whatever. I've never known her not to come to work without having studied the night before. She's rare in that respect."

"When you're sick, you can usually [work for] up to two and a half hours, and it usually makes me feel better," Lee said in the same article. "I've even gone to work with laryngitis. The guests do all the talking."

Not surprisingly, given her family background, flowers were a staple on the set of Lee's shows, as they've been on the sets of *The Young and the Restless* and *The Bold and the Beautiful.* "TV is such a stark genre," Schwartz says. "Flowers add warmth. They give you a perspective."

Lee encouraged interaction between her TV guests. "The point of the show is to get them talking to each other," Lee told the *Chicago Tribune* in 1971. "I always spend time in the dressing room before the show talking to the guests, to find out things they have in common that will be a basis of discussion for the show."

Lee excelled at in-depth, chummy interviews with A-list celebrities, but she was truly in her element when she took the show out of the studio and into the real world. Her visits to women's prisons and orphanages were groundbreaking in those days, paving the way for programs that followed—from *60 Minutes* to *Oprah.*

"The hardest people to talk to are celebrities," Lee said. "They've talked to so many people. You have to make it interesting for them, and you have to know their mood. They might be tired, or they [might] have received some bad news. The best thing to do is to ask them questions that are off the beaten show-business track."

CNN's Piers Morgan (*Piers Morgan Tonight*) has studied U.S. talk-show hosts, including Lee. "She's great," Morgan says. "The key to successful interviewing is [achieving] immediate empathy with your subjects. You have to make them feel that you're on their side even as they're talking and telling you stuff that they're not really sure they should be telling you. Part of an interview is always interrogatory, but the successful interviewers, like Lee, don't go too hard. They use charm. They use silence."

Lee's social-issue reporting garnered a slew of local Emmys. She addressed topics like breast cancer, teen pregnancy, and rape, which had never been tackled on TV. Her popularity and influence was such that she could have written her own ticket, choosing to do only cushy star interviews, but Lee has always opted to lead a life of social consciousness. She and Bill impressed this on their children, too.

"Lee paved the way not only for women journalists, but for all women to have a career and to be able to raise a family, too," says Eva Basler Demirjian, director of communications and talent relations, Bell-Phillip Television, and a mother of four. "Her children have told me that Lee said to them when they were young, 'Your homework's done? Great! We're going to the orphanage to visit underprivileged kids.'"

~

Lee told *Chicago's American* in 1964 that her goal was to give her "child all the love, attention, and affection that all mothers give." Despite her hectic schedule Lee was a hands-on mother. Lauralee had a nanny while Lee did her morning and midday broadcasts. "I must plan my schedule more carefully," Lee said. "Each morning Billy and I read and play together, and in the afternoon we go to the park. It's only after his bath in the evening that I start going over my work for the next day."

Lee's duties at WBBM-TV kept her from the occasional function at her children's schools, but if her children needed her, she'd drop everything. She once received a phone call from a local supermarket manager. Lauralee's nanny was being held for allegedly attempting a "five-finger discount." The police were on their way. So was Lee.

When she arrived, Lee saw Lauralee in her stroller, happy and smiling, blissfully unaware of what had prompted her mother's presence or why her nanny had disappeared. "We told her if she stole anything else that we'd have to let her go, so she stopped," Lee says.

Lee negotiated a deal with her WBBM bosses that she'd be able to be home by the time her children got home from school. She and Lauralee made a game out of it. If Lauralee arrived first, then Lee would drop a few coins in her daughter's piggy bank.

"Since the children were born, I haven't worked a full day," Lee told the *Chicago Tribune* in 1976. "When [our son] Bill was born, I thought I must quit. But Bill [my husband] told me to think about it. I guess he knows me better than I knew myself. He says quality is better than quantity. Our home life centers on the children. He knows that I love what I do, and he thought I could do both."

Schwartz was working in Los Angeles in the early '70s when he was hired to produce a national TV special for *Good Housekeeping*. His first thought was to hire Lee as its host. "I called the program director at WBBM," he recalls. "But he wouldn't let Lee do it. 'She's exclusive to us,' [they told me]." Schwartz pointed out that the syndicated special could very well end up airing on WBBM-TV, but the answer was still no.

"They were very protective of the people who worked for them. They didn't encourage them to do outside things," he says. Schwartz's special was produced without a host and wasn't picked up for additional episodes. He has no doubt that it would have succeeded if Lee had been a part of it and that Lee would have been a tremendous success if she'd gone national.

Comedian Danny Kaye was booked as a guest on Lee's show. The funnyman gave her a hard time during rehearsal. "He did everything he possibly could in order to shock her," Schwartz recalls. "But she never broke. She's a lady at all times. I met him again years later and asked him about his behavior that day. He said to me that he'd heard Lee was this perfect woman and he was intent on giving her a hard time. He couldn't understand why we were so enamored of her. I guess he was more used to being around 'broads.'"

"Lee doesn't like to talk about things that are tied into jealousy or envy," says Russ, Lee's brother. "She may not have appreciated certain things from a few guests like [foul] language, but she never tried to do anything more than be a friend to her guests. If they didn't get that on their first interview with her, then they would by the next one."

Lee found former First Lady Nancy Reagan and feminist Betty Friedan to be challenging interview subjects. Lee's policy was that children of celebrities were off limits, but she agreed to her producer's strong request that she ask Reagan about her controversial daughter, Patti Davis.

"Mrs. Reagan said, 'I don't talk about that,'" Lee recalls. "So I just changed the subject and we continued with the interview."

Friedan didn't warm to Lee at all. "She said during our interview, 'Those are kind of dumb questions!'" Lee recalls with a laugh. The *New York Times*' obituary on Friedan described her as "thin-skinned" and "famously abrasive."

Lee maintained her composure when Friedan displayed those qualities during their on-air chat. Perhaps the late feminist, who wrote in her memoir that she abandoned pursuing a PhD at the urging of a former boyfriend, felt that she didn't have much in common with the happily married Lee, who successfully balanced a husband, children, and career.

Another feminist, Helen Gurley Brown, had a different impression of Lee. Brown wrote to Lee after appearing on her show:

> Dear Lee,
>
> You are the most impressive lady and so is your show. Someone like me does dozens of shows in a year so I consider myself the old pro at

> deciding which ones are Really Something and which ones are just average. Yours is a 'super' Really Something and I'm honored that you let me be with you. I hope I'll see you again.

"I would never do anything to hurt or embarrass anyone on the show," Lee told the *Chicago Tribune* in 1976.

Lee always kept the show going. When the name of her lead guest, a singer, simply went out of her head one day, Lee improvised. "Today, you'll meet someone who I know that you'll just love," Lee enthusiastically teased. "I won't tell you who it is right now, but you will be surprised!"

Lee recalled the crooner's handle during the first commercial break and introduced him by name when the show returned, her audience (and the singer) none the wiser.

She encountered a bit of a language barrier when the British rock group the Rolling Stones sat on her sofa. "I had a little trouble understanding their 'English,'" Lee recalls of the interview. "But I made my way through and kept asking questions. I'd let their answers go on, and then, I'd just ask another one."

Lee interviewed Yves St. Laurent in Paris. The designer's limited English and Lee's one year of college French met in the middle. The *Chicago Tribune* ran a photo of Lee's trip to France titled, "Lee Phillip Is Faithful to Her Fashions."

"I loved meeting Yves," Lee recalled not long after. "His first showing a short time ago established him as one of the greatest of all Paris designers."

Bill tapped into his comedy-writing days by providing captions to accompany Lee's photos in a feature article called "Lee Phillip Is Faithful to Her Fashions," which ran in the *Chicago Tribune* in 1958. "In that picture, Yves looks like he has designs on you," Bill quipped.

It's difficult to imagine a more exciting or fulfilling career than the one Lee enjoyed as Chicago's top television personality. (*Gunsmoke* producers, for example, invited her to appear in an episode of the popular Western series, which she accepted.) Yet Lee closed a door on that part of her life so that Bill could become a more hands-on producer with *Y&R* in 1986, which necessitated relocating to Los Angeles. There Bill supervised the taping of *Y&R* from his office on the third floor at CBS Television City while still performing the endless task of plotting long-term and editing scripts. He continued to develop *B&B* at this time, too.

Lee foreshadowed the family's move west in 1976 when she told the *Chicago Tribune*, "I've been asked to go to Los Angeles and to New York. From a practical point of view, we should go to California because of Bill's work. He's [been] nice enough to stay here. Both our families are here."

A decade later, Bill, Lee, and their firstborn, Bill, were negotiating with CBS to start *B&B*'s production. Their younger son, Brad, was writing scripts at *Y&R* while attending UCLA. And their daughter, Lauralee, had become a contract player as ingénue Christine "Cricket" Blair on *Y&R*.

"Looking back, it was the biggest sacrifice that my mom ever made," Lauralee says of the family's move. "She had so many friends, roots, and contacts in Chicago. But she said, 'Don't worry! We're starting *Bold and Beautiful*.'"

"She was a very important lady in Chicago in so many ways, and still is," her son Bill concurs. "She was a celebrity, a TV personality with a daily TV show, involved in so many charities. It wasn't just her career. Her life was there."

"It was all right because we were coming to Los Angeles and it was going to be another step in our lives," Lee says.

"To hear Lee talk, she made no sacrifice whatsoever," says Jeanne Cooper, who's played Katherine Chancellor on *Y&R* since 1974. "I think she did. She's a woman who could name her own game. She could have gone national. She made it possible for Phil Donahue and Oprah Winfrey to have their shows."

Cooper experienced the weight of Lee's presence in Chicago when she appeared on her talk show. "Lee had Chicago in the palm of her hand, and Chicago had her in the palm of its hand. I saw the love the city has for this woman. People were asking me to sign things there, but many, many more kept coming up to Lee saying, 'Miss Phillip! Miss Phillip!' I relished her importance."

By moving gracefully from Chicago to Los Angeles, Lee created the setting for greater success for Bill and launched the careers of her children.

"Lee has three kids who are highly successful," notes Cooper.

While Bill Jr., Bill and Lee's son, supervised the remodeling of the Beverly Hills estate, Lee focused on deciding which lifelong possessions, furniture, and files would make the move from the family homes in Chicago and Lake Geneva.

Lee also sat in on final casting calls at *B&B* and was instrumental in developing the look and feel of the new half-hour soap opera, which has gone on to become the most widely watched dramatic serial in the world.

In addition to consulting on social issue storylines at *B&B* (Beth's breast cancer, Jake's childhood abuse), Lee assisted with character development and motivations. When *B&B*'s dying Caroline selflessly spent her final hours trying to mend fences among rivals Stephanie and Brooke, Lee provided the heroine with inspiring dialogue. She borrowed the following, which has been attributed to Stephen Grellet, a French Quaker missionary:

I shall pass through this world but once
Therefore if there is any good I can do,
Any kindness I can show,
Let me do it now; let me not defer it or delay it
For I shall not pass this way again.

Call the sentiment Pollyanna-ish if you will, but the moving words inspired Stephanie and Brooke to call a truce—at least for one night.

"Lee's always had a lot of empathy," Schwartz says. "If somebody was let go at the studio, Lee was always there to write a letter or do something for them. She's very supportive. I'd send someone to meet her who was trying to break into the business, and she was always willing to meet them."

While Lee shared cocreator titles along with her husband, it was Bill who was nominated and accepted awards for *Y&R* and *B&B*. Their coaccepting *Y&R*'s Daytime Emmy for Outstanding Drama Series in 1975 was a notable exception.

In the early '90s, *B&B* producers asked Lee if she'd play a reporter at a Spectra Fashions press conference, but she politely declined. With unassuming grace, Lee took to the podium at the Hollywood Roosevelt Hotel on October 28, 1993, when she was honored by the American Women in Radio and Television along with fellow recipient Leeza Gibbons.

Lee mostly kept a low profile presswise, but *Soap Opera Update* featured her in the early '90s in the article "Behind Every Great Man..."

The magazine's publisher, Angela Shapiro, added a personal note at the end of the profile: "As you know, ordinarily my comments are not a part of any interview in *Soap Opera Update*. However, in this case, I feel compelled to add a P.S. Speaking for all of us who futilely attempt to juggle family and career, I can't help but applaud one who has so brilliantly succeeded on all fronts. Lee is somewhat of an unsung hero. She's managed to carefully instill love, morals, and work ethics in her children, and her marriage to Bill is enviable. They seem the perfect family as they move through life as one. But Lee is a quiet storm—relentless in pursuit of her goals. She's really quite special, a person with whom one is proud to share the same industry."

Soap-opera writer and author Jean Rouverol echoed Shapiro's praise of Lee in her 1992 tome *Writing for Daytime Drama*. "Bill Bell is reported to get up every morning at 5 a.m. to write *The Bold and the Beautiful* breakdowns. And he is simultaneously driving *another* team of horses on *The Young and the Restless*. How, one wonders, can one man be so productive?

"Not surprisingly, there's a reason he is able to focus so much of his energy on the creative aspects of the two shows. Her name is Lee Phillip Bell. In addition to having been her husband's cocreator on both shows, she also handles the nuts and bolts—the research, the public relations, the promotion, and the headaches. Her contribution to the production machinery of the two shows is almost limitless. For instance, if there is an area of the country that *B&B* is not reaching, it is she who travels there, contacts the local stations, and rectifies the problem."

Viewers saw Lee on camera when she and famed pianist Van Cliburn taped cameo appearances in a party scene that aired on *Y&R* on September 11, 2006. Celebrity appearances on soaps can grind the action to a halt while awkward on-air introductions are made. (Unless, of course, you're Elizabeth Taylor and you're putting a curse on Luke and Laura at their wedding on *General Hospital*.) But in her scene with Cliburn, Jeanne Cooper, and Melody Thomas Scott (Nikki Newman), Lee kept the action moving just as she had for years on WBBM-TV.

In 2007 the daytime committee at the Academy of Television Arts & Sciences (ATAS) made a unanimous recommendation to its sister organization, the National Academy of Television Arts & Sciences (NATAS), that Lee be honored with the Lifetime Achievement Award at the *34th Annual Daytime Entertainment Emmy Awards*. The ceremony was set for June 15 in Hollywood.

NATAS concurred and Lee was announced as the recipient. Then, NATAS announced a corecipient—James Lipton, a former daytime head writer, actor, and host of *Inside the Actors Studio*. "We found out about it by reading it in *Variety*," an ATAS daytime committee member says.

Time during the Emmy broadcast is limited. The show was already dedicating a segment to honor CBS's Bob Barker, who was stepping down from his long-running gig as host of *The Price is Right*. Lee and Lipton received their statuettes during the non-televised Creative Arts ceremony the night before.

"I pled my case knowing that I didn't have the ultimate decision," says Schwartz, who'd been hired to produce a tribute to Lee for the broadcast. The tribute was cut from four minutes to one.

Calls were made to the network on Lee's behalf. Objections were raised, but fortunately, nobody lost his or her head.

"At one point I actually started following Lee's cue of grace and I let it go," says Eva Demirjian, *B&B*'s director of communications.

John McCook (Eric, *B&B*) and Peter Bergman (Jack, *Y&R*) introduced an abridged tribute to Lee during the Emmy telecast. A few lines from her acceptance speech from the previous evening were played on air.

"I give enormous gratitude to my husband, Bill," said Lee, who was joined on stage at the Creative Arts ceremony by presenters Susan Flannery and Katherine Kelly Lang from *B&B*. "We supported one another, built our dreams, raised our children, and created our shows together. And I know you're [watching] me now."

"It was a shame that they didn't let the audience in the auditorium and the viewers at home fully know just who Lee Bell is," says Demirjian.

Schwartz apologized to Lee after the broadcast, lamenting that his four-minute tribute was shown only at the non-televised Creative Arts ceremony. "But Lee didn't say anything bad," he says. "She's the consummate lady."

"Lee's the epitome of grace and elegance," adds Demirjian. "She proved it again on those two nights."

Any tribute to Lee would pale in comparison to the one Bill paid his wife at the Bells' annual Daytime Emmy press luncheon on May 14, 1998. To say that year's gathering, held at the Rainbow Room in New York City, was significant would be an understatement. Bill announced his retirement as *Y&R*'s head writer and named Kay Alden, his longtime cohead writer, as his successor.

"My name is Bill Bell and I've got a secret," Bill chuckled after stepping to the podium that day, knowing that his news had already been circulating throughout the room.

Bill could have taken the opportunity to reflect on his career highlights, which included writing top-rated *ATWT*, saving *Days* from cancellation, creating *Y&R* and *B&B*, and his work with social issues, but instead he chose to pay a heartfelt tribute to Lee.

"I felt I was long overdue in expressing my great admiration and, more important, my feeling of love for this lady, and you are my witnesses," Bill poignantly said.

"Lee is a loving, caring lady with no sense of celebrity or attitude. Everyone loves Lee. Much of her time was spent in the inner city where she would help and her efforts were invaluable. And you'll never find a more devoted mother than Lee is to our three children. They, and I, were always in the forefront of her life, which holds true to this day. While all this was going on in Lee's life, mine was spent writing and rewriting literally around the clock.

"These were the invested years. There were no shortcuts. You don't settle for second best or compromise when a rewrite or several will make a difference. Lee was so tolerant and understanding when I'd isolate myself up in our apartment. Lee, with the kids, would wait for her husband, who was doing yet another rewrite. This, in a nutshell, is Lee, the most fabulous lady I ever met.

"Within two weeks of meeting we knew we would marry, though it didn't happen for a year and a half," Bill continued. "Whatever I've done with my life is because of this beautiful lady—because Lee Phillip Bell made it possible. Thanks, sweetheart, for all you've done for me."

Looking up from his note cards, Bill said with a smile, as if Lee were the only other person in the room, "Now, I'm supposed to kiss you."

Bill crafted many love stories during his decades as a head writer of dramatic serials. They were all fictional. His life with Lee and their love were very real.

Susan Seaforth Hayes, who plays *Days'* Julie, wife of costar Bill Hayes (Doug), knows a thing or two about love and making a marriage work in show business.

"You're always fighting the world and the people who don't care or notice or listen, but in Bill and Lee's marriage there was always someone who cared and noticed and listened," she says. "When you have that, you're twice as strong because there are two of you."

"What a nice thought, that part of his success is their success," adds Bill Hayes.

Chapter 6

"LIKE SANDS THROUGH THE HOURGLASS"

If it hadn't been for Bill Bell's genius, Days of our Lives *would not be on the air today.*

—Ken Corday, *Days*' executive producer

Breakups on soaps can be explosive, but Bill's split with Irna in 1966, so he could become the head writer of *Days of our Lives*, was drama-free.

"She thought I'd be back after the show was canceled," Bill said.

Bill was deeply grateful to Irna for what he'd learned under her and the incredible opportunity that she'd given him, but he was fond of the Cordays, too, dating back to when Ted Corday, *Days*' cocreator, was a director at *As the World Turns*. Ted's wife, Betty, worked in the show's casting department.

"Ted was a superb director whose unique rapport and sensitivity with actors is legendary," Bill said. "His ability to extract every ounce of drama and emotion from the written word was a writer's dream. Betty, partner of Ted, was an equally dedicated mother, as well as [a] writer and producer, and a very powerful force in her own right. Each [was] the ultimate complement of the other."

Betty asked Bill to save her husband's show in 1966. He talked it over with Lee and got a good night's rest before accepting the position as *Days*' new head writer. He saw the offer as a great opportunity to implement everything that he'd learned from Irna.

Irna and executives at NBC asked Bill why he was risking the sure thing of working at top-rated *ATWT* to take on ratings-plagued *Days*, which was about to be canceled.

"I knew there was a chance of that happening," Bill said, adding enigmatically, "but what better time to take over a show?"

Bill and Lee had the safety net of her position at WBBM-TV for an income, but Bill was still taking a gamble.

Irna, Ted, and writer Allan Chase had cocreated *Days* but the show wasn't one of Irna's favored serials like CBS sudsers *ATWT* and *GL* were. "Irna treated *Days* like a stepchild," says Ken Corday, Ted and Betty's son, who became *Days*' executive producer in 1980. "Irna helped with the creation of the show, but she had her hands full with three other soaps."

Bill had to be thrilled that he no longer had to report to Irna's apartment each morning for work, indulge her whims, or take her late-night and weekend phone calls. He and Lee could plan Saturday and Sunday getaways to Lake Geneva with their children. They could enjoy uninterrupted meals at restaurants without having to switch tables.

One of Bill's first tasks at *Days* was to make some casting changes. He hired Susan Flannery to play Laura and Denise Alexander as Susan. He later recast the pivotal role of Julie with Susan Seaforth (Hayes).

Lee was the inspiration for the character of Laura. "Not her experiences, but the person, the being," Bill revealed in 1973.

"When Bill was in charge of the decision-making in casting, it was assumed that you were a good actress before you got there," Seaforth Hayes recalls. "This wasn't a training ground for neophytes."

There had been other "Julie's" on *Days*, but prior to casting Seaforth Hayes, Bill was frustrated that he hadn't found an actress capable of playing the pivotal role. "As for Julie," Bill wrote in 1967, "unless our next recast offers more than the preceding two actresses in the part, she will go to Europe...to await the birth of her infant son."

Seaforth Hayes was unaware when she met Bill during her audition that he'd end up changing not only her professional life, but her personal life, too. Bill cast her future husband, Bill Hayes, as Doug Williams and also hired her mother, Elizabeth Harrower, as one of his valued writers on *Y&R*. Harrower, shortly before her death, played the scene-stealing Charlotte on *Y&R* in 2003.

Seaforth Hayes recalls her audition scene—a confrontation between rivals Julie Williams and Susan Martin. "It was a very trying and emotional scene involving anger, threats, and hysterics. Julie was trying to give Susan a heart attack. Instead, she brought about her own labor pains." The actress won the part after delivering an emotional tour de force for Bill, who had come to Los Angeles for the talent test.

"I recall asking him years later why he hired me. He said it was my smile."

Bill could have indulged his star by saying that she'd given a dynamite reading, which, of course, she had. But he loved keeping people on their toes—not only his viewers, but the people who worked for him, too.

"Bill was the best actor of us all," Seaforth Hayes says of her boss. "He always had a princely quality that evolved up from that to monarch and god-like authority.

"I always felt working on Bill's show was like working on the manor of the lord. You applauded the family because they were your aristocrats. Weren't you happy to be on the property of an aristocrat rather than down with the other peasants fighting and struggling on the unemployment line? Bill and Lee had more to give us as far as opportunity and had the decency to be inclusive and kind to their employees."

As an employee of Corday Productions, however, Bill didn't have the free rein that Irna had at Procter & Gamble. His storylines for *Days* had to be submitted for approval to NBC. Bill pitched a story that involved Horton brothers Bill and Mickey being in love with the same woman, Laura. The sordid saga involved a questionable seduction and an illegitimate child. Bill was behind the story, but NBC Daytime executive Larry White rejected the idea. Too racy, he thought.

Bill was stymied—he'd been hired to do a job but was being told he couldn't do it the way he wanted. The way he knew it needed to be done.

While he didn't have Irna's power, Bill had experience and instincts. He knew from his days in advertising what to do when he knew better than the client did. He held his ground with White, just as he had with the Standard Oil executives.

"I said, 'Larry, let me put it this way. I want a release from you today that you will never use this idea on any other show on NBC.'" Bill's strong stand worked. White couldn't ignore Bill's passion or risk that he'd take the story to another serial or back to *ATWT*.

"That got to him," Bill recalled. The network approved the tale.

There were other battles with the neckties. "Bill told me about Lin Bolin [another NBC Daytime executive], who wanted him to do a story," recalls Susan Flannery. "Bill knew instinctively that it was wrong, but she kept at him—not unkindly, though. She had a genuine commitment to this."

Bill acquiesced to Bolin's wishes, but a few weeks into telling the story, he found that he couldn't continue. He simply didn't believe in this particular tale. "He told me that he'd never do that again," Flannery says.

Bill had a way of getting in the last word. As Ken Corday recalls, Bill asked Betty Corday to have an actor call and apologize because the performer wasn't saying his lines as Bill had written them.

"The actor couldn't get his mouth around the words," Corday explains. The star made matters worse by balking at Bill and Betty's request. Consequently, the character went upstairs.

For nine months.

"That was the power of the scribe then and now," Corday says. "As much as networks crow, 'We have creative say-so,' they never do with a strong head writer. They might have synergy, but they never have control."

Bill wisely chose which battles to fight while he was at *Days*. He recommended to the network and to the show's producers that they consider releasing a particular actress, one of the show's original cast members.

"[T]his actress leaves me a little cold," Bill wrote in a story proposal. "She's really dull. At least to me."

Ultimately, that performer remained with the show. Years later, Bill had much more authority. He recast a character, played by an original cast member, who had a pivotal role in a front-burner storyline on *The Bold and the Beautiful.*

He told the network about the decision a few days later.

Bill didn't clean house when he took over *Days* as some head writers do when they assume control of a show. Rather, he kept the Horton clan, led by America's grandparents Macdonald Carey (Tom) and Frances Reid (Alice), intact and mined characters who were already on the canvas.

He wrote a key scene that had Bill Horton at a bar, drowning his sorrows over Mickey and Laura's impending marriage. He enhanced the character's yearning for the woman he couldn't have by incorporating the haunting theme from the 1944 Gene Tierney film *Laura* into the episode. Bill Horton pushed a song on a jukebox, which played, "Laura, she's only a dream..."

"Bill walked out of the bar in a way that you knew he was going to make sure that she wasn't a dream," Bill Bell enthusiastically recounted. "Laura [a doctor] slept in the quarters in the hospital, and he went back there and said, 'You're not a dream! You're real!' By this time, Laura was waking up. They looked at each other." It was left open for interpretation as to whether or not the sex was consensual.

Was Laura willing? "I suspect that she was," Bill later said.

Laura, now pregnant, married Mickey, and the secret of baby Michael's paternity began. Again, NBC wanted a say in the story.

"The network sat down with Bill and said, 'You have to bring the story to a conclusion so that viewers learn that Bill is Mike's father,'" Corday recalls. "Bill said in his own inimitable way to the network chief, 'I'll conclude this story when I damn well see fit!'"

"Bill kept secrets," Flannery says. "His belief was, and it's quite true, [that] in real life, family secrets stay buried for years. He was tuned in to that."

The late Christopher Schemering, one of the industry's most respected historians, noted in his 1985 fact-filled tome *The Soap Opera Encyclopedia* that Bill, "who had been writing dialogue for ultra-conservative *ATWT*, made a 180-degree turn with *Days of our Lives*, creating potent, often shocking stories with strong sexual and psychiatric themes. Part grand opera, part French farce, *Days*' plotting played out in an atmosphere of somber verisimilitude; the show evolved into terrific melodrama."

Schemering added that Bill's stories created soap-opera stardom for Susan Flannery, Denise Alexander, and Susan Seaforth Hayes.

"Alexander's performance as the sensitive, confused Susan and Seaforth's vixenish portrayal of Julie became audience favorites, propelling both actresses into the pantheon of daytime superstars."

Bill learned a valuable lesson after he killed off Susan Martin's child. (The toddler died after falling from a swing set.) Viewers, mostly stay-at-home moms, found the death of a child to be too traumatic, and a portion of the audience tuned out. Alexander gave a compelling performance as Susan stood trial for killing her child's father, whom she blamed for the tragedy.

"Everything that Bill gave you to play was amazing," says Alexander, perhaps best known to soap fans for her role as *General Hospital*'s Lesley Webber. "Bill was never anything but complimentary to me. I felt cherished working for him. The trial storyline was amazing. The family dynamics were amazing. The show was in a class by itself. My awareness of how truly outstanding Bill was came years later. I just knew that I was having the best time while I was on *Days*. I was incredibly happy and loved what I was doing."

It wasn't long before Bill felt comfortable with his new role at *Days*. "Ours has become the quality serial on television," Bill wrote to NBC executives in 1967. "At long last it is a show of which I am tremendously proud. The marriage between writer and production has truly been consummated. Thank you."

Bill was writing *Days* in spring 1968 when Martin Luther King Jr. and Robert F. Kennedy were assassinated several weeks apart. Bill was deeply moved by the senseless killings, just as he was when Robert's brother, President John F. Kennedy, had been murdered. He took out a full-page ad in *Variety*'s June 6, 1968, edition, hoping to make a difference.

Bill's letter read:

> Open letter to the television and film industries,
>
> Within the past few months two insane violent acts have struck down two of America's most vital and dedicated young men. And worldwide the words "sick society" ring in our ears. Domestically, the cry is to stop this violence. The time is now for our industry and for each of us who are part of it to look deep within ourselves, recognize our responsibilities, and take decisive steps to temper and hopefully eliminate violence from our programming, violence that all too often is nothing more than gratuitous. As a writer, I know that wanton violence is the least creative and most obvious form of "drama" [and] that you can have conflict without violence. And that, invariably, is finer drama. I hope for your children and mine that this does not prove to be another cry in the wilderness.
>
> Bill Bell, Chicago, IL, writer, *Days of our Lives*, NBC-TV

Larry White wrote to Bill that his letter was not only "well-taken" and "pertinent" but also "needed."

Lee received similar praise from Chicago Mayor Richard Daley in 1972 when she spoke out on gun control. "Thank you for expressing your views," Daley said. "The stand you took was good and the conviction you demonstrated was admirable."

Of course, Bill wasn't able to totally remove violence or the threat of violence from his stories, but he kept such acts to a minimum. The ramifications of Thorne shooting Ridge on *The Bold and the Beautiful*, for example, played out for well over a year. Bill employed singular acts of violence that would propel story and character for months, sometimes years. He just didn't throw them into his shows as contrived plot devices on a weekly basis.

Variety reported in its December 1, 1971, edition that *Days* had claimed the number-one daytime spot from *ATWT*. "The NBC win was emblematic of the CBS daytime slide, which had been underway since the start of the current season. It is far more dramatic than many might think because 75 percent of NBC's and CBS's network profits come from the daytime lineup."

The trade publication went on to point out that "while nighttime may have the glamour and may draw all the attention in the rating competition, daytime's year-around daily grind and low production costs yield the hard cash, and a solidly sold single daytime hour can throw off $7 million to $8 million annually. The CBS slide means that NBC's daytime profits will be the best for the network in a decade..."

Flannery recalls Betty Corday making the announcement about *Days*' ratings victory after the show finished taping one afternoon and the cast and crew began rehearsing the next day's episode.

"Betty said she had mixed feelings about it," Flannery says. "She told us that she and Ted had been with everyone at *As the World Turns*. We allowed her that moment, but after she left the room, we all said, 'Yes!' It was great."

Meanwhile, Bill celebrated his accomplishment back in Chicago with Lee. After he moved to Los Angeles, Bill would come down from his third-floor office to the studio level for cake-cutting celebrations at *Y&R* and *B&B*. But the physical distance that Bill felt between Chicago, where Bill wrote the show, and Burbank, California, where it was taped, created an emotional separation, too.

"Every year there was an anniversary party for *Days*, and they invited me each time," Bill recalled. "But I'd just send a telegram. I never once went to a cast party. I love the show, but I was much more inhibited back then. I was immersed in my own world."

Bill knew that charismatic actors tend to descend upon visiting head writers at galas, ready to pitch storylines that would generate lots of work days for themselves in the process.

"You could be overwhelmed by talent, by personality. I was young then. I had this happy and secure life. I was still sort of an outsider."

In 1971, Bill made a rare trip to the NBC studios to celebrate the taping of *Days'* 1,500th episode. He and Betty posed with the cast for a photograph to mark the occasion. Later, Betty sent a copy of the photo to Bill. In it, he appeared to be hesitating from putting his arm around one of the show's actresses, who, in turn, appeared to be cozying up to the visiting scribe.

Betty's note read:

> Dear Bill,
>
> At long last, the "picture of the cast" you have wanted is enclosed herewith; only most important, this time it includes the "fountain-head of *Days of our Lives* Mr. William J. Bell..." I must give you two classic remarks from Susan Seaforth who stated:
>
> "Bill Bell is so handsome he outdoes the best leading men in Hollywood. My goodness, I look as if I were making a pass at the head writer, which was not my intention."
>
> I agree with both of her comments, but let me say your reluctant hand hesitating on Susan's back indicates your dignified rejection of her inadvertent "cuddling up."
>
> On second thought, maybe you better not show Lee this photo... seriously, I hope you get as big a kick out of this photograph as I did. It really is a nice picture and I am delighted to send it to you.
>
> Warmest regards to Lee and the children.
>
> Love, Betty.

Bill and Lee Bell formed a lifelong friendship with Bill and Susan Seaforth Hayes that began when Bill Hayes was a guest on Lee's talk show long before he was cast as *Days*' Doug Williams.

"Lee made her guests feel so welcome and wonderful," Hayes recalls. "She made [a person] feel like a king."

The writer saw great chemistry not only between Doug and Julie, but also between their portrayers. Bill originally planned to pair Doug with Marie Horton (played by Maree Cheatham), but he started putting Doug and Julie together.

"He saw something between us on camera," Hayes recalls. "He wrote a flirty scene for us and took the ball and ran with it. Bill was a genius. He knew just what to do."

"In our case, Bill didn't seem to be afraid of talking to his actors, even befriending us," Seaforth Hayes says. "We had the shocking pleasure of staying in their apartment when they were not there, which I thought was a great leap of trust."

"We saw Bill and Lee together, never on set, but at their home and out at dinner," Hayes recalls. "They were respectful and loving, very much in love and very close."

Bill had equal respect and fondness for the Hayeses. "'The Look of Love' is in their eyes, I'll tell you," he said in 1998, referring to the romantic couple's on-screen signature theme.

A former child actress, Seaforth Hayes has worked with heavyweight directors in films and big-name actors in episodic television. She acted for Bill not only on *Days*, but also on *Y&R* as Lauren Fenmore's jet-setter mom, Joanna Manning.

"Bill and Lee and their children have that Midwestern loveliness and elegance about them," the actress says. "It's a cut above."

The Hayeses also visited the Bells at their Lake Geneva home in Wisconsin. "We weren't married yet," Hayes recalls. "Bill wasn't sure if we were making out on the side. After he showed us to our separate rooms for the evening, he winked, 'I won't put the alarm on.'"

Bill encouraged Bill and Susan's romance off camera, but he couldn't come up with enough obstacles to keep Doug and Julie apart on screen, not the least of which was having Doug marry Julie's mother, Addie! In fact, Seaforth Hayes suspects that if Bill hadn't left the show after launching *Y&R* that Doug and Julie's October 1, 1976, marriage would never have taken place.

"In retrospect, he was right not to marry us," Seaforth Hayes adds. "Only dull things happen to married people on soap operas."

"Bill never would have married us," her husband concurs.

The Hayeses are correct about Bill's feelings on wedded bliss and his characters. "I don't like marriages," Bill wrote in his story projection for *Days* in 1967. "That is, in serials," he hastened to clarify. "Too often, it closes doors rather than opens them."

Bill was keenly aware that his goal as a writer was to keep viewers on the edge of their seats constantly, to keep them forever longing for that next development. He was unparalleled at creating drama and dilemmas that kept his couples apart.

He told stories of people searching for love and fulfillment. Is there anything more special, he rhetorically asked, than "that magic libidinous moment that you may have been building toward for weeks or months or even years [and] that, as a storyteller, you desperately would like to sustain 'forever' because you know that you [then] have your audience in the palm of your hand?"

When Bill allowed his star-crossed lovers to finally tie the knot, he wouldn't wait long before thrusting them into renewed jeopardy. A vengeful ex-wife who contested a duo's divorce was always great conflict.

Still, Bill made sure that he gave payoffs to his viewers who'd invested time and emotions in his serials. He wanted audiences to tune in every day, and he knew how to make that happen.

"The underlying psychology was to write episodes so that if you missed something it wouldn't matter because the plot would be summarized," Bill said. "Many [viewers] feel you [should] watch on Fridays because that's when everything happens. I don't go in for repetition. I want to have something important happen in every episode so that the viewers can't watch [the show] casually every other day."

Bill never wanted to be held to a timetable. He'd submit long-term storylines to network executives but never promised specifically when a story would climax. While he unfolded his stories in due time, he was also keenly strategic. For example, he scheduled peaks in Susan Martin's trial to air just prior to the debut of a competing serial on another network to keep his viewers from wandering over to the new program.

Bill had other compelling characters to write for on *Days* in addition to Julie and Doug, Bill, Laura, and Mickey. He brought Tommy Horton, Tom and Alice's firstborn son, back from the Korean War with plastic surgery, amnesia, and a new identity, Dr. Mark Brooks. Tommy, as Mark, fell in love with an unsuspecting Marie, his own sister.

No one in town knew Tommy's true identity, but a lab monkey in Salem that Tommy had encountered in Africa recognized him. "The monkey could smell or sense something about this man," Bill said. "[The animal] started going crazy [around Tommy]. One by one, characters started picking up on it."

Bill was a master at dropping clues in stories that would take years to unfold.

"We didn't tell our audience anything," Bill said of the monkey business, adding with a knowing lilt in his voice, "yet we told them everything."

As Salem's savior, Bill was riding high. The next logical step was for him to create his own show, but that would mean that he'd have to leave *Days*, just as he once left *ATWT*.

Understandably, NBC didn't want Bill to go and went so far as to sue him to get him to remain as Salem's chief scribe after he created *Y&R*. Eventually, a deal was hammered out where Bill would be able to write his own soap opera for CBS while continuing to provide long-term story for *Days*.

"Bill was under contract to Columbia Pictures Television [now Sony Pictures Television] and Corday Productions when John Mitchell [president of Screen Gems, CPT's TV division] approached him about writing a new show," Ken Corday explains. "But my mother didn't want to stand in the way of Bill doing it. She was fine with it."

Bill didn't exit Salem immediately. He remained as a consultant for *Days* until it went to an hour in 1978. His gratitude to Betty and Ted Corday lasted a lifetime.

"They were very precious to each other and to all of us who knew them," Bill said. "Betty and Ted, I will never forget you, not ever in all the days of my life."

The adult themes and sexual freedom that Bill brought to *Days* were just a warm-up to what he had in mind for his next dramatic serial.

"We knew that we were going to do something that was going to draw much more attention," Bill said about leaving *Days* to create *Y&R*. "We had that kind of confidence."

Chapter 7

"YOUNG AND RESTLESS" YEARS, PART 1

Bill had learned to do soap operas from Irna Phillips, but all the rest is his own smashing, sensational personal insanity.

—Robert LaGuardia, author, *Soap World*

Bill hadn't just saved *Days of our Lives* from cancellation. His dramatic and provocative storylines, pacing, casting, and, most importantly, singular vision, drove the show to the number-one spot in the ratings.

Irna's student had become the master.

Naturally, Bill's writing had made him a sought-after talent. John Mitchell, the president of Screen Gems, Columbia's TV division (and *Days* distribution partner), had worked closely with Bill in his role as *Days*' top scribe. The studio executive helped deliver classic nighttime hits like *Bewitched*, *The Flying Nun*, and *The Partridge Family* to networks. Mitchell encouraged Bill to develop his own daytime series.

"John had a gruff voice and was a very strong man," Bill recalled. "He called me one day and said, 'Get Lee off the air if you can for a few days, bring her and your kids out to L.A., and get a bungalow at the Beverly Hills Hotel. You're going to stay until we can make a deal.'"

Mitchell pitched Bill's soap opera to ABC, NBC, and CBS.

Michael Brockman, who has worked as a daytime executive at each of the big three networks during his career, recalls Mitchell meeting in 1972 with him and Brandon Stoddard, president of ABC Daytime.

"John walked into our office, sat down, looked at us, and said, 'Boys, I'm going to make your day! I have *Bill Bell* ready to do another soap opera, but I need from you an on-air commitment.' Mitchell added, 'Oh, and there's no show yet,' as if a network ordering a new series that hadn't been created yet were a minor technicality."

Normally, it would take a great deal of bravado to pitch a series that hadn't yet been developed, but Mitchell was armed with Bill's impressive track record. Bill had studied under Irna, written for ratings juggernaut *As the World Turns*, and made *Days* a top-rated soap opera.

When it came to Bill's success, the numbers told the story. *Guiding Light* rose from the number-two to the number-one spot in the ratings when Bill worked on the show with Irna, earning an 11.4 rating in 1956. Next, he wrote more than 2,500 episodes of *ATWT* from 1958 to 1966, during which time that show became daytime TV's top-rated soap opera with a ratings high of 15.4 in the 1963–64 season. As a solo artist, Bill wrote more than 3,000 episodes of *Days*.

Bill had the Midas touch. He knew how to tell stories that would engage audiences.

Despite these impressive facts and figures, ABC passed on the chance to work with Bill. The network was committed to Agnes Nixon's *All My Children*, which had launched in 1970. ABC's daytime lineup was comprised of sitcom reruns (*Bewitched*), game shows (*Let's Make a Deal*), and soap operas (*General Hospital*, *One Life to Live*).

NBC also said no. The peacock network's daytime lineup had a dozen series on the air, including a talk show hosted by Dinah Shore, six game shows, and five soap operas. Lin Bolen, said to be the model for Faye Dunaway's programming executive character in the film *Network*, was in charge of NBC Daytime and passed on Bill's untitled new soap.

CBS had twelve daytime programs during this time, too, but executives found a Bill Bell-written soap opera simply irresistible. The low-rated serial *Where the Heart Is* was canceled to make room for *Y&R*. Bill returning to CBS was serendipitous. He'd started his TV career writing comedy sketches at WBBM-TV, the network's affiliate in Chicago where Lee broadcast her live talk show.

"I had worked with Irna on *As the World Turns*, and the CBS management was from Chicago," Bill said. "These were all our friends, Lee's and mine. It made sense to go to CBS."

Fred Silverman, who'd been promoted to the head of all CBS programming, and Bud Grant, vice president of CBS Daytime, gave Bill's dramatic serial the green light.

"As soon as Bud said, 'Bill Bell,' I said, 'Make the commitment,'" Silverman recalls.

"I started in CBS Daytime," the executive adds. "It was my entry to the network and I never lost interest in it. It was a big loss when Bill left *As the World Turns*. You hate to see someone that talented go to a competitor. There was a standing offer from CBS for Bill to do his own show. Naturally, we jumped at the chance. *Y&R* was by far the classiest show in the whole daytime schedule. From the theme song to everything else, it was right on the money."

After CBS gave the go-ahead, Mitchell had an important question for Bill. "John said to me, 'Bill you do have a show, don't you?'" Bill recalled, chuckling. "I said, 'John, would I lie to you?'" But Bill hadn't even begun to write his new show yet. Ideas may have been in his head for the new serial, but he was so invested in his characters that he wanted to make sure that they would have a home before he began their conception on the printed page.

Bill faced an incredible challenge by remaining at *Days* while creating and executing his new show. He had written two programs for most of his career, but those experiences had been either collaborating with Irna (*ATWT*) or redefining an existing canvas of characters (*Days*). Creating a brand-new daytime show without Irna was going to be a first.

"Lee and I realized the moment of truth had come," Bill said. "We were committed to a show and we didn't have one."

Bill and Lee went to the Beverly Hills Hotel's famous Polo Lounge and began writing their new show's characters and long-term story projections on cocktail napkins. "We were challenged," Bill revealed. "We were a little scared by what was facing us."

The fear was unfounded. In a few weeks, Bill and Lee had created a sixty-five-page proposal for *Y&R*. The title page read: "'A New Dramatic Serial for Daytime' by William J. Bell and Lee Phillip Bell."

Since Bill was still under contract at *Days*, Screen Gems used Corday Productions as the original producing entity for *Y&R*. Corday Productions didn't have an ownership stake in Bill's serial; however, contracts for actors, producers, and directors were issued in the name of Corday Productions. Betty Corday served as a consultant on *Y&R*, for which she was credited on-screen until her death in 1987.

Corday Productions continues to share a "produced in association by" credit at the end of every *Y&R* episode.

Bill devoted the first ten pages of his brilliant treatment for *Y&R* to explaining how his and Lee's serial would be different from all the other soaps on the air.

Bill's passion, knowledge, and confidence leapt off the pages of his proposal. Surely a bidding war would have ensued for the rights to

Bill's show if Mitchell had been armed with the document, dated with a copyright of September 25, 1972.

"It's time that the daytime serial changes," Bill wrote. "That we update and innovate!"

Bill felt it was vital for viewers to identify with a serial's characters and storylines, even though the on-screen personas often seem larger than life and therefore are, in a sense, unapproachable.

"However," Bill maintained, "it is also my unequivocal belief born of seventeen uninterrupted years in this field that the serial is also an escapist form, one in which the viewer can become very deeply involved in the lives of some very stimulating and/or provocative people who dare to live a lifestyle that they, the viewers, perhaps secretly envy."

Bill believed that chemistry between characters, not hospital or law-office settings (though his characters would work in and interact in those specific locales), was the prime emotional force of daytime. "Man-woman chemistry. Live, flesh-and-blood people who can get the adrenaline flowing. Damn nifty people who can turn you on and keep you turned on. That's what it's all about today as never before."

Bill wanted to draw his viewers so deeply into his fictional world that the outside one would cease to exist.

"You don't quite make it by taking a 'beat' or a pause, nor via the cliché, or what by now has become cliché in these very precious moments. But—there is a way.

"The answer is—music. The dimension of music to enrich the moment...music mooded to the moment—either voiceover—or sung very intimately by one or both of our principals."

The most important music associated with the show would be its opening theme. "We spent hours and hours listening to music to find just the right songs," Lee recalls. When the couple heard a theme in the 1971 film *Bless the Beasts & Children*, they knew they'd found their show's signature tune.

"The *Y&R* theme is bittersweet," says Jack Allocco, a veteran composer for *Y&R* and *B&B*. "It has a sense of sadness to it, yet there's a hopeful side to it, too. It's haunting and mesmerizing. It sweeps the viewer into the show and sets the tone for what's to come.

"Bill showed an incredible instinct with his choice. He just knew that was the right song, intuitively."

Bill felt that music, like his actors, would play just the right role in his show. Themes would score dramatic moments, but not in every scene or in every episode. "We'll use music in situations...that lend themselves to it," he said. "We'll search for those moments when both mood and story will prove much more exciting and compelling—because of the lyric."

Bill didn't overwhelm his audiences with music. "Through the Eyes of Love," the love song in the feature film *Ice Castles*, serves as the love theme of *Y&R* star-crossed lovers Victor and Nikki. The show has used it sparingly over the decades, but the tune, which has been played during the couple's weddings and at one of their divorces, is unmistakably recognized as the duo's theme. It never fails to resonate with *Y&R* viewers.

Bill's working title for his and Lee's show was *The Innocent Years*, but he decided that wasn't going to fly in the decade that followed the turbulent '60s. "I realized that there were no more 'Innocent Years,'" Bill said. "They'd been left behind. The world had become much more sexual and sensual."

Choosing the exact title for the show was a process. The first few scripts, in fact, had the title "Young and Restless Years" on them.

"I knew I wanted 'The Young and the...' in the title. 'Restless' was a long time in coming. We tried a lot of different words. We didn't come up with the title easily," Bill said.

Ken Corday recounted in his 2010 memoir, *The Days of our Lives*, that his mother, Betty, suggested "Restless" to Bill. She was greatly talented, Corday wrote, "especially when it came to titling a new daytime drama."

There was no question as to where the series would take place—Genoa City, Wisconsin, a town that Bill, Lee, and their children passed through on the way to their summer home in Lake Geneva. Bill's description of his serial's locale read that it would be "urban in some respects, small-townish in others, population of around a quarter of a million."

Bill enigmatically added, "Beyond this brief description, Genoa City will be everything we want it to be."

Bill's document outlined the show's original characters and families, which included the Brookses (Stuart, 48; his wife, Jennifer, 48; and their four daughters: Leslie, 24; Lauralee, 21; Chris, 19; and Peggy, 16); the Hendersons (Bruce, 50; his wife, Regina, 43; and their sons Jim, 21, and Russell, 17); and the Fosters (Liz, 38, and her three children: William Jr. "Snapper," 21; Greg, 20; and Alison [later renamed Jill], 18).

Rounding out the cast were leading man Brad Eliot, 29, and restaurant owner Frenchie, 40.

Bill became immersed in his new show, a new life, and new challenges while still providing the big picture for the citizens of Salem. "Bill wrote long-term for *Days* and gave it to head writer Pat Falken Smith to flesh out while he wrote *Y&R* every day," Ken Corday explains.

When *Days* expanded to an hour in April 1975, Bill officially turned over the reins to his protégée. "Patty and I worked together for a long time," Bill recalled. "She's an excellent writer and was always a special favorite."

Despite being in Smith's capable hands, *Days* cast members did not want to see Bill leave the show. "*Days of our Lives* was his baby, but he had a new baby in *Y&R*," recalls Suzanne Rogers, an Emmy-winner for her role as *Days*' Maggie Horton. "It was as if a little sibling had come along. I'm sure it was a bigger blow to the rest of the cast that had known him longer."

Bill transitioned from Salem to Genoa City via Manhattan. He presented the *Y&R* proposal (aka "bible") to more than two dozen CBS executives at a meeting in New York. He wasn't sure that they'd understand why much of his treatment was devoted to the origins of the Fosters and the Brookses.

"A nighttime show has a beginning, middle, and end," Bill explained. "But here we have a treatment that tells them what happened before the story even begins." Bill surmised that the executives' expressionless faces betrayed that they didn't quite comprehend the intricacies of serialized storytelling. "They didn't understand why I was telling them about what happened to characters prior to the show starting," Bill said, chuckling.

Next, Bill traveled 3,000 miles across the country to meet with Charles Cappleman, longtime head of West Coast Operations at CBS Television City in Hollywood. Despite its name, CBS Television City is not truly a city, but rather a studio facility in the Fairfax district of Los Angeles. Cappleman (aka "Cappy") showed Bill the studios where *Y&R* is still produced today.

"I can't tell you what a wonderful man Charles Cappleman is," Bill said.

Bill recruited John Conboy, who produced the short-lived CBS soap opera *Love Is a Many Splendored Thing*, to produce *Y&R*. Conboy, along with the late Bill Glenn, a director whom Bill later hired as a director and production consultant for *B&B*, defined *Y&R*'s lush and sophisticated look, a style that made daytime richer and more adult.

Conboy, who'd been based in New York, told *Variety* that working with Bill was the reason he came to Los Angeles. "It's a very viable story, which doesn't rely on sensationalism," he said of Bill's show. "The story comes out of people reacting to each other, and the emphasis is on character and relationship. The story is not built on incidents. This is one of the best [serials] I've come across as far as the way it's constructed."

Conboy was responsible for the show's daily production, but the ultimate vision of the show came from the top. Bill had final say in casting, personnel hiring, and of course, the story.

The Young and the Restless debuted on March 26, 1973, at 12:30 p.m. Eastern Time. The show opened with mysterious Brad Eliot hitching a ride with a trucker as they passed through Genoa City. Other dynamics included Stuart Brooks grilling potential son-in-law Snapper Foster, who was dating his daughter Chris but seeing waitress Sally McGuire on the side, and sisters Leslie and Chris having a heart-to-heart talk about love. Also, Brad's fiancée, Barbara, was told erroneously by the police that Brad had died. Bill incorporated music into his premiere by having pianist Leslie play "The Look of Love," a tip of the hat to the Burt Bacharach tune that he'd given plenty of airtime on *Days*.

The show's opening credits included black and white sketches of the show's characters, drawn by famed artist Sandy Dvore. He later created the famously recognizable *Y&R* logo using red lipstick, a nod to the show's backstory about Jabot Cosmetics.

Over at ABC, Brandon Stoddard and Michael Brockman watched the premiere of the show on which they'd taken a pass. "We didn't say a word to each other after it was over," Brockman recalls. "We just looked at each other. There was a silence between us, as if to say, 'Oh, dear. We've got a *big* problem ahead of us.' You knew right away that the show was very different, very appealing."

"Bill took the soap-opera concept and jazzed it up," says Meredith Berlin, former editor-in-chief of *Soap Opera Digest*. "He made it 'Hollywood.' His characters weren't just great-looking, they were stupendously great-looking." Berlin cites William Grey Espy, the original Snapper, as an example. "Did it get any better than that? Bill put so much glamour into everything. He made characters *mesmerizing*. *Y&R* was revolutionary."

How did the name "Snapper" originate? Bill explained that the young man was so angry in life because his father had walked out on the family. He "snapped" at everyone. "He was arrogant, so the name stuck," Bill said.

Bill introduced provocative sex scenes on his new show, including a steamy shower scene sequence with Jaime Lyn Bauer and Tom Selleck's characters.

"It was wonderful," Bill said of the increased sensuality. "It caused people to respond and discuss it. [But] I don't think we were responsible for all of it."

Irna's characters tended to lament their woes over coffee in living rooms and kitchens. Bill led his characters into the bedrooms, but *Y&R* isn't just beautiful people making out in boudoirs. From the beginning, *Y&R* tackled social issues including rape, breast cancer, and alcoholism. Bill drew heavily on Lee's knowledge and expertise about societal concerns that she had addressed on her talk show and in her award-winning documentaries. Daytime had never taken on certain topics until Bill and Lee brought them to the airwaves. Brad Eliot flashing back to asking his girlfriend, Barbara Anderson, to get an abortion in *Y&R*'s premiere episode was groundbreaking.

"There was valuable information in Bill's social-issue storylines, but they were also still dramatic," says Margot Wain, a veteran executive at CBS Daytime. In one scene, two of the show's more attractive players, Snapper and Casey, enacted a comical and provocative demonstration of the Heimlich maneuver.

A more dramatic incident involved Victor Newman using infant CPR on his daughter Victoria, bringing awareness to viewers at home on what to do if they ever found themselves in a similar crisis.

"I hope we're more than storytellers," Bill said. "We have the ability to influence people's lives. We feel it's a mandate of writers, programmers, and storytellers to do more than tell story, to impact people's lives."

Bill praised Lee's influence on his storytelling as "totally invaluable. Lee added contributions to what we were doing. It was very collaborative."

In 1993, Bill revealed to *Soap Opera Digest* that *Y&R*'s first year had some discouraging moments. Viewers had fourteen different soaps from which to choose when *Y&R* debuted, and many of those serials had loyal followings, some dating back to the 1950s. Getting viewers to turn the knob (ask your grandparents, kids) or add a new soap opera to their daily viewing habit wasn't going to happen overnight.

"Everyone was a little depressed because [the show] wasn't doing as well as we thought," Bill revealed. However, he was ultimately confident that the show would succeed.

"I remember talking to Bill after *Y&R* premiered," recalls Paul Rauch. "I said, 'It's really good. It'll go a long way.' Bill said, 'It's going to be number one.' He was absolutely dead certain about that early on, and he was right. Bill had total confidence about what he was doing. He knew what he was doing better than anyone."

Viewers who sampled *Y&R* quickly became hooked. By 1976 *Y&R* had moved up to the third spot in the ratings, not far from *AW* and *ATWT*.

The network, in turn, supported Bill by giving him carte blanche to tell his stories. The only "notes" he got from executives were of the thank-you kind. Mark Waxman, CBS Daytime director, wrote to Bill on February 22, 1979:

Dear Bill,

Bravo on today's share/score. Pound for pound, you are the king of the day mountain, and for those of us who take your bows every Thursday morning, much thanks.

Mark Waxman

In 1975, *Y&R* won the Daytime Emmy Award for Outstanding Drama Series. Bill had truly beaten the best in the business, given that the other two nominees were *AW*, which was enjoying critical acclaim and high ratings under executive producer Paul Rauch and head writer Harding Lemay, and *Days*, which was, of course, still riding high on the long-term story that Bill himself was supplying.

Critics were on board from day one. "*The Young and the Restless* is the most modern, elaborate, and 'slick' serial yet produced on daytime television," wrote Robert LaGuardia, soap opera historian, author of the 1977 tome *The Wonderful World of TV Soap Operas*. "Its cast reeks of California-tanned good looks, good health, and good spirits." LaGuardia also praised the serial's lavish sets and well-rehearsed acting, noting that *Y&R* was breaking ground in its treatment of sexuality.

"There is at least as much lovemaking on screen as there is talk of sex," he wrote. "The scripts abound with special contemporary sexual problems: premarital sex, sexual inhibitions, rape, and the fears women have of testifying against rapists. All this is new, very new to daytime television."

The historian heaped additional praise on Bill and *Y&R* in his next book, *From Ma Perkins to Mary Hartman: The Illustrated History of Soap Operas*. *Y&R*, LaGuardia wrote, "doesn't really use different stories—the brutal truth is, they are soap clichés—but different methods. The phantasmagorical lighting of a Hollywood studio sculptures the actors' faces with Ingmar Bergman-esque sensuosity. The actors themselves are fashion plates out of the pages of *Vogue* and *Esquire*—even the older characters are pretty.

"These gods and goddesses, who supposedly are content to live in a nowhere town like Genoa City, dress in high-fashion boutique wear. They all talk a lot about sex, with the suffering Hollywood sex kittens showing provocative décolletage and the religious and/or terminally ill studs flexing good pecs around oft-naked chests."

"*Y&R* within the context of daytime television has amazingly high-quality writing," wrote Norman Mark, television columnist for the *Chicago Daily News*. "The scenes are shorter than most on daytime dramas and the cast is very attractive, but it is the storyline that I found to be quite involving."

With *Y&R*, Bill was taking the genre into the future, but he never forgot the essential roots of serialized storytelling.

"In some ways, *Y&R* is not new or modern," LaGuardia observed. "Its theme concerns young people finding themselves, and love as well, in a contemporary world. [The characters] are above all concerned with marriage and their relationships with their families, as has been true of young people on daytime since the early days on radio."

Bill had the first few months of scripts for *Y&R* written before the show began production. He doled them out slowly to keep storylines from leaking out in the media or at the studio. Even in a pre-Internet age, daily newspapers and weekly tabloids could give away key plot points.

Bill would have preferred having direct autonomy over the show, but he opted to remain in Chicago, helming *Y&R* from his East Lake Shore Drive apartment. He watched the show daily, just as his audience did. He made occasional visits to Los Angeles to check on the show's production, and he and Lee and the children would attend the show's anniversary parties.

Meanwhile, Lee's star as the top TV personality in Chicago continued to rise and shine. Bill, Brad, and Lauralee were still in school. It wasn't the right time to relocate to the West Coast.

"Bill writing from Chicago was a good thing because it gave him a perspective of the real world, not life in Los Angeles, not the 'L.A. world,'" offers Margot Wain. "Bill being in the Midwest served the show well because he was in touch with the values and the issues that are important to our viewers."

Bill relaxed his policy on attending show anniversary and holiday parties once he launched *Y&R*. He was no longer an employee, as he had been at *Days*, but rather a partner in the show. Melody Thomas Scott, who joined *Y&R* as Nikki Reed in 1979, recalls meeting Bill at the show's anniversary gala at the Beverly Hills Hotel's Crystal Room.

"Bill Bell himself asked me to dance," says the actress. She sensed that the scribe was studying her during their twirl around the dance floor. "He was looking at me and also thinking of Nikki. He sat me down after the dance, thanked me, and said, 'Captivating. Simply captivating.' It's like he had a split appreciation for both the person and your character. His wheels were always turning. He may have been thinking of some story with Nikki dancing with Victor. Bill was always halfway in work mode. The great head writers have to be. They must always be thinking about story."

Y&R's sophomore season in 1974 heralded the arrival of two important "Kays" in Bill's life. Katherine "Kay" Chancellor, played by Jeanne Cooper, made her Genoa City debut in January. Also Kay Alden, who was doing her thesis on soap operas, showed up at Bill and Lee's apartment for an interview.

Cooper, a veteran actress from nighttime and film, was vacationing in Hawaii when she learned that Bill was offering her the role of the show's matriarch.

"I kept hearing, 'Bill needs to know! Bill needs to know!'" Cooper recalls. "I knew Bill had created the show along with his wife, but I wondered since when does a writer have such control? His name wasn't Procter & Gamble. I asked John Conboy, 'Who is this Bill Bell again?' John said, 'He's the man who controls it all.'"

Bill created one of the greatest rivalries in serialized drama with Katherine Chancellor and Jill Foster. Kay's husband, Phillip, who'd fallen out of love with his wife, left her and took up with the much younger Jill, Katherine's companion. Alcoholic Kay drove her car off a cliff. She survived, but her passenger, Phillip, died, leaving behind Jill, his pregnant mistress.

Phillip was gone, but the animosity between the two women raged on and continues to be a dynamic on the show today. It is daytime drama's longest-running conflict.

Bill took a few hours of his busy time one day to meet with Alden, just as Irna Phillips had met with him. Alden shared with Bill her passion for the genre, citing a storyline on divorce Bill had told on *ATWT*.

"I'd grown up in a small town in Kansas," Alden says. "I'd never seen what a divorce does and just how it impacts a family until I'd seen Bill's storyline."

With Bill, every facet of the diamond was displayed, held to the light, and examined for his audience's viewing pleasure. It's why he loved serialized storytelling. Events unfolded in real time, and viewers experienced every emotional moment along the way.

"Bill played every beat," says Wain. "You never said, 'Hey, I missed where someone found something out.' You didn't wonder what someone's reaction was to something. You got every single one of those beats."

Bill accurately sensed an innate talent and a true dedication to the genre in Alden. He offered her the opportunity to write a sample script. Later, the graduate student accepted, putting her thesis on hold. She soon became Bill's right arm, aiding him with writing and plotting the show on a daily basis. She reported to his apartment for work, just as Bill had done with Irna.

"Unlike Bill's affiliation with Irna, Bill was very kind to me," Alden asserts. "He was always seeking to help me learn. He was the ultimate teacher and I was the consummate sponge. He could pour into me every ounce of wisdom and experience that he had and I was the grateful recipient."

"Bill and Lee were both very protective of Kay," Sherman Magidson recalls. "Kay drove in every day from Northbrook. It was a long drive, so what did [Bill] do? He and Lee bought her a new car. Kay served the same purpose to Bill that Bill did to Irna. Kay got the job done. He could trust her."

"Bill trusted Kay," concurs Tom Langan, former *Y&R* producer. "I never really knew her while I was at the show. I just knew what Bill would tell me. Bill knew that Kay would fill in the blanks and that she knew intuitively the emotional life of his characters. Those two were a marriage made in soap-opera heaven."

Bill wrote long-term story projections for *Y&R*. He created an eighty-page document detailing what would unfold in Genoa City during 1977.

The treatment outlined Bill Foster's mercy killing, the developing animosity between Lorie and her new mother-in-law, Vanessa Prentiss, and Leslie Brooks miscarrying Brad's baby.

Bill knew what he wanted so intimately that he included particular scenes in his projection. "Let me take a moment to delineate Leslie's state of mind regarding the loss of her baby," Bill wrote. "She will be stoic. This isn't to say she wouldn't be filled with all the inevitable emotion. But we want Leslie to keep her head, not to be emotionally debilitated in any way. Her love for Brad remains stronger than her bond to any unborn child.

"I'm extremely sensitive that the Brad-Leslie storyline now and ahead could easily translate into something very depressing. We must, instead, look upon this as a love story. The trap would be to write and interpret Leslie's aborted child in the more traditional manner, i.e., to pull out all the emotional stops. Indeed we want to play for emotion until Leslie loses her baby. But afterward, we want to play her more together. A woman saddened yet undeterred."

While he left himself open to byroads in his treatment, Bill felt that every show needs one couple that endures. For *Y&R*, that couple is Chris and Snapper. "Let there be no doubt that there will never be a divorce between Chris and Snapper while I have anything to do with these storylines," Bill wrote. "Granted, never is forever, but we've seen over and over again how much the audience welcomes a young couple being able to handle their problems without resorting to divorce."

Bill continued to let executives know that his stories would unfold as he saw fit. "It's virtually impossible to suggest how long these storylines will last. Obviously, some longer than others."

Bill ended his treatment on a wry note: "Until we meet again—keep young but not too restless."

As *Y&R* was thriving, NBC was failing to find a successful program to follow the popular *AW*, so in the mid-1970s the network expanded Irna and Bill's cocreation to an hour. Other networks took note of the economic benefits of hour-long soaps and began reformatting their shows to sixty minutes in length.

Irna hadn't lived long enough to see soaps expand this way, but she likely would have felt, as her protégés Bill and Agnes did, that the half-hour format was better. It's wise to leave your audiences always wanting more.

Finding airtime to expand the soaps to the hour form meant cancelling some shows that were languishing at the bottom of the ratings. In 1970, there were nineteen soap operas. By 1981, that number had decreased to thirteen. *The Secret Storm* and *Love of Life* were among the shows that got the ax so that *GL*, *ATWT*, and others could switch to an hour.

For as long as possible, Bill vehemently resisted making the transition.

Alden recalls visiting CBS Television City in the late 1970s and seeing that a new studio was being configured to accommodate the additional stories that *Y&R* would be telling as a sixty-minute serial. Back in Chicago, Bill reassured her that it wasn't happening. "He put his hand on my shoulder and said, 'Kay, honey, calm down,'" Alden says. "'They can't do it without my say-so and I have not yet said yes.'"

Bill used the word "honey" all the time, but he never meant it in a sexist way. "He called everybody 'honey,'" says Cindy Popp, a veteran *B&B* producer-director. "It was his term of endearment for everybody—male, female, old, young—everybody was 'honey.'"

Meanwhile, CBS was planning to take *Y&R* to an hour as surely, if not as nefariously, as terminally ill socialite Vanessa Prentiss schemed to frame daughter-in-law Lorie for her "murder."

The network planned to announce *Y&R*'s expansion at its annual affiliates' conference in Century City in late spring 1979. Bill asked the neckties to hold off. They later called Bill, interrupting his tennis game in Lake Geneva, to lay down the law.

"I was on the phone for a total of four hours with several people, including Bud Grant [CBS Entertainment president]," Bill recalled. "They wanted me to agree to the hour, but I just couldn't go there."

Brian Frons, former ABC Daytime president and then a programming manager at CBS, recalls the intense negotiations. "I was standing next to Michael Ogiens [CBS Daytime president], who was on the phone with Bill at the Century Plaza Hotel where we had the affiliates' conference," Frons says. "He was telling Bill that they were about to announce the show going to an hour."

It wasn't often that anyone got the last word in with Bill, but this time CBS did. "Finally, they said, 'Bill, just know this: the ship is going to sail—with or without you,'" Bill recalled.

Upon accepting CBS's mandate, Bill, Lee, and Kay did what most people would do when faced with a crisis—they ordered a pizza. "We proceeded to commiserate," Bill said. "We knew we had to go ahead with it." The crusts from Gino's East (Bill's favorite pizzeria) were no sooner in the box than Bill began conceiving new characters to add to the canvas. They included Paul Williams, Paul's family, and Victor Newman.

Eric Braeden inhabited the iconic Victor from the beginning. "When he came in to audition, it was almost like we, not him, were the ones being scrutinized," recalls Edward Scott, then an associate producer at the show.

Bill recalled in the tome *Worlds without End* that Victor's run was originally intended to be short term. "It would last between eight to twelve weeks, at which time he was to be shot by his beautiful wife," Bill said. "In short, Victor Newman was in concept a despicable, contemptible, unfaithful wife abuser."

However, when Bill heard Braeden's voice on screen everything changed. "I knew immediately that I didn't want to lose this man. He was exactly what the show needed. Not the hateful man we saw on screen, but the man he could and would become over time."

"Bill was a 'man's man,'" Braeden says. "He understood my character and what I would and would not do. Victor is a 'man's man,' too. We were cut from the same wood. We had an interesting relationship in that he knew I would make certain changes [in the dialogue] and he pretended not to know. But he trusted those changes because they were always in the best interest of the character."

Prior to joining *Y&R*, Braeden was enjoying a successful career in films (*Escape from Planet of the Apes*) and in episodic television (*Mary Tyler Moore*, *Kojak*), most often playing gruff antagonists. He found the character development on daytime appealing and wanted to continue playing Victor.

"The Bells are a rare exception in this business," Braeden says. "They are from the outside. They aren't from Hollywood. In some ways, that has an enormous advantage.

"Lee," the actor adds, "is one of a kind."

Braeden made two requests of his boss. He asked that Victor not suffer a heart attack when he collapsed during a heated argument with Jack Abbott in the early '90s, but rather a "coronary episode."

"I asked Bill not to make it that," Braeden says, "because my father died of one. I didn't want to play that."

Braeden's other request was that Victor be humanized. Bill fulfilled that by revealing the mogul's painful and lonely childhood. Victor, born Christian Miller, was left in an orphanage by his destitute mother, Cora, on Christmas Eve. Rather than be defeated, Christian grew into adulthood and created a financial empire, changing his name to Victor Newman.

"There was a mixture of anger, sadness, loneliness, and fury all at once," says Braeden, recalling a scene in which Victor blasted Cora, played by Dorothy Maguire, for her actions. "It is still my favorite scene, that and the scene where Victor told Nikki about his childhood. They were brilliantly conceived and written. I had expressed my concern to Bill about playing these dehumanizing bad characters. He listened carefully and came up with a brilliant solution. We understood from then on why Victor was the way he was."

The hour-long version of *Y&R* premiered on February 4, 1980. As Bill had predicted, viewers took a while to adjust to the show's new format and embrace the new faces.

"We lost four share points when we went to an hour under protest," Bill recollected. "It took us three years to get them back."

As *Y&R* inched back up in the ratings, Bill was faced with another dilemma—cast defection. Actors were not contractually obligated to remain on *Y&R* if it were to expand to an hour. When it did, some took advantage of that and exited the show, hoping to parlay the popularity they experienced as one of Bill's characters into primetime and films.

Bill preferred not to recast. He understood that his audience was deeply invested in not just his characters, but also in the actors that brought those roles to life. In *Y&R*'s relatively short history, viewers had welcomed into their hearts two versions of Leslie, Lance, and Snapper as well as four different Gregs.

"I was at the point where I knew I'd have to do something if one more person said to me that he or she were going to leave," Bill said.

A day later, veteran cast member Jaime Lyn Bauer contacted Bill. She informed him that she wasn't going to be renewing her contract when it expired later that year.

Bill had an important decision to make: recast Bauer's role as heroine Lorie Brooks Prentiss, or jettison her along with the other actors related to her since he would no longer have Bauer there to anchor them?

The decision that he made changed the landscape of *Y&R* forever.

Chapter 8

"YOUNG AND RESTLESS" YEARS, PART 2

I thought this is an actor we could ill afford to lose when we lost Terry Lester [ex-Jack], but Bill's attitude was, 'This is not going to affect us.'

—Jack Smith, senior *B&B* writer, formerly *Y&R*'s head writer, coexecutive producer

Bill found himself at a crossroads when Jaime Lyn Bauer told him in winter 1982 that she wasn't going to sign a new deal when her contract expired in the summer.

As heroine Lorie, Bauer had spent nearly a decade in tears, turmoil, and tragedy, winning both a loyal following and Bill's admiration in the process. Bill loved writing for her because she always delivered the goods. Bauer, however, was a mother of two young children. She told Bill that she needed a rest and asked him not to try to change her mind.

Bill decided that if Lorie, a character named after his own daughter, Lauralee, was going to leave, then he'd write out many of the characters involved in her storyline, most of whom had already been recast.

"I thought, 'I cannot recast Lorie. I just cannot,'" Bill recalled to Linda Susman in *Soap Opera NOW!* in 1987. "I looked at her and said, 'Jaime, I'll tell you what—as of this moment I will never once mention it to you again about staying. If you want to stay, you come to me.'"

The future of Bill's story canvas, not to mention the livelihoods of many actors, hinged on Bauer's decision. Bill didn't burden her with this knowledge, however. In fact, she didn't even learn for certain the impact her departure had on the show until March 1990 when Bill shared what it meant with her at a tribute to *Y&R* sponsored by the Museum of Television and Radio and held at the Los Angeles County Museum of Art.

"I didn't know," said Bauer, who was grateful to Bill for not telling her. "I had gone to Bill and told him I really wanted to leave. I said, 'Please don't do anything to try and get me to stay.' It was so easy for me to put someone else first, but I was exhausted and needed a break."

Bauer marvels at how Bill masterfully kept *Y&R* going, despite sweeping change. "He re-invented the show under two new families, which was brilliant. It must have taken a lot for him not to say anything to me. I am forever grateful from the depths of my heart. Had I known, I would not have left. I would have felt too responsible for all the other people who would have lost their jobs."

Many actors did lose their steady gigs, but other performers found employment after Bill hired thespians to play new characters. Bill repopulated his canvas by fleshing out two island characters—Paul Williams (some of his family members had made sporadic appearances) and Jack Abbott. Bill cast Jerry Douglas (who bears a resemblance to Bill) as patriarch John Abbott, Eileen Davidson as heroine Ashley Abbott, and Beth Maitland (who became *Y&R*'s first Daytime Emmy acting winner in 1985) as insecure Traci Abbott.

Just as the wealthy Brooks family contrasted with the poor Foster clan, the well-to-do Abbotts were juxtaposed against the working-class Williamses. Bill tied the clans together via Jack's reluctant marriage to young Patty Williams. Jack's philandering ended the union and scarred Patty deeply, a dynamic that Maria Arena Bell, Bill's daughter-in-law, revisited as the show's head writer a quarter of a century later.

Bill knew that getting his viewers to shift their emotional allegiance to new characters was asking a great deal. Making sweeping changes to a show has been known to drive viewers away.

"If someone said today that there won't be any more Chandlers or Martins on *All My Children*, your jaw would drop," Brian Frons, former president of ABC Daytime, said in 2009. "But Bill didn't have a fear of turning his whole show over."

Bill embraced his new characters with the same passion and devotion that he had brought to his first days of *Y&R*. Viewers accepted the Abbotts because Bill tied them to a character they already cared about via John's marriage to social-climbing Jill. Soon, fans were equally invested in seeing if Katherine was going to ruin Jill's romance with John, just as they were when Kay tried to destroy Jill and Phillip. Audiences gladly pulled a chair alongside the Abbotts for their famous family breakfasts.

Bill shifted the Foster and the Brooks families off the canvas like a master chess player, keeping familiar faces, including Victor, Kay, and Nikki, on the canvas while he enforced the transition.

"That's one of my proudest moments in this business," Bill said. "I built a sister, mother, and dad for Paul, and the crossover came with Patty and Jack and their relationship. Over the next four months, I backed away from the Brooks and Foster families and moved forward with the Williams and Abbott families...we never lost a share point. In fact, we gained three or four points."

"It was seamless," recalls Edward Scott, who spent more than twenty-five years on *Y&R*'s producing team.

The industry agreed. By creating new families, Bill reinvigorated the show. The following year, *Y&R* won its second statuette for Outstanding Drama Series at the Daytime Emmys.

Bill was still living in Chicago when the Abbotts were established. Beth Maitland, in fact, didn't even realize who her boss was when he visited the set one day or how fond he was of her performances, especially her singing on the show.

"I saw this handsome, blond, dignified man wearing a cream white suit talking to Patty Weaver [who played Gina Roma]," Maitland recalls. "He leapt up and came running over to me and hugged me. He didn't realize that I didn't know who he was. Then I heard Patty say, 'Bill,' and I figured out in a flash who he was. It was a time when he was far away. He was like the voice of Charlie on *Charlie's Angels* to us."

Having his actors not recognize him wasn't the only limitation Bill experienced by living in Chicago. By the early 1980s, shows were being taped two to three weeks in advance. Bill would watch the show daily on-air, just as Irna had with *ATWT*, but because several episodes were already shot, it was more difficult for Bill to correct any misdirection that he saw in terms of actor performances.

Bill hired Sally Sussman Morina as a story consultant in 1982. She watched the show daily in Chicago alongside her boss.

"Bill knew that calling the studio and yelling about something was futile because the next set of shows had already been taped," Sussman Morina recalls. "But he needed to get his point across. We were watching the show one time when Nikki was driving home." Instead of a car engine, however, the sound effect of a jet taking off was played. "Bill turned to me and said, 'Oh, good. Nikki's driving home—on her jet.' We laughed. Bill would call up executive producer Wes Kenney and start screaming his head off. He'd say, 'My Christ!' That was Bill, but then it was over. He asserted his authority and vented, but he got over it pretty quickly."

Bill more fully played air traffic controller in 1986 after he, Lee, and the family moved to Los Angeles. From his office in *Y&R*'s production suite, Bill was able to monitor the show as scenes were being taped, making sure that actor performances and character motivations were aligned.

Christina Knack was Bill's executive assistant from 1987 to the mid-'90s. "Bill was a genius and gracious," she says. "He always knew where he was going when he introduced a character or a new family. He was very organized."

Bill could have had his lunch ordered in every day from nearby five-star eateries like The Ivy or the restaurant at the Four Seasons Hotel in Beverly Hills, but he was content with a frozen Healthy Choice entrée that Lee would bring from home and prepare in the production office's microwave for him. Lee kept a close eye on what Bill ate to control his type 2 diabetes.

"He also loved the turkey club sandwiches from the CBS commissary," Knack recalls. "He was more than happy with that, and he'd offer half to Jerry Birn."

Knack recollects Bill laughing more after Birn joined the show's writing team and took an office next to Bill's in 1988. "They had the greatest regard and respect for one another, both personally and professionally. They each had a dry sarcastic wit and they really connected."

Bill was a history connoisseur, collecting letters and signatures from entertainment and political figures, including Judy Garland, Abraham Lincoln, and Winston Churchill.

"Bill loved history and was very passionate about it," Knack says.

Knack's duties included screening Bill's telephone calls. When Bill had time, and sometimes even when he didn't, he'd take inquiries from aspiring soap-opera writers who were seeking advice on how to break into the industry.

"If people weren't too pushy, he'd take the time with them," Knack says. "He supported people trying to get into the industry, but as soon as they started not being pleasant, he wouldn't give them the time of day."

Bill understood that it was frustrating for actors who were used to working a lot to work less often, but he had no tolerance for rudeness. He was approached in the CBS hallway once by an actor's representatives who were displeased that their client had shifted to the back-burner, a place where all characters spend time sooner or later. The actor's handlers wanted to talk to Bill about their client's future. Bill suggested that they set up a meeting to discuss the matter.

"No," one of the representatives rudely stated. "We want to talk *now*." Not surprisingly, the character, who wasn't working out anyway, soon shifted off the canvas entirely. The ill manners cost the actor an official farewell scene. He was just never mentioned again.

Bill chose former *Days* director and executive producer H. Wesley "Wes" Kenney to take over as *Y&R*'s producer after John Conboy left the show to start up *Capitol*. In 1999, Kenney wrote Bill a thank-you note that read, in part:

> Bill, we had our differences on *Days*. You said, "I know, but we got the job done because of our mutual respect." So true. Thanks, Bill. For hiring me. For trusting me and for giving me five great years.

Kenney left the show in the mid-'80s and took over the reins at *General Hospital*. Then Edward Scott assumed producing duties in the control booth.

"I couldn't do what Bill did, and he couldn't do what I did," Scott says of his relationship with Bill. "The guy was such an interesting dichotomy in terms of emotions. If you met him in person or went out to dinner with him, he was very comfortable to be around. The whole family is the most congenial group. But when you were in a business situation, there was an amazing difference.

"There were times when I'd call him after we shot a scene and I'd ask him if that's what he was looking for. He'd say, 'Yeah, that's fine, Eddie.'"

Melody Thomas Scott recalls that Bill trusted her husband to experiment at times. "Bill used to tell Edward on the phone, 'Just because I wrote it that way doesn't mean that they have to *play* it that way.'" The actress adds, "At first I didn't understand that, but now, I do. Bill and Edward were a great team."

Cooper says that Bill's presence on the West Coast made him appear less imposing. "When he spoke from Chicago it was like a voice coming out from the clouds that said, 'You will live to regret f—ing up that script the way you did!' He became less of a threat after he moved to Los Angeles."

The mid-'80s were an incredibly successful era for CBS Daytime. It surpassed ABC as the top-rated network in viewers. And *Y&R* was narrowing the gap with ABC's first-placed *General Hospital.*

Susan Banks, who was the director of CBS Daytime promotion, produced sizzling campaigns featuring characters from all four CBS soaps in varying states of duress and undress. The sexy promos were set to the pulsating tunes of "Some Like It Hot" by the Power Station and "Addicted to Love" by Robert Palmer.

CBS Daytime was on fire and Bill's storylines supplied endless fuel, keeping the flame an eternal one. His golden touch hadn't gone unnoticed by the other networks.

Frons, who had moved over to NBC Daytime, and NBC Entertainment president Brandon Tartikoff had hoped to lure Bill back to the peacock network with the promise of a new show. "Anything but *Days of our Lives* or *Wheel of Fortune* could have gone away for a Bill Bell show," Frons says. "Brandon and I paid a visit to Bill and Lee's home in Lake Geneva. They had directors' chairs that said on the back of them 'The Old and the Pooped.' Bill and Lee couldn't have been sweeter or more charming, but they said that they were exclusive to CBS."

As the World Turns, under head writer Douglas Marland, and *Guiding Light*, written by top scribe Pamela Long, were also enjoying a golden age in the mid to late '80s. However, the jewel in the CBS Daytime crown, if not the crown itself, was *Y&R*. The show won additional Outstanding Drama Series honors two years in a row at the Daytime Emmys, starting in 1985.

Soap Opera Digest named *Y&R* the top soap in its annual Best and Worst issue of 1986. The show, which had undergone sweeping changes four years earlier, was now being heralded by editors for its consistency. The magazine lauded *Y&R* for taking time to develop and enrich characters and stories, noting that other serials lacked *Y&R*'s finesse in successfully introducing new romantic duos to their canvases.

"A week later, viewers are expected to wildly root for this instant couple," the magazine's editors wrote. "Not so on 1986's best show, *The Young and the Restless*...once you find characters and stories you like, you can sit down, relax, and enjoy. They'll be around for a while."

As *Y&R* continued its climb to the number-one spot, three immensely popular performers vacated their front-burner roles. Brenda Dickson (Jill), Eileen Davidson (Ashley), and Terry Lester (Jack) left Genoa City, respectively, in 1987, '88, and '89.

Each actor was uniquely important to *Y&R*. Dickson, who had returned to play Jill in 1982 after a four-year absence, was an original cast member. Davidson, the definitive Ashley, played the one true threat to the show's supercouple, Victor and Nikki. ("Ashley," in fact, became the fourth most popular name for girls in the '80s. The handle's popularity is attributed to Bill's character.)

At the time, Lester was one of the show's few Emmy nominees. Strong leading men are difficult to come by in soaps, and Bill knew he had a great one in Lester. One critic wrote that the actor combined the perfect amount of "snake oil and charm" that made Jack simultaneously loveable and despised.

"Terry was the biggest loss, with Brenda being the second biggest," head writer Jack Smith says. "But as I got to know Bill better, I realized that we could lose anybody."

"Terry could be a pain in the ass," recalls Tom Langan. "But Bill really loved that character."

Top talent exiting a soap opera can be catastrophic to a show's ratings. ABC Daytime lost five million viewers after Anthony Geary and Genie Francis, legendary supercouple Luke and Laura, checked out of *General Hospital* in 1983. *Y&R*, however, kept going up in the rankings even after losing three top-tier players in the late '80s. The reason? Bill's storylines never wavered.

The popularity of the performers he was losing could have inspired Bill to shift the Abbotts off the canvas and revamp the show, as he'd done earlier when he jettisoned the Foster and Brooks clans.

"Bill always said that recasting comes down to whether it's the actor or the character who is more important," Kay Alden says. "In the case of Jill, Ashley, and Jack, Bill was simply not ready to say good-bye to those characters."

Instead, he recast the trio, with the sensational Jess Walton, fresh off a successful stint as reformed hooker Kelly Harper on *Capitol*, as Jill, newcomer (and Davidson look-a-like) Brenda Epperson as Ashley, and, on the advice of Melody Thomas Scott, fan favorite Peter Bergman as Jack. Bergman had just concluded an Emmy-nominated ten-year run as good guy Dr. Cliff Warner on *All My Children.*

"I may be doing actors a disservice, but you could replace anybody as long as you give them good story," Bergman says. "That's how you keep it going."

Soap opera historian Christopher Schemering credited Bill's loyalty to his characters as a reason for his success. "Just when you think characters like Paul or Nikki are 'played out,' Bell comes up with tantalizing ideas for audience favorites," the critic said. "It's uncanny. Other soaps take heed."

Brad Bell says his father had a term for mining another aspect of veteran characters. "He'd talk about 'folding it back in,'" Brad says. "People talk about stories having beginnings, middles, and endings, but when my dad would get to the middle of a story, he'd take a diversion, which would start a whole new story. He'd have mini-payoffs but never full conclusions. The story would fold back into another character. Stories were less linear and more complex."

Bill was never at a loss over what to do with his creations. In 1993, Victor Newman alienated his family and loved ones by attempting to control their destinies one too many times. So Bill had Victor get carjacked, just as Brad Eliot had been in the show's premiere.

Like Brad's attacker, Victor's assailant was killed in a fiery crash. In the days before DNA testing, a burnt driver's license and charred body remains was all the evidence a TV coroner needed to state with enough certainty that someone had perished.

In reality, Victor had wandered onto a farm in Kansas, unaware that his loved ones thought he'd been killed. The mustached mogul showed a sensitive side as he befriended a blind farmer, Hope Adams (whom Bill named after *B&B* producer Hope Harmel Smith). Upon learning from confidante Douglas Austin that everyone back in Genoa City thought he was dead, Victor asked him not to reveal to anyone that he was alive. The ruse inflicted greater agony on Victor's loved ones, but the audience couldn't wait to see what Victor had up his sleeve.

His eventual return to Genoa City brought tears to his loved ones, shocked his enemies, and shot *Y&R*'s ratings up to an impressive 9.1.

Victor was single when he met Hope, but a few years earlier Schemering had criticized *Y&R* for glamorizing adultery. (Victor was married to Nikki when he had an affair with Ashley.) The critic also felt that Bill's characters often took too long to get to the point, happily conceding that it worked well in some instances.

"Major players like Eric Braeden's Victor are masters of this kind of ambiguity; Braeden gives such bemused reactions to Nikki's baby-doll mischief that even the quiet scenes are eerily tense," Schemering wrote.

The critic also said he had seen quite enough of fantasy scenes that had characters doing something provocative only to have the moment quickly dissolve back to reality. However, the critic had more praise for *Y&R* than negative comments, noting that Bill had ingeniously rejuvenated the Kay-Jill feud by having the two women team up against upstart Nina.

"Overall, *Y&R* is a winner," Schemering wrote. "It's the oddity of daytime—it makes its own rules and looks like no other soap." He gave thumbs-up to the show's structure, direction, and production values.

"The show is like a big, juicy blockbuster beach novel which never ends. Pass the champagne and chocolates."

Soap Opera NOW!'s Linda Susman pointed out to Bill that he was revisiting Leslie's breakdown by having Ashley go through a similar ordeal. "I can't believe people remember, and I won't deny it," Bill told the respected journalist. "I am very complimented that it had that kind of impact."

Bill never consciously set out to repeat his storylines. Yes, characters at his different shows would take similar paths, but each journey was unique. "Characters dictate their own story to me, and all stories emerge from those characters," he said. "You can't just superimpose any story over any character."

"There are only a certain amount of stories available to you as a writer," Langan concurs. "But each of Bill's characters was so distinct that [their individual tale] didn't appear to be the retelling of the same story. And, of course, it wasn't. There were similar setups, but how [each story would] unfold would be completely different."

After NBC was unsuccessful in getting Bill to create a new show for its daytime lineup, executives there reached out to Sally Sussman Morina, one of Bill's writers. She was also pursued by ABC, but NBC's offer to start up her own show was irresistible. Just as Bill had left Irna to go to *Days*, Sussman Morina also flew the nest.

"I'm sure it was easier for Bill to leave Irna than it was for me to leave him, but it was, in its own way, identical," the scribe reflects. "Bill was disappointed, but he understood."

Generations, Sussman Morina's series, launched on March 27, 1989. Ironically, like many serials, the program had worked out its kinks and had come into its own just as the network pulled the plug. *Generations* aired its last original episode on January 25, 1991.

Sussman Morina and cast member Jonelle Allen (whose dynamic character Doreen had a memorable catfight with Vivica A. Fox's Maya on the show) gave a post-mortem to *Soap Opera Digest*'s Roberta Caploe. "I believe that if we weren't opposite the second half of the top-rated show in daytime [*Y&R*], we would have done much better," Allen theorized.

"Creatively, we did something that nobody's ever tried before,"

Sussman Morina said, referring to *Generations* including so many African American characters. "I had my little piece of TV history."

Thanks to Bill, Sussman Morina actually has two. He was famous for naming characters after relatives and family friends, (Yes, Virginia, there is a "Ridge.") Soap insiders picked up on an inside joke between the Generations' creator and Sally Spectra (played by the late, great Darlene Conley), whom Bill created for *B&B* in 1989. Spectra ran an upstart rag competitor that challenged established fashion house Forrester Creations on *B&B*. A parallel could be drawn between that dynamic and *Generations* competing against *Y&R*.

"I asked Bill if he named Sally Spectra after me," Sussman Morina shares. "He said that he had. I asked him why. He said, 'Because she gets things done!'"

With his successful recasts at *Y&R* in place, Bill continued to tell the stories of the Abbotts, the Newmans, and the rest of his characters. *Y&R* had been beating *GH* in the ratings as the most-watched soap opera on occasion during the mid-'80s. Bill's show claimed the top spot on December 4, 1988, and has remained there ever since.

Bill's stories around this time included Brad Carlton being kidnapped and held in a cage by his deranged ex-wife, Lisa Mansfield; Victor taking control of Jabot Cosmetics to even a score with Jack; and Leanna Love (the former patient of Ashley's psychiatrist husband) trying to poison her rival with a lethal lei in Hawaii. Romantic weddings (Scott and Lauren), social issues (Jessica having AIDS), and lavish galas at the Colonnade Room remained staples of the show.

In the early '90s, a masquerade ball brought nearly the entire cast together, a rare occasion. Kay dressed as the Queen of Hearts; Jill entered as Cleopatra; and young lovers Ryan and Victoria portrayed

Romeo and Juliet. The extravaganza brought overdue Emmy gold to the show's costumer, the late Greg York.

Bill wrote Danny Romalotti's rock concerts into the summer months when younger viewers were more able to watch. Michael Damian (Danny) put in long hours taping the musical extravaganzas, but as far as he was concerned, Bill was the one who had the nonstop work ethic.

"Bill amazes me," Damian told *Soap Opera Magazine* in 1997. "I drive in early in the morning and his car is already there. I leave and he's still there. He's writing and writing and writing. I've always been impressed with him."

"Bill was obsessed with the show," Braeden offers. "'Obsession' connotes something negative, but with Bill it was a positive. It was 'magnificent obsession.' Only someone who felt that way could write something that has been so enduring."

During Danny's concerts, Bill would have either Nina or Cricket address concertgoers about a social issue—the dangers of drunk driving or guarding against date rape. Teenagers don't like being told what to do, especially at concerts, but Bill made the sermons seem logical.

Critic John Kelly Genovese echoed Schemering's positive sentiments about the show. "*The Young and the Restless* is an old-fashioned soap opera," Genovese wrote. "But it works. It presents compelling stories about fascinating people who are products of their backgrounds, emotions, and values—not pawns in ill-conceived flights of fancy, manipulating characters for the sake of plot. It makes us feel for the characters. And it carries it all off with the ultimate in production values and finely tuned performances from a talented cast."

Lee, Mary (Bill's sister), Brad, and, of course, Lauralee all appeared on *Y&R* in front of the camera. Bill himself came close to making a cameo appearance. He taped a walk-on role when the show went to Hawaii to tape Cricket and Danny's wedding in 1991. "Would you believe it? I ended up on the cutting-room floor," he chuckled to *Soap Opera Digest* in 1993.

Bill was once asked the impossible—could he choose a favorite storyline? "I'd never get it down to one," he replied. "I might get it down to a dozen."

One tale that would make his list and was instrumental in driving *Y&R* to the top spot was the George Rawlins murder mystery. Bill introduced the compelling crime story in 1988. It was the first adult storyline for Emmy-nominee Doug Davidson, who plays private eye Paul Williams.

In the tale, Paul learned that Cassandra, the beautiful woman he'd become captivated with, was also "Sandy," the young wife of his elderly new friend and client George, an impotent millionaire who'd come to love Paul like a son.

Ironically, George asked Paul to find out who his wife was seeing behind his back. The riveting plot thickened after he asked Paul to be the surrogate father for his and his cheating wife's unborn child. Later, George learned of the duo's betrayal and also that he was dying. He hired an assassin to do him in so Paul would be jailed for his "murder."

Sensing his audience's involvement with the story and impressed with the acting improvement of Nordic beauty Nina Arvesen (Cassandra), Bill not only extended the saga but also altered its outcome.

"Nina started out with beauty and some performance, but the performances were getting better," Bill said. "They improved during the year, and we had to ask ourselves if we were prepared to lose her."

The answer was no. Bill changed his original ending, which would have revealed that the killer was indeed Cassandra. Just as he had with Barbara Crampton's Leanna, Bill softened Cassandra to keep her on the canvas. "He loved what Barbara did on screen," recalls

Christina Knack. "He loved Nina Arvesen, too. She was the most beautiful woman we ever had on *Y&R*. She gave off an aura that was just mesmerizing."

Critics felt that the Rawlins mystery was taking too long to conclude, but Bill wrote for his audience—not magazine editors.

"I never put a timeframe on anything because you're only going to inhibit the story [if you do]," Bill said. "I take no pleasure in 'stretching' stories. I promise you that there's either story movement or character movement in every scene, or there's something that if you don't [watch], you're going to miss.

"To show you that I don't write for time, I would have wrapped up the [Rawlins murder mystery] during February or May sweeps," Bill added. "I'm doing it in April. The middle of April. That should tell you something."

Cassandra went from suspect to victim after Adrian Hunter, George's killer and Cassandra's lover, drugged her, which left her temporarily paralyzed. Adrian placed a gun encased in dry ice by her head. His scheme was for the ice to melt and then the gun would fire, killing George's widow in the process. Everyone would think that she committed suicide because of her guilt over "murdering" George. Later, Adrian returned to find a bloodied and seemingly lifeless Cassandra on the floor.

Sherman Magidson concocted the deadly dry-ice device. "Los Angeles had an ordinance where you couldn't buy a toy gun so my wife, Gail, went outside of L.A. to find one," the criminal attorney recalls. "Ron Linder [husband of *Y&R* actress Kate Linder] and I got the dry ice. We set up the cap gun and went out to the movies. When we came back, the ice had melted; the gun had fired and landed on the floor. I called Bill and told him this would work."

The audience and Adrian, however, didn't know that Paul and Victor had arrived in time to save Cassandra. One of the most chilling moments in *Y&R* history, directed by Frank Pacelli, occurred when an incensed (but very much alive) Cassandra, covered in fake blood, popped up into frame over the shoulder of a raving Adrian.

"Nina is just a wonderful actress," Bill praised. "Doug Davidson has been his very best. Eric has done a wonderful job, as always."

Ironically, Cassandra suffered the cruelest of soap-opera fates a year later when she was killed (off camera!) by a runaway vehicle. Brad Carlton inherited the Rawlins fortune, which set him on the path to become a major financial player in Genoa City, someone who would compete against power moguls Victor and Jack.

Bill produced between fifteen and ninety minutes a day of dramatic television during his five decades as a television writer-producer. He didn't have time to watch the other shows with any kind of regularity, but he was aware of who the key players were on other serials. He hired actor Kristoff St. John from *Generations* in 1991 to play rising Jabot executive Neil Winters.

The actor's run began with a four-episode tryout. "I didn't know that Bill was famous for bringing actors on for a few episodes to see if he liked them or not," St. John shares. Bill called St. John on the set after he finished taping his second show. "I liked your scenes," Bill cheerfully said. "How'd you like to stay for three years?"

"It was a dream come true," says St. John, who felt that with the demise of *Generations*, soaps weren't featuring African American characters as much as they could. "Yes, *All My Children* had had Jesse and Angie, but that's all they had. Nobody was doing it on the scale that Bill was."

Bill was turning more of the creative reins at *B&B* over to his son Brad in 1992, which was good timing because Bill's social calendar had never become more jam-packed.

A plethora of tributes to Bill began that year. First up was Bill receiving the Editors' Choice Award at the eighth annual Soap Opera Digest Awards in January.

The following month, on February 10, a rainy Monday night, Columbia Pictures Television hosted a roast of Bill at Chasen's restaurant on Beverly Boulevard. Actors, network and studio executives, producers, directors, and other invited guests paid homage to Bill with tributes that ran from heartfelt to tongue-in-cheek. Many execs went for humor, but most ended up showing why they had careers behind the scenes. Ed Trach, executive in charge of production for Procter & Gamble, however, was very funny as he pretended to have a phone conversation with the late Irna Phillips, who was still being bossy in the hereafter.

Also, Mike Ogiens told a funny tale about how Bill had been a problem child. The former CBS Daytime executive said that Bill's parents even threatened to send him away to live with his grandfather—but Bill didn't think he'd learn anything from his elderly relative, who'd been married many times and lived among scandalous, sex-addicted, eccentric characters. "Fortunately," Ogiens deadpanned, "Bill's parents sent him away anyway."

"Poor Bill, poor Bill had so much on his mind," lamented Jeanne Cooper, adding, "Bill, you haven't seen 'poor' in twenty years!"

"If all his Emmys were laid end to end, I wouldn't be a bit surprised," said a smiling Susan Seaforth Hayes, putting her own spin on the Dorothy Parker quip.

Next, a pretaped musical tribute to Bill performed by the *Y&R* cast and crew was shown. Lee's heartfelt words wrapped up the presentation. "You're a wonderful husband, a great father to the children, and my best friend," Lee said. "I love you."

Then it was Bill's turn to speak. With Lee at his side, he let loose with a few remarks of his own.

"I haven't had this much fun since my circumcision," Bill quipped. "I do want to set one record straight once and for all. No matter what he says, I do not, repeat, I do *not* look like Jerry Douglas! Will you help me get that out of his head?"

On a serious note, Bill added, "I'm glad Lee's here beside me. There's where she's been all these years. Without Lee, nothing would have been the same. The shows wouldn't have been the same, and, God knows, the kids wouldn't have been the same!"

Next, Bill introduced Bill, Brad, and Lauralee. "Every father's dream is to have a son follow in his footsteps. I'm lucky enough to have two—Bill, who runs our shows both domestically and worldwide, and Brad, who works as a writer and associate producer of *B&B*. We have a daughter, who's followed in her mother's footsteps. I'm so damn proud of all three of them—Brad, Billy, and Lauralee."

Bill also singled out six members of his inner circle, whom he described as being "very important to the show."

First up was Kay Alden, "the brilliant young writer, who came to interview with me nineteen years ago," Bill said. "I was impressed with her, suggested she contact me if ever she was interested in writing. Six months later, I did hear from her. Kay, I still don't know what took you that long! But she's been Lee's and my right hand ever since."

Bill introduced Jack Smith, calling him "a very talented man." Jerry Birn, Bill said, "was our best man at our wedding, and he's joined us at *Y&R* and he's doing a hell of a job.

"Certainly, I want to mention Maria Arena, who is also a part of our writing team on *B&B*, very talented, and God knows the prettiest part of the *B&B* writing group," Bill said of his future daughter-in-law.

"Ed Scott, I wrote this before I had the Martini, but I have never in my career felt a closer relationship with a producer than I do with you today." Bill hastened to quip, "Yesterday was something else. It's a joke! It's a joke!

"Nancy Wiard, my irreplaceable left and right arm, I don't know what we'd do without you."

Bill also thanked his actors from both shows. "Your contribution is enormous," he praised. "Each of you is my extended family. I spend more time thinking about you than I do my own family. Mostly because they don't get themselves in the goddamn messes you do!"

Tributes to Bill continued that year. He received the Lifetime Achievement Award at the Daytime Emmys on June 20 in New York City. On October 29, CBS dedicated Stage 43 to Bill and *Y&R* at CBS Television City in Hollywood. The ceremony was held in the area which connects four soundstages. You couldn't see the floor that night, however, because of the hundreds of people that filled the hallway.

"Bill Bell is responsible for shows on three of our four stages," Charles Cappleman said. "We're all happy to see Mr. Bell's car drive safely on the lot each morning."

Y&R celebrated its twentieth anniversary with an all-star gala at the Four Seasons Hotel in Beverly Hills in March 1993. Cast members past and present joined the show's writers, producers, and directors and the Bells to celebrate. David Hasselhoff hosted the event.

Bill began writing soaps in 1956 with *Guiding Light*, but he showed no signs of slowing down as he continued into the '90s. Exciting new characters (Malcolm, Sharon, Phyllis) and plot twists (Victor's shooting, Chris and Danny's split, Nathan's affair with HIV-positive Keesha) were on the horizon.

But not even Bill could have foreseen the real-life soap opera that was going to explode in the mid-'90s and would deal a crushing blow to the daytime serial genre.

Chapter 9

TAKE YOUR DAUGHTER TO WORK DAY

I'd tell people who were new at the show, 'Hi, I'm Lauralee,' and someone would say 'This is Lauralee Bell.' I'd think, 'Argh! Give me a chance! Would it hurt if people didn't know for a week?'

—Lauralee Bell (Christine "Cricket" Blair), *Y&R*

Lauralee Bell wasn't above engaging in some un-Cricket-like behavior to spend time with her dad, who wrote from home each day, creating stories for Leslie, Lorie, the Fosters, and Kay Chancellor.

In a move worthy of Cricket's rival-turned-pal Nina Webster, Lauralee used a household thermometer and a few glasses of hot water to fake a fever and stay home from school.

Like a lavish gala at the Colonnade Room in more budget-friendly times, her ruse lasted a week.

"The longer I stayed away from school, the more I didn't want to go back," Lauralee recalls. "I wanted to hang out with my dad, learn and watch what he did."

Sensing Lauralee's interest in the soap world, Bill and Lee gave their daughter her first professional opportunity, a non-speaking role on *Y&R*, during a family trip to Los Angeles. After working as an extra in a scene on board an airplane with David Hasselhoff, Lauralee got the bug—in more ways than one.

"It was easy and fun," Lauralee recalls of her one-day gig. "But my dad told me I hadn't gotten the full impression. He asked, 'What if we had you do a few more days?' I was excited, but by no means did we think it would ever be much more than that."

Bill created the role of ingénue Cricket Blair, named after a childhood friend of Lauralee's, for his daughter in 1983. Soon, newcomer Thom Bierdz and Tricia Cast, fresh off a stint on *Santa Barbara*, were hired to play angst-ridden teen Phillip Chancellor III and the previously mentioned Nina, a girl from the wrong side of the tracks. Nina had not one, but two out-of-wedlock babies. The two teen girls, like all of Bill's characters, were clearly defined: Nina couldn't do anything right and Cricket couldn't do anything wrong.

Meanwhile, Phillip battled the bottle, just as his surrogate grandmother Katherine had.

"Good girl" characters have always been a staple on soaps, and there were plenty of them in the mid-1980s. *Guiding Light* had saintly Beth Raines; *Days of our Lives* showcased virginal Jennifer Horton; and *All My Children* featured innocent Julie Chandler. But none of these ingénues held a candle to Cricket when it came to goodness. Bill had his young heroine tackle and often conquer every social issue under the sun with the exceptions of lupus and leprosy.

"It might have been hard for him to envision me as anything else," says Lauralee, who appreciates her father's position. "I can't ever see saying to my daughter, Samantha, 'Well if you want to be the fun character, you should play the bitch!'"

Cricket's virtue made her an easy target for critics who took the young actress and Bill's writing to task for what appeared to be the character's incessant goodness and regular presence on screen. "Gimme a Break!" "Make Room for Cricket," and "Most Over-Exposed Heroine" were just a few of the barbs and blurbs about Lauralee's alter-ego that were printed in the pages of *Soap Opera Digest*.

It wasn't the first time Lauralee had faced ridicule after appearing on TV. When the King Tut exhibit came to Chicago in the late '70s, Lee taped a spot on her show about it, in which Lauralee was a makeup model.

"Everyone at school the next day was walking around doing the Steve Martin 'King Tut' dance," Lauralee recalls with a groan. "It was mortifying."

Lauralee handled the attacks on Cricket with a grace and maturity that belied her teen years. She was hardly the only offspring of soap creators to go into the suds business. Her two brothers took positions at their parents' shows. Other head writers including Bridget and Jerome Dobson (*Santa Barbara*) and Claire Labine (*Ryan's Hope*) hired their children, too, but because they'd played behind-the-scenes roles, their feet weren't held as closely to the fire.

Lee gave advice to Lauralee on how not to be offended by the printed word when the fifteen-year-old was reading a celebrity magazine.

"I was crushed that someone was getting reamed in an article," recalls Lauralee. "My mom said to me, 'Turn the page. Your thoughts will go to the next person and then when you close the magazine your thoughts will go to your life.'"

Terry Lester, *Y&R*'s Jack, was unhappy that Cricket was getting a lot of airtime even though story for his character never seemed to wane. He opted to air his frustrations in the press.

"Lauralee handled that beautifully," Tricia Cast recalls. "I never saw it get to her." Given that the soap opera press is dependent on cooperation with the shows it writes about, Bill was certainly in a position to suppress negative items about his daughter. And who would have blamed him if he'd picked up the telephone and made a friendly request to an editor or two?

"I received a few strange phone calls from producers of other shows," recalls Meredith Berlin, *Soap Opera Digest*'s editor-in-chief. "Bill would call or send a note if he liked something that he'd read about the show in the magazine, but he never called about anything that was written negatively about Lauralee."

Bill drew the line, however, after a tabloid reported that Lauralee's costars didn't like her. He told Linda Susman at *Soap Opera NOW!* that the rag's attack was part of a Terry Lester backlash.

"It stems from Terry leaving," Bill said. "There are about twenty gross errors in the story." Among them, Bill noted, was a connection between Lauralee being cast and the family's move to Los Angeles.

"All that stuff is ludicrous," said Bill, both the protective producer and proud parent. "Whether I lived in Chicago or L.A., I have made every major casting decision. Lauralee's performance speaks for itself. The truth is she is among the top three every week in fan mail, positive fan mail. And I would challenge some of those so-called quotes from [anonymous] cast members. She's very popular among cast mates."

"It was hurtful, mostly because I respected him," Lauralee said of Lester's remarks. "He apologized to me before he died. He said he was being an insecure actor. If you understand where people are coming from, it doesn't make it fully better, but you understand it."

Ironically, Lester once had a great relationship with *Y&R*'s creator. The actor wrote to Bill on March 8, 1986, after Bill had left him a message on his answering machine, praising him for giving a powerful performance.

The letter read:

Dear Bill,

You sure know how to make a guy's day. That message couldn't have meant more to me than if it'd been delivered to my doorstep. An actor couldn't ask for more from his boss, nor could a friend ask more of a friend. Thank you from the bottom of my heart.

Terry

Arguably, the Cricket attacks in the press technically were directed at the show's writing, but when they'd run next to a photo of Lauralee, how could she not take it personally?

"Lauralee was put in the difficult position of being given entire storylines as a teenager when she had far more experienced actors around her," Berlin says. "She's very much like her parents in that she's a secure person. You don't find many actors who are."

"Lauralee managed not to become hard-shelled and full of herself," says Susan Seaforth Hayes, who played *Y&R*'s Joanna from 1986 to 1989. "I've seen quite a few ingénues who've gone directly to 'divadom' within a few weeks. It's miraculous how it can happen."

"Lauralee's a joy to work with," adds Eric Braeden. "She's the daughter of one of the wealthiest men in the business, but you never would know that. She has a grace and a sense of professionalism about her. That says a lot about her parents."

While the press was taking shots at Lauralee, critics raved about her costar Cast and her ability to go head-to-head against powerhouse actresses Jeanne Cooper and Jess Walton. In 1988, *Digest* dubbed Nina one of two "Most Intriguing Characters" out of the hundreds of characters that appeared on daytime and nighttime soaps combined.

"[Nina] is pathetically self-sufficient, her own worst enemy, and precisely because she doesn't want anyone's compassion, she earns ours," wrote the magazine.

Nina, who became pregnant after seducing Phillip, Cricket's fiancé, regularly fired off zingers to Kay and Jill. "It ain't over 'til the fat lady sings," a knocked-up Nina snarled at the overprotective women. "And, boy, is she gonna get fat and is she gonna sing!"

Meanwhile, Cricket had the more reserved duty of reciting statistics on social issues and giving advice to older characters. She remained the good girl.

Cast, who won a Daytime Emmy for Outstanding Younger Leading Actress in 1992, believes, however, that Nina and Cricket's differences made the duo more dynamic.

"We were each other's complements," she says, adding that magazine items were never a source of friction between the two ingénues. "There's a danger in believing both good and bad press."

Three thousand miles away in New York City, Martha Byrne, who played ingénue Lily Walsh on *ATWT*, could relate to Lauralee's position.

"I thought how hard it must have been for her to read what was being written about Cricket," recalls Byrne, whose character became *Digest*'s "Most Over-Exposed Heroine" in 1988. "Lauralee probably had one hundred times more pressure that I had. People would say, 'Oh, she's Bill Bell's daughter.' But I don't see anyone in that family giving anyone opportunities that doesn't deserve them. You have to earn your place at the table."

"Lauralee Bell is my great example of somebody who was handed a giant opportunity that she had not yet earned and then proceeded to earn it," says Peter Bergman, who succeeded Lester in the role of Jack. "Stunning. Terrific to watch. I watched her do that and thought, 'Good for you.' She made the job everything she could and turned into a lovely actress."

"Bill did his daughter a great favor, and she paid him back tremendously by succeeding," Byrne adds. "That must have made him feel extremely proud."

Cricket may have had her detractors, but Lauralee's fans and the show's ratings told a different story. The actress received approximately five hundred letters a week from young girls who wanted to be like Cricket and grandparents who adored her. Viewers found it refreshing to see a teen character be played by, well, an actual teen (and not a thirty-one-year-old star, claiming to be twenty-four!).

"Most of Lauralee's fan mail didn't even mention that she was the boss's daughter," says Cathy Tomas, the actress' fan-mail coordinator. "We especially got letters during the date-rape storyline."

Not all the critics were unkind either. "Bell and Bierdz were handed some of the most difficult, long-winded material in the past year," wrote Christopher Schemering in 1988. "And if they sputtered from time to time, chalk it up to a production that was pushing too hard, too fast."

Two of Cricket's most powerful storylines aired soon after *Y&R* took the top spot in the ratings on a regular basis. The Jabot model was date-raped, and she also discovered that her estranged mother, Jessica, played with sensitive reserve by Rebecca Street, had been diagnosed with AIDS. Cricket went public with her date-rape ordeal at one of Danny's concerts. Her sermon prompted a young woman (played by Lisa Rinna) to think twice about going home with a man whom she'd just met. The man was Derek Stuart, who was none other than Cricket's attacker.

Next, Bill switched Cricket's name to Christine and her profession from modeling to law. The courtroom provided an arena where the heroine could tackle even more social issues including illiteracy, sexual harassment, and senior-citizen rights.

Even Bill, who made the change, had to get used to his daughter's new handle. "Bill told me a funny story about himself," Linda Susman recalls. "He was watching the show after the name change, and Bill turned to Lee and said, 'Who's Christine?' And Lee said, 'It's Cricket—your daughter!' We had a good laugh about that."

Bill wasn't alone. To Nina, Danny, and many, many diehard fans, Lauralee will always be "Cricket."

With Nina reformed, Bill introduced a new adversary for Christine in 1994. Phyllis Summers, played by the dynamic Michelle Stafford, wrecked havoc in Chris's life in ways that Nina had only dreamed of doing. The red-haired vixen drugged Danny while he was performing in a production of Andrew Lloyd Webber's *Joseph and the Amazing Technicolor Dreamcoat* in New York and lied that he was the father of her son, which prompted the duped rock star to break up with Christine via overnight letter.

Their love, however, didn't die. After Danny and Phyllis split and Chris's wedding to Paul was delayed, Christine, for once, did something selfish. The skies opened and the seas parted when Chris had a one-night farewell stand with Danny just before her rescheduled wedding to Paul.

"Any little bit of badness was so exciting to play," Lauralee recalls of the fling. "Some viewers were shocked, but I think most were cheering."

It was also, perhaps, Bill's acknowledging that his little girl was growing up.

Lauralee was a star on TV's top soap, but she was always too busy memorizing the next day's script (especially those lengthy courtroom speeches) to warrant any Shannen Doherty-type or Lindsay Lohanesque hijinks. Though, Sally Sussman Morina, with whom Lauralee stayed one summer, recalls covering for her with her parents when she had some late-night dates with Michael Damian. There were also celebrity romances with John Preston (*General Hospital*), Stephen Gregory (Chase, *Y&R*), and, briefly, Scott Baio, who appeared on *Diagnosis Murder* with Lauralee's *Y&R* costar Victoria Rowell (Dru).

"Scott was very intriguing to me, but it was short and sweet," Lauralee says of dating *Happy Days*' Chachi. "He was good in that I was around someone who was very matter-of-fact. We'd be out to dinner and he'd say, 'Do you want the steak or not?' He helped prepare me for my Scott."

Lauralee reconnected with childhood friend Scott Martin when she was looking for a date for the 1996 *Soap Opera Digest Awards*. "Lauralee and I had friends in common," Scott says. "But we didn't know each other that well." He admits that getting a call to attend a Hollywood gala was a tad nerve-racking. "But it wasn't what I feared. Lauralee was still totally normal despite being in L.A. and working in Hollywood. I was amazed. It gave me a desire to get to know her on a different level."

"A sense of serenity came over her when she started dating Scott," Cast says. "It was lovely. Scott's just a cool guy. Lauralee went from being a young adult to a woman."

Scott and Lauralee soon began dating exclusively. They commuted between Los Angeles and Chicago while Scott supported his photography career by bartending. A year later, he proposed.

"My parents had seen me go through some heartbreaking relationships," Lauralee says. "They knew Scott was such a good guy. When you can count on someone, which I can with him, it's worth everything."

The couple wed in Santa Barbara on October 4, 1997, in an intimate affair attended by family and close friends. Bill couldn't help but have a little fun with the bridegroom at the rehearsal dinner.

"Scott's walking around like this is a done deal," Bill joked. "Scott, you never once, not once, asked me outright for my daughter's hand in marriage—much less the rest of her!

"I couldn't be happier, Scott, at Lauralee's choice," Bill poignantly hastened to add. "Next to her mother, Lauralee is the most precious girl I have. The greatest wish I could have for the two of you is that you have the kind of marriage that Lee and I have. We love you enormously."

"Lauralee and Scott had the most beautiful wedding," recalls Cast. "It wasn't 'industry' at all. She kept it small. She'd done all the work beforehand so when the weekend came, everything just fell into place." Father and daughter danced to Bob Carlisle's "Butterfly Kisses" at the reception.

Lauralee's hard work at *Y&R* was paying off, too. She was a nominee at the 1999 *Soap Opera Digest Awards*, along with *B&B*'s Bobbie Eakes and *ATWT*'s Lauren Martin for Best Supporting Actress. *GL*'s Grant Aleksander and Beth Ehlers read Lauralee's name as the winner. Her classy speech hit all the right notes as she thanked the magazine's editors, the fans, *Y&R*'s producers, writers, directors, Cathy Tomas, cast and crew, Scott, her "wonderfully protective brothers," and also "Mr. and Mrs. Bell, whose greatest success is in being 'Mom and Dad.'"

Soon, Lauralee and Scott began planning their own family. "I said to her, 'Just do it,'" recalls Byrne of advising her pal over lunch at the Formosa Café in Hollywood. "You'll be so happy you did. Show business doesn't go away, but the opportunity to have children does."

Lauralee returned to *Y&R* after she gave birth to son Christian James in 2001 and daughter Samantha Lee in 2002. On the show, Chris and Paul's relationship survived her one-night stand with Danny as well as Phyllis's other machinations, but the couple's marriage was torn apart courtesy of temptress Isabella Brana.

Even after having Paul's baby, Isabella was threatened by Chris and Paul's undying love. She tried to frame Chris for her "murder."

Later, a knife-wielding Isabella attempted to drown the legal eagle in her own bathtub.

Michael and Paul saved Chris. Isabella was institutionalized while her portrayer, Eva Longoria, went on to find fame on Wisteria Lane as one of ABC's *Desperate Housewives*. Chris broke things off with fiancé Michael after he confessed to once being in cahoots with the sociopath. Soon, Chris moved overseas to work in corporate law while Lauralee happily reported for duty at her children's kindergarten classes. She opened a clothing store on Beverly Boulevard (aptly named "On Beverly") not far from CBS. She later moved her boutique to Sunset Boulevard for a few more years.

Brad lured his sister to *B&B* for a series of episodes in 2007 when character Ridge was in a legal jam. Lauralee returned to *Y&R* for a short stint in summer 2010 as Christine reunited with Paul and Nina, who were then dating, and Phillip, who turned out not to have died back in 1989. She reprised the role again in 2011.

Lauralee has stepped behind the camera, too, as creator and producer of the Web series *Family Dinner* and *Just Off Rodeo*. The former has attracted guest stars including Shirley Jones and Cloris Leachman. Lauralee maintains her parents' work ethic, sensibilities, and attention to detail.

"My dad was always approachable and still maintained being the boss," Lauralee says. "He never made anyone feel like a certain job was more important than another."

Chapter 10

FROM "RAGS" TO RICHES

Bill said to his father, "We should own our own business and leverage your standing in the creative community." That's how The Bold and the Beautiful *came to be.*

—Maria Arena Bell, executive producer and head writer, *The Young and the Restless*

Michael Brockman missed out on a chance to work with Bill Bell while at ABC Daytime in the early '70s when ABC passed on *Y&R*.

He wasn't about to let that happen again in his new position as head of CBS Daytime. After joining CBS in 1982, Brockman examined the network's soap-opera lineup. He saw a potential weak link in *Capitol*, which had debuted a few weeks before his arrival.

Stephen and Elinor Karpf, *Capitol*'s creators, tapped into the country's fascination with celebrity politics in creating the half-hour serial. Former movie star Ronald Reagan was president of the United States. His ex-wife, Jane Wyman, headlined the nighttime soap *Falcon Crest*.

The political-themed soap opera was owned and helmed by John Conboy, who'd been instrumental in developing the groundbreaking and critically acclaimed "look" of *Y&R* for Bill.

Capitol debuted with an hour-long primetime special on Friday, March 26, 1982 (coincidentally *Y&R*'s ninth anniversary), and began airing in its regular time slot the following Monday between *ATWT* and *GL*. The glitzy serial had all the elements of a successful soap opera—warring families (the Cleggs and the McCandlesses), star-crossed lovers (Trey and Sloane), and powerful matriarchs (played by Constance Towers and Carolyn Jones).

The show taped across the hall from *Y&R* at CBS Television City. The two soap operas had similar tones in terms of direction, lighting, and production design.

"If you didn't know better, you'd think that *Capitol* was a Bill Bell show," says Meredith Berlin.

However, the sudser had five different head-writing regimes in its five-year history. The constant turnover contributed to instability.

Brockman was concerned about the show's long-term viability. "John Conboy has a unique touch, a distinctive eye in look, casting, and style," the executive says. "Despite a certain appeal about the show's design, there was enormous confusion, disorganization insofar as the writing went. The core of the show was in trouble. We tried to fix it."

As those efforts were failing, Brockman approached Bill. "I said, 'Not now, but very probably, somewhere in the next few years we may need another show, and I don't want it to be from anyone else. I want it to be you.'"

Initially, Bill wasn't interested in creating another show. Brockman said that his door was always open. A few years later, Bill let him know that the time had come. "I've been thinking about it," Bill said. He handed the exec some pages.

Brockman wanting another show coincided with the younger Bill Bell's idea that his father's writing talent could and should serve as the foundation for a family business.

"My father's hope was always to be able to have a real ownership stake in a show," Bill Jr. says. "He once said that he wished we could all have a business together, maybe own a restaurant."

Father and son fleshed out the idea when they drove from Chicago to Los Angeles in fall 1985 for the wedding of *Y&R* producer Edward Scott and Melody Thomas, the show's beloved and impulsive Nikki since 1979.

Despite having parents and two siblings in the creative end of show business, Bill Jr. always gravitated towards the business end. "It's more than just numbers," he clarifies. "I'm connecting to all aspects of the production. It's not the same feeling you have when you're performing or writing, but it's really been satisfying for me."

"He's a business guy at heart," says Maria Arena Bell, who wed Bill on September 11, 1993, in Aspen. "He's a numbers guy. I would never do a business storyline without Bill's input."

Bill is an interviewer's dream, highly quotable but, ironically, preferring to keep a low profile. He even had his name removed from the title page on all *B&B* scripts in the early '90s after learning his handle appeared on them as director of business affairs. Bill sampled performing in high school with a role in a production at the Lyric Opera in Chicago. As a toddler, he also made a few appearances on Lee's talk show.

"I learned very early on that I have no talent at all for performing," Bill says, chuckling. He says he has vague recollections of visiting his mother at the studio and remembers seeing a copy of a Chicago newspaper's TV guide that he was on the cover of with his mother.

Bill and Lee encouraged their firstborn's financial acumen. "They turned to him for business advice even when he was a teenager," Maria says. "They'd ask, 'What does Bill think?' It was to everyone's benefit that Bill had the ability to utilize his dad's talent. Bill and Lee empowered Bill as a young man in a way that I don't think many parents would."

Prior to the creation of *B&B*, Bill hadn't fully owned his own show. "Soap operas weren't a business to my father. They were his career. He was a highly talented and well-paid writer."

After the Scott wedding, the younger Bill decided to remain in Los Angeles and study the business end of soap operas by observing production at *Y&R*.

"I told my father, 'I'll learn as much as I can, and you create the show.'" However, Bill made one creative contribution to his parents' new serial. Inspired by Palm Beach neighbor Leslie Wexler, who created The Limited clothing line, Bill suggested to his dad that the new show be set in the universe of high-end clothing. "I thought there was wealth and glamour in that world," he says.

Fashion wasn't a totally unfamiliar backdrop in soaps. Colleen Zenk's character, Barbara Ryan, had created the label "Simply Barbara" on *ATWT* in 1985. Also, NBC's failed sudser *Morning Star* featured designer Katy Eliot in the mid-1960s. But no drama had utilized the world of first-class couture the way *B&B* has, as evidenced by the show's new opening titles where the main characters are literally watching a fashion show.

The fashion backdrop prompted Bill to use a working title of *Rags*, slang for the garment industry, for the show. He later decided it was too irreverent and came up with *The Bold and the Beautiful*.

"I started trying it out on people and got not just favorable response[s], but very, very positive responses," Bill said.

The show was originally set in Chicago, but Bill and Lee moved the locale to Los Angeles to take advantage of glamorous exteriors in southern California. (The Bells' Beverly Hills home serves as the exterior of the Forrester mansion.)

Bill and Lee wrote the *B&B* bible in Los Angeles, just as they had done with *Y&R*'s treatment. The new document, dated January 1986, was shorter (thirty-nine pages compared to *Y&R*'s sixty-five), had wider margins, and contained handwritten notes.

"It was not a huge document," Bill Jr. said. "If you took my parents' names off it and made a judgment on the material alone, CBS would have had a harder time building confidence in it."

Brockman says that anyone else who'd submitted a document with handwritten edits on it would have prompted him to say, "Next!" *Rags*, however, had nine irresistible words on its title page—"Created by William J. Bell and Lee Phillip Bell."

"Bill didn't just hand me the pages," Brockman recalls. "He talked me through it."

Brockman did what he thought any smart executive would have done with Bill Bell in his office pitching a new soap opera.

"I just sat back and let him talk. I got out of his way."

Bill and Lee's show was given the go-ahead. They reached out to Bill Glenn, a former *Y&R* director, to serve as director-production consultant and also to Gail Kobe, fresh off an executive producing stint at *Guiding Light*. Bill was getting a top-notch talent in Kobe, who, along with head writer Pamela Long, had brought *GL* to the number-one spot for three weeks in 1984, displacing *GH* as the ranking champ.

Kobe and the three Bills (Bell, Bell, and Glenn) met at Le Dome restaurant on Sunset Boulevard to get things started. Bill Jr. began negotiating the licensing deal for the series with CBS.

Brad Bell, who'd been writing at *Y&R*, became a member of *B&B*'s original writing staff, which Bill limited to himself, Brad, senior *Y&R* writer Jack Smith, and actress-writer Meg Bennett, who had played Julia Newman on *Y&R*.

"It was a juggling act, writing both shows," Bill recalls of his father turning out ninety minutes of daily drama. "But he could work with

Jack in a very shorthanded way. He could give Jack a brief outline, and [he'd] turn it into a script."

Capitol went out with a bang, figuratively, if not literally, on Friday, March 20, 1987. Head writer James Lipton deliberately kept the finale open-ended. Viewers never knew if Sloane was executed by a firing squad in a foreign country or if she somehow survived.

"I'm never telling!" Lipton groused about the heroine's final fate in the press room at the Creative Arts ceremony for the 2007 Daytime Emmys in Hollywood, apparently still peeved over the show being axed. It was tough for the *Capitol* gang to be voted out of office, but Conboy knew that he'd been replaced by the best.

"For a show to be number one," he told *Soap Opera Digest* in 1992, "it takes a lot of things, the first being wonderful storytelling. You need Scheherazade, and if you can't get her, you need Bill Bell."

The Bold and the Beautiful debuted on Monday, March 23, 1987, at 1:30 p.m. Eastern Time. There were minor changes made to the show's original treatment. The Forresters were first called the "Chandlers." Bill planned to call the Logan clan the "Stevens" family. Ex-college sweethearts Eric and Beth, torn apart in college by Eric marrying his pregnant girlfriend, Stephanie, were set to become a front-burner couple on the show. Viewers, however, quickly became more interested in seeing Stephanie succeed in keeping her marriage intact than they were in witnessing Eric and Beth's reunion.

The middle-aged Forrester matriarch used her wits, wealth, passion, and persistence to keep the couple apart. Stephanie found an unwilling ally (and punching bag) in her quest—Beth's own daughter Brooke. If she didn't convince her mother to move on from Eric and reunite with her estranged husband, then Stephanie would alienate her son Ridge from Brooke. Beth and Brooke were sympathetic, but the audience saw Stephanie's point that they were both "consummate opportunists"—out to snare men who arguably did not belong to them.

Bill not only had Stephanie win, but he made sure that she succeeded in style. First, she hired private eye Conway Weston to locate Stephen, Beth's wayward husband. Then, Steph urged her pal Bill Spencer, a publishing magnate, to offer the Logan patriarch a lucrative job in Paris. Finally, she tactfully urged Beth to go there with him by pointing out to her how romantic it would be to be in Paris in the spring with a man who loved her.

"Viewers related to Stephanie having control," says John McCook, who plays Eric. "Women at that age don't always feel that they do. Stephanie is fiercely protective of her family. Bill Bell saw Susan [Flannery] playing that and he ran with it." Beth was out of the picture, but the intense rivalry between Brooke and Stephanie became—and remains—*B&B*'s dominant relationship just as the Kay-Jill and Victor-Jack dynamics are at *Y&R*.

The greatest challenge a new soap opera faces is getting viewers to feel like the characters on it are relatable old friends so they'll want to tune in tomorrow. *Capitol* concluded with long-running couple Sam and Myrna Clegg headed for a bitter divorce. Bill quickly conveyed to his audience that the union between Eric and Stephanie was equally miserable in *B&B*'s first few episodes by inserting the word "malaise" into the couple's dialogue:

> "Do you get anything out of our marriage? Anything at all?" Eric asked Stephanie in the series' second episode.
> "For you to ask—suggests that you don't," Stephanie replied.
> "I asked for your honesty," Eric shot back. "Don't you feel it, too? The apathy? The malaise?"

"When I saw the word 'malaise,' I thought it was something you put on a sandwich," McCook quips. "As it turns out, it's not. Bill had us saying that word, and it was capitalized in print in the scripts." The word appeared in on-air promos that CBS broadcast to introduce the series to viewers, too.

The uncomfortable moments between husband and wife, which took place in the landmark Forrester living-room set, spoke instantly to the couple's strained union. The pair was brand new to daytime, but Bill made viewers feel as if they were eavesdropping on private conversations between familiar favorites, a husband and wife who were more than ready to call it a day.

"Many writers can't do this, but Bill was able to establish the real depth of history between these characters within three or four episodes," McCook says. "If you watched them, you understood everything that you needed to know about Eric and Stephanie."

The matriarch could have easily become universally despised, but she—and her portrayer—gained a loyal audience as Stephanie continued to scheme and manipulate. "What was strikingly original was the performance of Susan Flannery as Stephanie Forrester—a fascinating alabaster sphinx of a woman," wrote Christopher Schemering in 1987.

Bill originally conceived Caroline Forrester, played with Grace Kelly-perfection by Joanna Johnson, as a short-term character. He changed his mind upon seeing Johnson's nuanced performances. Critics applauded his choice, and *Soap Opera Digest* called Johnson's Caroline "Best Daytime Casting" in 1987.

"It's a big mistake to commit too far in advance," Bill said of planning how long a character might be around. "You're closing opportunity. You're going along a course [with] many byroads that could end up becoming a heck of a lot better than the road you were going to initially take."

An original concept that Bill had in *B&B*'s proposal and brought to its full potential is the character of Ridge, played by Ronn Moss. The affable actor's chiseled cheekbones and ability to seem enigmatic have helped make him a domestic fan favorite as well as an international superstar. Viewers in Barbados followed Moss as if he were the Pied Piper when the show shot on location there in 1996. Moss and other cast members of the show require bodyguards when they visit Italy, the show's most popular international market.

"Ridge should emerge as the super-stud of daytime," Bill wrote. "Ridge has a little black book that Warren Beatty would kill for."

Bill may have wanted Ridge to give Beatty a run for his money, but, as far as Moss was concerned, Bill was the movie star. "Bill reminded me of Paul Newman," the actor says. "He had the same intensely blue eyes that seemed to look through to your soul."

As for his first impression of Lee, Moss says with a smile, "She reminded me of an angel. Still does."

Bill Jr. didn't work creatively with his father the way his siblings did, but they had their own dynamic. "My father and I totally trusted each other," Bill said. "I never wanted to tread on his area and he never wanted to tread on mine. He wasn't someone who liked the financial issues of the soap-opera world. He was much happier being in the creative domain."

The younger Bill explored the show's international potential. "The timing of *B&B* and world history was very good," Brad explains. "The world was opening up to democracy and capitalism."

New World Television, *B&B*'s original overseas distributor, was also selling an eight-hour miniseries *Queenie*, which starred Kirk Douglas and Mia Sara. As a bonus to stations that bought it, New World also gave them the first 250 episodes of *B&B*—for free. "We sat on shelves across the world, and eventually they'd try us," Brad says. "We caught on here and there."

And, soon, everywhere! *B&B* has become the most widely

watched dramatic series in the world. The show hit in Greece first, then Italy. The show was named the "Most Popular Daytime TV Soap—Current" by Guinness World Records in May 2010.

Bill's dramatic-serial writing and Lee's broadcasting career provided a solid income, enabling them to raise a family, build a summer home in Lake Geneva, and live in the coveted Gold Coast section of Chicago. *Time* magazine speculated in 1976 that Bill alone was earning more than a million dollars a year.

Creating the international hit *B&B*, however, catapulted the Bell family into a new financial realm.

"Financially, it's been a great savior to us," Brad says.

"It's a tremendous thing," Bill Jr. concurs.

But Bill and Lee taught their children to always stay grounded, emphasizing morals, values, and a strong work ethic.

"Money has never been stressed in our family," Lee said. "We don't think, 'how much are you making?' All we know is we're fulfilling what we want to do. That is one of the greatest luxuries in the world."

After moving to Los Angeles, Bill Jr. entertained the idea of finding an apartment for his family to live in, but he says, "It didn't take long to realize that L.A. was a city of homes."

He helped his parents select a property that was connected to Hollywood lore. The new family home, once owned by actor Charles Boyer, had many other famous occupants including Katharine Hepburn, Clare Booth Luce, and Cary Grant. Howard Hughes is said to be a former resident, as well. According to *Los Angeles* magazine, Gower Champion bought the estate in 1973. The Bells acquired it from European Asian Bank for $3.5 million in 1986.

The family moved into their new home just in time to celebrate Lauralee's birthday in December. The entire family lived at the same residence, just like the Abbotts do on *Y&R* and the Ewings on *Dallas* did, though Bill Jr. and Brad each had their own guest houses on the property.

"It was so ironic and hilarious that the Bells lived like a real soap-opera family does," says Maria, who met Lee and Lauralee first at a luncheon before meeting her future husband at a birthday party for a mutual friend.

Upon learning of Maria's background in fashion (her stepfather worked in the fashion industry as a *garmento*), Lee recommended her future daughter-in-law for a consulting gig at *B&B* to lend additional authenticity to the show's fashion backdrop. Meanwhile, Lauralee fixed Maria up with her brother. "They were all always so relaxed and lovely," Maria says. "It felt natural and comfortable being around them."

In 1989, Bill teamed Brad and Maria as writers at *B&B*. Jack Smith turned out four scripts a week while Brad and Maria collaborated on the fifth. They were a team but also independent of each other. Maria, an art aficionado, is the former chair and current president of P.S. Arts, which provides art instruction for schoolchildren, and also cochair of the board of trustees at the Museum of Contemporary Art in Los Angeles. She jokingly hung a copy of artist Roy Lichtenstein's "Drowning Girl" over her desk at *B&B*. The print shows a troubled woman being swept up in waves, proclaiming in a thought bubble, "I don't care! I'd rather sink—than call Brad for help!"

Being tied to Bill and Lee's children through marriage, work, and friendship gives Maria a unique perspective on the Bell siblings. "Bill and Lauralee are more similar, despite the fact that she's an actress and he's behind the scenes. Lauralee doesn't crave attention. She's very shy and quiet, but to know her is to love her. She doesn't let a million people get too close. Brad is more gregarious and friendly. Anyone who's a friend to any of them is lucky because it takes some work to get to know them. They grew up in a unique setting."

B&B climbed quickly in the ratings. In May 1990, the show took the number-three spot, an impressive accomplishment given that the show was still a relative newcomer to the daytime scene.

Bill dipped his toe into uncharted waters on the July 4, 1991, episode of *B&B* when he had Felicia Forrester comment on sister-in-law Macy's bathing suit at a pool party.

"Thanks," Macy replied. "I got it at Fenmore's West."

"Fenmore's West?"

Y&R viewers know that Fenmore's is the name of the department store run by Tracey Bregman's character, Lauren Fenmore, in Genoa City. With that one reference, Bill established that his two shows existed in the same universe.

A year later, Bill decided to firm up that connection by bringing Sheila Carter, one of his most successful characters, from *Y&R* over to *B&B*, unleashing her on the unsuspecting Forresters in the process. The deadly but sympathetic antagonist was given a portion of screen time that had been, until now, reserved for *B&B* characters only. Asking his half-hour soap's fans to accept a persona from another show was asking a lot.

As usual, though, Bill had a plan.

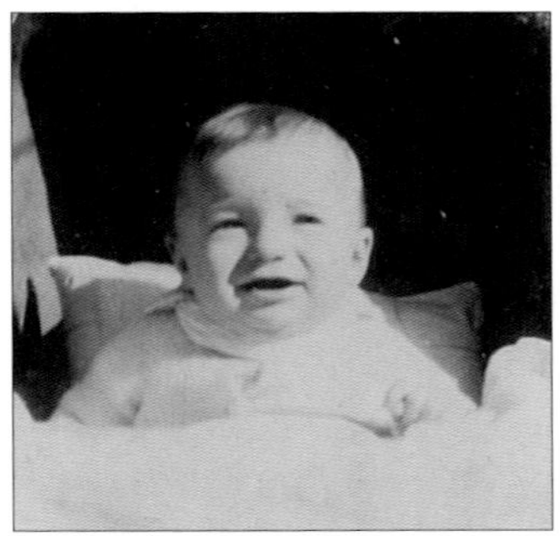

Bill at seven months old (1927)

Bill in his Navy uniform (1945)

Bill with best man Jerry Birn (1954)

Bill and Lee's wedding (1954)

Cast of As the World Turns *(early 1960s)*

Bill and Lee with Bill, Jr. (1962)

Lee with Lucille Ball on her Chicago talk show

Bill with cast of Days of our Lives *(early 1970s)*

Bill at his typewriter with Bill, Jr., Brad, and Lauralee in the background (early 1970s)

The cast of Y&R *(1974)*

Bill, Lee, and John Conboy at the Daytime Emmys (1975)

Lee outside Chicago's Water Tower in a WBBM-TV advertisement

Bill and Lee dancing (1980s)

Bill and the Y&R company at the 1986 Daytime Emmys celebrating their win for Outstanding Drama Series and their (short-lived) victory for Outstanding Drama Series Writing

The Bold and the Beautiful *cast photo (1987)*

One of Bill's most popular storylines on Y&R *was the George Rawlins murder mystery, featuring the characters of Paul (Doug Davidson) and Cassandra (Nina Arvesen) (late 1980s)*

Lauralee on the cover of Soap Opera Digest *"Soap Sweeties" issue (1990)*

Bill Bell with his Daytime Emmy for head-writing Y&R *(1992)*

"Past and Present" cast photo from The Young and the Restless *twentieth anniversary party (1993)*

Bill walks Lauralee down the aisle (1997)

Lee, Bill, Patty Weaver, and Jerry Birn (1997)

Jeanne Cooper, Bill, and Jess Walton celebrate a Y&R *milestone (1998)*

Bill Bell and Kay Alden, celebrating Y&R *being rated #1 for 500 weeks (1998)*

The Bell family's holiday card (2004)

Photo of Bill and Lee that hangs in the hallway at CBS Television City

Chapter 11

THE SON ALSO WRITES

I'm fantastically proud of Bradley.

—Bill Bell to *Soap Opera Digest* in honor of *B&B*'s tenth anniversary, 1997

While playing outside, an eight-year-old boy chases his older brother into the street. He's struck by a car going 40 miles per hour. The boy sails into the air and strikes the pavement—head first and hard. A grief-stricken father races to his son's side.

At the hospital, a doctor tells the father he can't come into the operating room while a surgical team attempts to save his son's eye.

This sounds like a dramatic set-up that came from Bill's typewriter, but it was, in fact, a real-life drama that occurred when Brad and his brother were playing outside in Chicago near the family's apartment. A car came racing along East Lake Shore Drive and hit Brad. Fortunately, unlike Addie Horton's on *Days of our Lives*, Brad's auto incident wasn't fatal.

The apartment doorman quickly informed Bill and Lee of the accident. While Lee stayed with Lauralee, shielding her from the tragedy, Bill, still in his bathrobe and slippers, raced out into the street.

"I saw my father's Gucci loafers coming toward me," Brad recalls. "He couldn't stop sliding and he fell right on top of me. My dad said he wanted to go into the surgery room with me but they told him no, he couldn't.

"I remember being in the operating room. I felt the surgical thread on my face. I looked up and saw my father wearing a mask. My mom was there, too."

Brad stayed out of school for a few weeks while his eye made a full recovery, but the pre-adolescent didn't yet have an interest in his father's soap operas. "They just weren't meant for someone my age," he muses. A few years later, however, Brad's interest began to grow. Bill gave his son his first job in soap operas—collating *Y&R* scripts.

Bill used to type his scripts on a form that had six copies underneath, separated by pieces of carbon paper. "The last one was so faint you could barely read it," Brad says. "Whoever got that one had to use a magnifying glass."

Bill promoted Brad to a summer job of sitting in on story conferences with his writers when he was sixteen. Brad reported for work each morning at 8 a.m. and worked until 6 p.m., just as his father had with Irna Phillips.

"You had to be brave to get a word in or throw out an idea," Brad said. "It became fascinating for me. I liked exploring the interactions between families and lovers."

Mostly, he listened and absorbed. "There wasn't time for me to say anything," he laughs. "They didn't want to hear what I had to say."

After high school, Brad enrolled at the University of Colorado. He attended the University of Wisconsin and also UCLA, so he could be closer to *Y&R*. Brad got a feel for what went on at the show by doing extra work. He wrote for *Y&R* before joining *B&B* as a writer and later became associate producer.

When Brad wrote some sample sitcom scripts for *Charles in Charge* and *Family Ties*, Al Burton, executive producer of the former series, offered him a three-script deal. Brad proudly shared the news with his father, but Bill wasn't laughing—or even smiling.

"I thought my dad would be thrilled by the offer, but he wasn't," Brad shares. Bill told his son that he had to make a choice—either commit to the family business or don't. Brad took a few days to think it over before selecting soaps over sitcoms.

"More than anything, I loved working with my father," Brad says. Bill was, of course, thrilled by his son's choice. "All right," Bill said. "Let's get to work!"

The two scribes became inseparable. Two heads of blond hair could be seen popping out of a white convertible as father and son drove from Beverly Hills east along Beverly Boulevard and into the CBS parking lot. Along the way, they'd talk about the Forresters, the Logans, and Sally Spectra.

"We spent so much time together," Brad says. Bill would work on one of his shows until the early afternoon and would then switch over to the other. They'd write until 5 or 6 p.m. Then it was time for Martinis. They'd watch tapes of the shows during dinner.

"He'd yell at the TV," Brad recalls. "Episodes were either wonderful or horrible. He'd say, 'How the hell can they do that? The pacing is so slow!' Or he'd say, 'That's beautiful!' He had strong opinions about everything."

Brad was always taking notes, scrambling to find any scrap of paper on which he could write. He'd relay his father's thoughts and decisions to *B&B*'s control-booth producers on what needed improving, which characters had to change, and occasionally, which ones had to be recast. "My dad was involved in every element of production," Brad says.

"For about the first year, I frustrated the hell out of Bradley," Bill said. "I didn't use any of his stuff because I didn't feel he was quite ready for it."

Brad turned to Lee when he and his father had conflicts. "She's great because I could talk to her and say, 'Look, he's driving me crazy,'" Brad told *Soap Opera Digest*'s Roberta Caploe in 1993. "My dad would do the same thing with her, so she was the person in the middle saying, 'This is where your father is coming from, and I know you're working hard, but he feels you need another couple of months before he's ready to entrust you any further.' She functions as the quiet voice who always keeps everything running well."

"Being my son was, in many respects, a disadvantage for Bradley," Bill mused. "His work was more closely scrutinized than it would have been if he were someone whose name wasn't Bell. By the time everything connected, it was great, because there was minimal editing and rewriting."

Bill groomed Brad to become both head writer and executive producer of *B&B*, but Brad didn't wait for his father to hand him the gigs. He initiated the transition soon after his 1991 marriage to childhood sweetheart Colleen Bradley.

"Our honeymoon was very brief," Brad says.

The show lost valuable lead time when Bill and Lee took a rare vacation to attend the 1992 Winter Olympics in Albertville, France. While Bill and Lee watched ice skater Kristi Yamaguchi and other pros compete for world records, Brad was back in the United States going for his own gold. He and Jack Smith decided to write the next ten episodes of *B&B* without Bill's input.

"We almost felt like criminals," Brad says of the semi-subterfuge. When Bill returned, anxious to get moving on scripts, Brad told him they were actually further ahead than Bill thought they were. "I know where to take these characters," Brad confidently assured his father.

Bill read the scripts and was impressed with what Brad had written. He not only agreed that his son was ready to take the show over, but he also decided to become a coconspirator. Bill continued to give Brad more control, but he didn't tell the network—not right away.

"Eyebrows would have been raised by CBS executives if they'd known," Brad says. "They would have asked, 'Is he qualified?'" In time, Bill went to the network and told them that Brad was taking over as head writer. Later, Bill turned the executive producing reins over to his son, too. The network had no objections since Brad was already effectively performing in those capacities.

"They were fine with it," Brad recalls. "The show was doing well and we were inching up the ratings ladder."

Bill and Brad brought *B&B* to the number-two spot in the ratings in fall 1992. An explosive confrontation between two characters from *Y&R*, Lauren and Sheila, moved the show up to a 6.8 rating with a 25 percent share of the audience. Bill threw in a twist nobody saw coming—the fight was in reality a nightmare of Sheila's, which allowed the two women's actual reunion to take place over on *Y&R*.

Delaying a payoff, as Bill had done with Lauren and Sheila, was one of the many disciplines that Brad learned from his father. Keeping a healthy distance from his actors was another.

"That was very beneficial to my father," Brad says. "A lot of writers feel this way. The character is the character. There is no one else. Sometimes it's helpful to meet with an actor so you can notice something organic about them, but it's better to keep a distance and see Eric Braeden as 'Victor Newman.'"

This philosophy is one of the reasons that Bill referred to actors by their character names. "He knew the characters intimately," Brad says. "He didn't want to go any further, not because he didn't like them personally, but because he loved the characters.

"My father was passionate, outspoken, and he brought in the

ratings," Brad adds. "He had a vision and the networks could see that. He knew soap operas better than they did, and they wisely let him do what he did."

Bill's decisions were final. He cast Hunter Tylo on *B&B* in the role of Dr. Taylor Hayes to help fill the void left by Joanna Johnson in 1990.

Bill had Tylo read for him both as a Caroline replacement and as her doctor during the audition process.

"I came into the room, and there was the whole Bell family and some of the producers," Tylo recalls. "They asked me if I were willing to dye my hair blond. I said, 'No, I'm trying to change my image.' There was an awkward pause. Later, Bill said to me, 'Has anyone ever told you that you're beautiful?' I still laugh about that today. It wasn't a pickup line. It sounded like a young man who had just gotten out in the world and was meeting people. It was sweet and innocent. He genuinely meant it."

Shortly into her tenure as Taylor, Tylo contracted the chicken pox and was temporarily recast with Sherilyn Wolter, best known for her turns as heroine Celia Quartermaine on *General Hospital* and the evil Elena on *Santa Barbara*. The amicable actress walked into the role, playing key scenes related to Ridge and Taylor's developing romance with Ronn Moss admirably. She had proven chemistry with Taylor's other love interest Storm Logan, played by her former *GH* leading man Brian Patrick Clarke. In fact, Wolter fit in so easily and so quickly with everyone at the show that personnel began wondering if Bill would keep her on in the part. After all, viewers hadn't yet become too invested in Tylo's portrayal of Taylor, and the actress's unique personality hadn't quite yet meshed with the show's tight-knit cast.

"Hunter is Taylor," Bill said, squashing the speculation of a permanent switch.

"That's awesome," Tylo says, learning that Bill was on her side. "It's very flattering."

"My father had fallen for Hunter's beauty and confidence," Brad recalls. "After her reading, he said, 'Did you see who just walked out of the room? That's our Dr. Taylor Hayes.'"

"I remember loving having Sherilyn with us and wishing they'd find another part for her," Ronn Moss recalls. "I don't remember anything about anyone wanting to 'replace' Hunter. As Bill said, 'Hunter is Taylor.'"

Tylo returned and went on to emerge as one of *B&B*'s most popular stars. The Brooke-Ridge-Taylor triangle became a focal point of the show in the '90s (and continues today), just as the Caroline-Ridge-Brooke story had been in the '80s.

"My dad would think long and hard about something and then make his decision," Brad said. "People would say, 'Okay. Bill knows. He sees something.'"

Just as his parents' courtship began with a miscommunication, so did Brad's adult relationship with his wife, Colleen. The two had shared a teen romance and were "completely, madly, and innocently in love," Colleen recalls. They drifted apart after Brad moved to Los Angeles. He called her one day to wish her well on her upcoming wedding. Colleen, however, hadn't gotten engaged.

She told him that she was coming to L.A. on business and a dinner date was made. By the time the appetizers arrived, the former teen sweethearts knew they were getting hitched.

"It was this underlying thing that we both felt," Colleen says. "Neither of us liked the long-distance thing."

Brad and Colleen wed on October 4, 1991, at St. Athanasius Roman Catholic Church in Evanston, Illinois. Colleen's sister, Shannon, who later joined *B&B*'s production and writing staffs, was maid of honor. Brad's brother was his best man. After their brief honeymoon in Hawaii, Colleen, who'd given up a lucrative position in marketing, joined the *B&B* production staff in the show's most demanding position (short of her husband's position as head writer). Colleen worked at the show's reception desk. After a short stint of fielding telephone calls, greeting visitors to the show, assisting Lee, and performing a myriad of other challenging tasks, Colleen quickly moved up to positions in casting and production in the control booth.

"I was the most inspired and fulfilled working in the booth," Colleen says.

Brad and Colleen have four children: Chasen, Caroline, Charlotte, and Oliver. After Charlotte was born, Colleen took a step back from working daily at *B&B*. In 2012, Colleen rejoined the show's production team as an associate producer. She serves a role similar to the one Lee did with Bill by providing Brad with information he can incorporate into the show's social issues, such as for Agnes Jones' DNA rape-kit storyline.

Colleen also consults with the show's costumer and donates time with various social organizations, including Best Buddies. She's lobbied on behalf of legislation to combat mercury poisoning and support climate control.

"Brad's first priority is to entertain," she says. "He brings light to issues he cares about, too." Brad's tackled alcoholism, gambling, HIV, child abuse, Alzheimer's disease, and the plight of the homeless, but he's careful not to turn the half-hour soap into a public service announcement. "There have been many things presented to him over the years, but he won't do them if it feels contrived," Colleen says.

Bill certainly told provocative storylines. He had Marie Horton fall in love with her own brother on *Days* and wrote Vanessa Prentiss jumping to her death on *Y&R*. Jack Smith feels that Brad has taken even greater risks as a writer, citing Bridget falling for her former brother Ridge (a man she once thought was her father), Amber not knowing if Rick or Raymond had fathered her child, and Brooke having accidental sex with Oliver (her daughter's boyfriend) as examples.

Bill served as executive story consultant on *B&B* after Brad took over as head writer. He approved of his son pushing the envelope. "Bill was always proud of the job that Brad was doing," Smith says.

"Bill saw a natural talent in Brad," concurs Colleen. "It wasn't just because he was his son. Bill truly respected Brad as a writer and a colleague."

Chapter 12

BILL AND JILL WENT UP A HILL

On Y&R, *Bill has employed 38,596 extras, 7,904 actors with under five lines, 9,984 day players, and 324 contract players. And he remembers only one name—Brenda Dickson [ex-Jill,* Y&R*].*

—John McCook (Eric, *B&B*) at a roast of Bill Bell at Chasen's restaurant on February 10, 1992

If Bill had continued to write comedy instead of going into advertising and soap operas, he still would have ended up hiring both John McCook and Jeanne Cooper. The two actors are blessed with the ability to make biting remarks that might sound mean if they came from anyone else. But with McCook and Cooper, well, they're just plain funny.

So Bill chuckled heartily at McCook's quip over him only remembering Dickson's name, (A) because it wasn't true and (B) because of the actor's deadpan delivery.

Plus, Bill had successfully recast the seemingly irreplaceable role five years earlier.

Soap Opera NOW! reported in its June 15, 1987, issue that Dickson was out at *Y&R* and that Jess Walton was in as the new Jill Foster Abbott. Bill wasn't in the habit of going public with backstage dramas (he once initiated a press blackout after an immensely tense incident occurred at the studio), but he knew that fans were going to wonder why Katherine was bantering with a new Jill.

"Suffice it to say there were differences in the interpretation of the character [of Jill]," Bill said in a statement.

Letting Dickson go wasn't easy for Bill. "Brenda was an original cast member, and Bill felt a certain loyalty to that," recalls Sally Sussman Morina, who wrote for Bill for five years. "He liked what was being done with Jill, but at some point you can't sacrifice the company for one actress."

NOW! reported that Dickson's "well-publicized prima donna routine, complete with temper tantrums, finally got the better of the powers-that-be." The publication added that Dickson and the soap had always managed to kiss and make up—until now. "When any performer's on-set behavior—be it temperament or preparedness or whatever—becomes a financial as well as emotional burden, meaning long delays in tape that add up to $$$ down the drain, that's usually the last straw."

Cooper recalled sparring with Dickson in the show's early days. "There was a particularly heavy show one day and she was late," Cooper told the author for TVGuide.com in 2000. "After I yelled at her, she said, 'No one's ever talked to me that way.' I said, 'Get used to it. If you don't like it, pretend I'm Shelley Winters.'

"Brenda wouldn't speak to me for three days. I went to her and said, 'Brenda, this is ridiculous. The reason [I yelled] is because you were late and we shoot the show live. Being on time is just professional, honey. If you pull that outside, they'd get rid of you.'"

Kay Alden recalls an instance in which Dickson and the show

weren't on the same page. Bill had written a scene that had a contrite Jill testifying in court so that her illegitimate son, Phillip, could use the Chancellor name.

"We put in the script that Jill needs to dress like Madonna here," Alden recalls, so that the judge would see Jill's motherly love and deep concern for Phillip. "Instead, she came in wearing a low-cleavage, totally inappropriate outfit."

How did Dickson respond to Jill's wardrobe not matching what the script called for?

"You told me to dress like Madonna!"

The ousted actress presented her side of the story in an E! Television episode of *True Hollywood Story* in 2001. She claimed that her firing was the result of being caught in a political war between Bill and two of his West Coast-based writers over how Jill would be portrayed.

"I'm in the middle of all of this," Dickson told E! "It's a tremendous amount of pressure."

While the conflict may have sounded plausible to the casual E! viewer, it's common knowledge in the soap world that Bill's word with the storyline was law.

"It was more in her mind that there were problems between Bill and his writers," Wes Kenney told E! "There is no writer that works for Bill Bell that isn't in complete agreement and understanding of what he's after."

"Bill Bell said that if she stormed off the set, which she had done several times before, she needn't bother coming back," recalled Marguerite Ray, *Y&R*'s original Mamie Johnson.

Dickson recounted becoming ill one day at the studio after banging her side on the edge of a desk after her blocking was changed. She says that William Bell ("She always called Bill 'William,'" recalls one of Bill's writers) and producer Edward Scott came to her dressing room, insisting that she return to the set for taping.

"I tried to tell William Bell, 'Look, I can't even remember the lines at this point,' and that I needed help. They're not going for anything I'm doing. They wanted me out on the set."

Next, Dickson, who had eight weeks left on her contract, was informed by the show that Jill had been recast.

One of Bill's scribes recalls Dickson meeting with Bill, hoping to rectify the situation.

"This was really difficult for Bill," recalls the writer. "He liked Brenda and he knew that she was compelling on screen, but they couldn't work with her at the studio. Bill had no choice. He didn't want to get rid of her, but he wasn't going to enable what was going on. He was smart enough to know that he had to let her go. "The truth is, he kept her on longer than people at the studio wanted him to."

Dickson walked away with a consolation prize. In early 1988, she won the Soap Opera Digest Award for Outstanding Villainess, beating out fan favorites Andrea Evans (*One Life to Live*) and Elizabeth Hubbard (*As the World Turns*).

Dickson wore a sparkling red gown to the televised awards show. On her way to the podium she shared a warm embrace with Cooper, who was on stage ready to present the next award.

"I'm really surprised," Dickson said. "I didn't expect to win. I'd like to thank Jeanne Cooper, who's given me the incentive in many scenes to be a super bitch!" Dickson also thanked the magazine and Dick Clark Productions, which produced the awards show. Her speech, however, made no reference to Bill, *Y&R*, or any of her former coworkers except Cooper.

E! reported that Dickson later filed an $11 million lawsuit against the show for wrongful termination. The suit was dismissed. Years later, Dickson and Bill ran into each other at a restaurant in Chicago and the two shared a cordial reunion.

Dickson's exit came at a time when the show could ill afford to lose

Jill. She was in the thick of the storyline—the rivalry between Kay and Jill had never been greater, and Phillip, Jill's teen son, had been introduced as the show's newest heartthrob. Also, Jill was scheming with her male secretary, David Kimball, to hire a homeless man to romance Katherine.

Bill didn't realize that the answer to his casting conundrum was sitting right on his desk in the form of a demo tape labeled "Jess Walton." He thought Jess was a man. Bill didn't know that was the name of the actress who'd been playing Kelly on *Capitol*. Ironically, Walton's dressing room was right next to Dickson's at CBS.

After viewing Walton's tape, Bill knew immediately that he'd found his new Jill. "We are thrilled to get a talented actress like Jess Walton to play the role of Jill Abbott," he said.

Walton initially mistook her new boss for Tom Palmer, the show's then-casting director. "After I was hired, I'd see Tom in the office and he'd say to me, 'Have you heard anything about how you're doing as Jill?' Thinking he was Bill, I said, 'Well, no. Have *you*?' He said, 'I guess you're doing fine.'"

After Walton finally met Bill, she inquired as to just how dastardly Jill could become. "I asked Bill if Jill could ever kill anyone. He said to me, 'Well, we like to think she wouldn't.'"

Bill's instincts in hiring Walton proved to be correct. The actress's interpretation of Jill has proven to be one of the most successful recasts in daytime serial history. *Soap Opera Digest* proclaimed Walton "Best Recast" of 1987.

Soap Opera NOW! praised Walton's performances in its March 14, 1988, issue, which reviewed Jill's attempt to marry Rex, Kay's beau. "Watching Walton and the gloriously expressive Jeanne Cooper bring the complex Jill-Katherine history to a gripping pre-wedding confrontation, one would never sense that Ms. Walton didn't begin laying the groundwork fifteen years ago and only took up Jill's mantle fairly recently. These two highly skilled actresses are exquisitely matched, nuance for nuance, word for word."

Walton's fellow actors have nominated her five times for Daytime Emmys. Jill was a focal point in the two episodes *Y&R* submitted for Best Drama at the 1999 awards, too. Walton has taken home the gold twice—in 1991 for Outstanding Supporting Actress and in 1997 for Outstanding Lead Actress.

"All I've ever wanted to do in my whole life is to be an actress," Walton said in her 1997 acceptance speech. "I've got you, Mr. Bill Bell, to thank for that. Bill and Lee, thank you for the gift of Jill!"

There was only one instance in which Walton ever, pun intended, pissed Bill off.

"I received a script that had Jill saying to Katherine, 'You are going to tell me where Nina is, but first I need to step away. You've got me so upset my bladder is distended!' I was *horrified*. The convent girl in me didn't want to say that I was going to the bathroom on national TV."

Walton called Bill in his office to discuss her uneasiness. "Bill told me that he'd been saving that line for years," the actress recalls. "He knew someone in the soap opera world who suffered from that condition and he'd always wanted to put it in one of his scripts. But I wasn't sure. I practiced it, but I told Bill I just couldn't say it."

Walton was unaware that Bill's patience—like Jill's bladder—was about to burst. "He says to me, 'Cut the f—ing line.' I hung up and told Jeanne what he said. She looked at me and said, 'Well, now you have to say it!'

"I said it in the scene and took off. Jeanne was in the foreground writing at Katherine's desk. She was brilliant as she looked up into the camera as if to say, 'Did I just hear that?'

"Bill never swore," Walton reflects. "But he did that one time. It was the angriest I ever saw him get. It was so unusual for him."

Bill and Walton's collaboration brought Jill to new heights. He created Jill and Kay's unlikely but logical alliance against Nina, remarried John and Jill, gave her another son (Billy), and linked her romantically, albeit briefly, to Victor. The Kay-Jill feud has never wavered and continues today.

"You never went up to Bill's office and his TV wasn't on," Walton marvels. "He was so connected with what was going on both on the air show and with what was being taped. If you asked him about the story, he'd know exactly what you were talking about. He had his finger on the show. He knew it all. The man was magnificent."

"If Bill saw something he didn't like, he'd call down to the control booth and question it," Christina Knack says. "He was very hands-on every single day. That's a unique quality, to have one eye and ear on one thing and still be able to create and discuss storylines."

In spring 2009, *Y&R* put out a casting call for Jill Abbott after renegotiations with Walton reached an impasse. *Soaps In Depth* magazine contacted Dickson to see if she'd been approached about reprising the role. She had not been, but the actress said that she loved the show and wished it well. Later, that same day, Walton's rep announced that she and the show had come to terms and she'd be continuing on as Jill.

Dickson's exit had been one of the more publicized events in *Y&R*'s history. Producers and writers at every soap opera have had their days interrupted by off-screen conflicts among their stars. One show's executives, in fact, had to deal with the reality that they couldn't pair a romantic duo on screen any longer because the couple's off-screen union had ended badly.

Bill wasn't a fan of having to deal with backstage dramas that took him away from his typewriter. He asked actors to put aside their personal differences, show up on time with lines memorized, and be professional.

Real-life conflicts, while unpleasant, can generate story ideas for writers. Did Bill ever use what he learned about actors' personal lives as jumping-off points for storylines?

Yes. He once wrote a pregnancy into an actress's storyline even though she'd suffered an off-screen miscarriage and she asked Bill not to in case she lost the second baby. Also, Bill wrote marital disharmony into an actor's story after rumors started circulating that the performer's real-life mate, also a performer, had been unfaithful. (And, in fairness to Bill, what character doesn't eventually experience marital infidelity?)

"Bill was great at picking up what was going on with a person and finding a way to incorporate that in the character," says Heather Tom, who played *Y&R*'s Victoria for over a decade and joined *B&B* as Katie in 2007. "We almost felt like our dressing rooms were bugged," the three-time Emmy winner chuckles. "There's definitely intuitiveness with Brad, as well. Bill really cared about the people who worked for him. Brad does, too."

"I don't think if Bill ever heard about something that was going on in an actor's personal life that he'd say, 'Aha! Now, I can mess with this actor,'" says John McCook. "He'd always be thinking of the character. 'Wouldn't this be cool if it happened to the character?' He wasn't about manipulating the actor. If he ever wrote something into the show that was parallel with what was going on in the actor's life, it was done on a subconscious level. It was never done with malice."

But it was still done. "A good writer writes what he knows," says Linda Susman. "The soaps are about the human condition. Writers can't fully divorce themselves from what they may know about actors who bring their characters to life. They'd be passing on opportunities to use raw material to help build stories."

In a perfect world, Bill would have preferred that the actors' private lives remain private, despite the occasional inspiration he'd mine from them.

"Bill was happiest when he was just being inside the characters," Sussman Morina theorizes. "The personal lives were a bit of a hassle to Bill. Writers want to live in the universe they've created. Bill never wanted to deal with issues that took him away from that. When he moved to Los Angeles, it was harder for him to avoid that."

Chapter 13

CHASING EMMY

The Emmys is one evening, and you have the rest of the year where you have the Nielsen's [ratings] once every week, and you go back to your stories and your characters.

—Bill Bell to *Soap Opera Weekly*'s Mark McGarry, 1997

Bill was a celebrated writer who deservedly won many awards during his career, including four Daytime Emmys for Outstanding Writing in a Drama Series (1976, '92, '97, and 2000) and six for Outstanding Drama Series (1975, '83, '85, '86, '93, and 2004).

Those statues, along with Lee's seventeen regional Emmys from Chicago, and her Golden Mike awards, as well as numerous other honors from civic organizations, stand proudly in lit display cases in Bill's study.

There's a recipe for winning in the categories for best show, writing, and directing at the Daytime Emmys that many in the daytime community follow, and they have the golden girls to show for it.

What is that magic formula? Climax multiple stories simultaneously, blow the budget on special effects, and write your episode as succinctly and self-contained as possible. That way, voters who aren't familiar with your show will be able to better follow it and, as a result, will be more likely to vote for it.

Speculation that soaps have been doing this dates back decades. *Soap Opera NOW!* commented in its July 9, 1990, edition that "there's a growing resentment that some shows do one episode a year specifically to enter in the Emmys if the show gets a nomination."

"We don't do that," Bill told the popular newsletter. "We don't do any special episodes for that reason. We submit a typical episode of our show, and I really believe that's what the award should be based on."

Yet some shows have submitted tailor-made episodes for years. Lather. Rinse. Repeat? Not so fast. Savvy soap-opera writers, like Bill, know not to climax all of the storylines at the same time.

"Bill won Emmys, but he didn't write a specific self-contained show to do that," says Margot Wain, CBS Daytime executive. "If you pile everything into one episode, what are you going to do tomorrow? Bill knew the ebb and flow of storyline. As one [storyline] was reaching its climax, another was at the beginning and another was in the middle."

"Bill didn't give a crap about [the] blue-ribbon panels that judged the Emmys," Ken Corday bluntly states. "He wrote for the viewers. Sometimes he'd frustrate them in taking a long time to peel that onion, but as long as they weren't turning away, and they weren't, it was to his advantage.

"Bill's great talent was sprouting a story, [while] bringing another one along that was half grown, but still bearing fruit. [Yet another] story would be at its fruition. That's what he taught [*Days* head writers] Pat Falken Smith and James Reilly. That's the craft. You can't be a one-trick pony because then you're left with a void."

Y&R first took Outstanding Drama Series honors in 1975. Emmy gold came again for Bill the following year when he won for writing

Days. Alas, that win was somewhat bittersweet. While Bill was still a part of the show's team and had contributed long-term story projections, he felt that *Days* was Falken Smith's by this point.

"She had taken control and wanted to do her show," Bill said.

Bill and his scribes, Kay Alden and Elizabeth Harrower, were nominated for *Y&R* in 1979. He and his team received another nod in 1986. That year, he was up against formidable talent, including Falken Smith (now at *GH*), three-time Emmy-winner Douglas Marland at *ATWT*, and former actress Pamela Long, who was *GL*'s top scribe.

It appeared to be a good omen at the *13th Annual Daytime Emmy Awards* on July 17, 1986, when two actors from *Another World*, which Bill had cocreated, stepped on stage at the Waldorf Astoria Hotel in New York City to present the award for best writing.

Y&R's writing clip was a winner. In it, Jack blackmailed Ashley into letting him run Jabot Cosmetics or else Jack would tell John that he wasn't Ash's biological father. Ashley was both sickened and shocked by her half-sibling's cruelty, but Jack wasn't backing down.

The acting, directing, and writing in the clips for the other nominated series were all excellent, too. After the scenes were broadcast, actor Stephen Schnetzer opened the envelope and read, "And the winner is...the writing team from *The Young and the Restless*."

Y&R's trademark opening theme was played as a smiling Bill and his writers left their seats and maneuvered their way through the maze of banquet tables. Fashions that day ran the gamut. *Miami Vice* was a popular show at the time so there were a few Sonny Crockett imitators among the male presenters. *Santa Barbara*'s A Martinez and Marcy Walker wore matching tuxedos. Bill's look, however, was, as always, timeless and classic. He wore a navy-blue sports coat and tie. He walked up the stairs to the podium, his arm around writer Jack Smith, who'd traveled from Honolulu to attend the ceremony.

"Who says writers don't have fun?" Bill chuckled after giving a few congratulatory kisses to his female scribes. "This is how we write the scenes!"

Emmy in hand, Bill proudly turned to his writers and, referring to a popular storyline that was currently airing, teased, "Behind me are the only people who know who really shot Jill Abbott!

"We've put in long hours and many years waiting for this moment," he said. "It has arrived and everything I planned to say has gone right out the window! I can certainly empathize with our actors more and more. Thanks very much!"

Bill was joyful, beaming, grateful, charming, and humble. He didn't take the honor of winning the award for best writing lightly.

As it turned out, he wasn't taking it at all.

The next day, in his suite at the Park Lane Hotel, Bill received a call from Michael Brockman, CBS's Daytime chief. Brockman had the unenviable task of informing Bill that there'd been a tabulation error with the accounting firm hired by NATAS. Long and her scribes at *GL* had won the award for best writing—not Bill and his team.

"The snafu was unprecedented in the history of showbiz awards and has not been repeated at another trophy show since," says Tom O'Neil, author of *The Emmys*.

"*Guiding Light* had won the award, but because of a mistake made by the firm, Coopers & Lybrand, tabulating the results, the prize was wrongly bestowed to *Y&R*. Only after the show did some people start to notice that the winner announced at the ceremony didn't match the champ listed in the official press release."

"The mix-up occurred at the accountant's level," confirmed the academy's Michael Llach.

"The academy called and said a horrible mistake has been made," Brockman recalls. "I said, 'Don't do anything. I don't want Bill to hear this from anyone but me. I don't want his shock or emotion to hit anyone else. Let him yell and scream at me.' That was my instinct."

Bill couldn't believe it when Brockman gave him the news.

He hadn't walked away Emmy-free that day. *Y&R* also won the award for Outstanding Drama Series, its fourth in that category, but Bill felt that award belonged equally, if not more, to the show's control-booth producers.

"Although I'm a producer and have been for many, many years, I consider myself more than anything a writer, a storyteller," Bill said. "I take great pride in the stories we tell and how we tell them."

Therefore, if NATAS was going to ask Bill to return one of the two Emmys from that day, Brockman says with a knowing sigh, "They asked for the wrong one."

Joseph V. O'Donnell, the regional managing partner for Coopers & Lybrand, sent Bill a mailgram in Chicago on July 21 that read: "Coopers & Lybrand deeply regrets the circumstances which led to incorrectly awarding the Emmy for 'Outstanding Drama Series Writing Team' at July 17th's Emmy awards presentation. We sincerely apologize for the clerical error that occurred and for any embarrassment it caused you and your associates."

Bill spoke to the *Los Angeles Times*' Lee Margulies about the incident. Telling his writers that they hadn't won "was the most unpleasant job of my life," Bill said. "From a night of triumph you just go to a moment of humiliation...far better that nothing had happened than that this happened."

Bill realized the error wasn't made intentionally; however, he noted that the firm's credibility was damaged if one person's tabulating hadn't been double-checked. "The greatest impact is that a group of awfully fine, talented people were hurt the way few people can be hurt because ultimately it became a great indignity and it never should have happened," he said.

Paul Rauch spoofed the travesty done to Bill in a 1989 episode of *One Life to Live*, the soap he was helming. A soap opera within a *OLTL* storyline, *Fraternity Row*, was nominated at the fictional "Daisy Awards."

After the writing award was given to some scribes, an actor playing an accountant told host Robin Leach that there had been an error and the scribes had to give the award back.

"We had felt so badly for Bill," Rauch says. "That was our way of making a statement that the academy had really screwed up."

Bill, however, was getting the last laugh with the ratings. In summer 1986, *Y&R* began overtaking first-place *GH*. He threw a party to celebrate the show and *Y&R*'s other Emmy winners (for directing and videotape editing) back in Los Angeles.

"I had T-shirts made up for the writers that said, 'And the winner is *The Young and the Restless*,'" Sally Sussman Morina says. "On the back, they read, 'Just kidding!'"

It's been debated if Bill ever returned the tainted Emmy to the academy. At the time, Llach told *Soap Opera NOW!* that he assumed the awards from the *Y&R* writers would be given back. They were not. It wasn't a case of the scribes refusing to do so, but rather NATAS deciding not to make the request, given the incident's embarrassing nature.

One writer's statue was damaged in an earthquake years later. Rather than repair it, the remains were tossed.

"I didn't like what it represented anyway," the scribe said.

Bill put the matter in the past and traveled to New York for subsequent Emmy broadcasts. In 1992, NATAS bestowed its Lifetime Achievement Award on Bill. He was also a double nominee for writing and producing *Y&R* that year. The tribute to him that night began with a clip package that showed highlights from Bill's social-issue storytelling. Jeanne Cooper, *Y&R*'s longest-running cast member, presented the Emmy to "Mr. William J. 'Beloved' Bell."

Notes in hand (Bill almost always came to awards shows with note cards), he stepped to the podium, while receiving a standing ovation. Bill expressed his deep thanks to the academy's governors, the Cordays, and John Mitchell.

"If you want to see a grown man cry, keep it up," Bill emotionally said. "It's wonderful. I thank you from the bottom of my heart."

Bill shared with everyone gathered for the awards and with the viewers at home that his characters are his extended family, but joking about the distinct difference between them and his real family. "Fictional characters will do everything I tell them to do, say what I want them to say, react as I expect them to, [and] will obey everything I ask of them, unlike my own family which seems to want to write their own scripts sometimes!

"I shouldn't be up here alone tonight," Bill added. "My wife, Lee Phillip, should be standing beside me. Without Lee, nothing would be the same. The show wouldn't be here. Come to think of it, neither would the children!"

Bill also acknowledged members of his writing team, including Kay Alden, Jack Smith, and Jerry Birn. "We have other writers," Bill noted, adding with a wry tone, "I hope you'll have the opportunity to meet them later in the show."

Later on in the broadcast, two actors from *AW*, Tom Eplin and Judi Evans, read the nominees for best writing. Bill's impressive competition included Agnes Nixon for *AMC*, Lorraine Broderick, Nancy Curlee, Stephen Demorest, and James E. Reilly for *GL*, and Michael Malone for *OLTL*.

This time, having two actors from Bay City proved to be serendipitous. "And the Emmy goes to," Eplin said, "*The Young and the Restless*."

Six years after the embarrassing snafu at the Waldorf, Bill won the Daytime Emmy for Outstanding Drama Series Writing Team, this time for real. Like his audiences, Bill had learned what it was like to wait for the payoff.

Having said everything that he wanted to in his lifetime achievement speech, Bill kept his second one short and humorous.

"In our nineteen years, this is the first time we've won the writing Emmy so it makes us especially proud," Bill said. "Well, that's not true. Years ago we won, and I got a call the next morning from Michael Brockman, who was in charge of CBS Daytime. He said, 'Bill, I'm going to tell you a story that you're not going to believe.' I said, 'Sure, what is it, Michael?'

"He said, 'You didn't win the Emmy. They're taking it back.' I said, 'Oh, sure, Michael.' We went back and forth for twenty minutes and I finally believed him. The point of the story is this—if anyone calls me tomorrow at 8:30 in the morning, I ain't picking up the phone!"

The audience roared with laughter and cheered with applause. Bill had made two speeches that evening, one heartfelt and the other comical. Bill may not have considered himself a performer, but he always entertained when he appeared on TV.

There were future accolades from the NAACP Image Awards, the SHINE Awards (which honor the presentation of social issues in media), and the California Governor's Committee for Employment of Disabled Persons.

Bill's Emmy win for writing again in 2000, which head writer Kay Alden accepted, was especially poignant because Susan Flannery, long overlooked by the academy for her powerhouse performances as *B&B*'s Stephanie, also won that year. The duo had taken home their first Emmys twenty-five years earlier at the *2nd Annual Daytime Emmy Awards* in 1975.

"I was with Susan the first time she won," Bill recalled. "You can't know what a strikingly beautiful girl she was then. Just a terrific lady, as she is still today."

"That was a sweet moment," Flannery recollects of the wins that took place twenty-five years apart. "Bill came to look for me in the pressroom. I have a photograph from the first time we won, just the two of us. It's a little black and white photograph. Bill used to have it up on the wall in his office."

"The Emmys mean recognition, prestige, something in which everyone in the business takes great pride," Bill said. "But we're in the business of presenting a program every day that has an impact on our audience. That's where our focus is, day by day. Certainly, I'm not going to say that the Emmys aren't important. Of course, they are. But the most important thing for any and all of us [is] the impact we have on our audience, and the numbers we produce. That's where it's at."

Soap Opera Digest bestowed its Editors' Choice Award on Bill twice, first in 1985. He received it again on January 10, 1992, at an all-star tribute that was broadcast from the Beverly Hills Hilton Hotel, home of the irreverent Golden Globes.

The magazine and Dick Clark Productions put out the call to six of Bill's on-screen leading ladies to help do the honors.

The 8th Annual Soap Opera Awards got off to a great start with Doug Davidson winning his third consecutive award for playing *Y&R*'s Paul.

"I would like to thank Bill Bell," Davidson said. "I don't know what you write with, but you have my undying respect. And, Lee, I honestly think that you care about people's feelings and I carry that with me, always."

Later, Lauralee kicked off the segment devoted to Bill. "Imagine a person with enough talent and dedication to have created more than ten thousand episodes of soap opera, someone who started as a writer in 1956 and then worked his way up to become one of the most influential people in soaps," she proudly stated. "Well, there *is* such a person...he's the man who created three successful daytime soaps, gave life to over 285 characters, and even had a hand in creating me. I am very proud to say he's my dad, Bill Bell."

Tom Selleck appeared next in a pretaped tribute. "Not only did the job you gave me give me a regular paycheck, but it also gave me the opportunity to learn and work and grow with some terrific professionals," said Selleck, who played *Y&R*'s Jed from 1974 to 1975. "I'd like to join all the actors, writers, producers, [and] directors of all the Bill Bell shows [in] saying, 'Congratulations, boss.'"

Next, actresses representing Bill's time at *GL*, *ATWT*, *Days*, *Y&R*, and *B&B* spoke, each pointing out Bill's specific contributions to their shows.

"It was Irna Phillips who taught Bill the ropes of writing soap operas," said Ruth Warwick, who played Janet Johnson, a nurse, on *GL* in 1956, before moving on to her iconic role as Phoebe on *AMC*. "He couldn't have had a better tutor because he went on to write a script a day for the next thirty-five years!"

"Coming from a strong family background himself, Bill brought an even greater emphasis on the family to *As the World Turns* and to all the marvelous interactions between our characters," praised Helen Wagner, who played matriarch Nancy Hughes.

"I'll always think of Bill for bringing music to soap operas," recalled Susan Seaforth Hayes. "But most people credit Bill Bell for bringing something else to daytime—sex! Once viewers who had never witnessed such adult storylines in soap operas got a look at Bill's adult plotlines for *Days of our Lives*, there was no turning back."

Next, Jeanne Cooper pointed out Bill's accomplishments with *Y&R*. "It's hard to imagine what else he could contribute to daytime soap opera," the actress mused, tossing the next part of the tribute to Susan Flannery, who, not surprisingly, knocked it out of the park.

"William, you are a weaver of tales and a spinner of stories, brother to that distant storyteller who told around the tribal fire his or her people of their trials and travels in history," Flannery said. "You are inextricably linked to the weavers of *Beowulf*, *Canterbury Tales*, and *Great Expectations*. You have weaved tales of love and hate and life and death, and your stories have seeped into the consciousness of millions and millions in our global village. You have done this with wit, wisdom, and a higher sense of moral purpose."

Then Bill was invited up to accept his statue. He was, as always, gracious in his speech, making sure to pay tribute to those who'd helped him along the way—Irna and the Cordays.

"I don't know that I deserve all this, but I accept it with great pleasure," Bill said. "This is all very exciting to all of us. Thank you."

Bill genuinely enjoyed seeing others walk to the winner's podium. In 2000, he attended the Writers Guild of America Awards in Los Angeles and watched former protégé Sally Sussman Morina accept the Daytime Serial award for head-writing *Days*.

"I saw Bill smiling, looking right at me as I thanked him in my speech," Sussman Morina recalls.

Bill didn't have to be nominated for him to attend a ceremony either. He and Lee went to a banquet in Chicago in the late 1970s that honored Illinois natives who'd appeared on the cover of *Time* magazine. Bill Hayes was among the honorees, courtesy of *Time*'s January 12, 1976, cover story on daytime dramas, titled "Soap Operas—Sex and Suffering in the Afternoon."

"Bill Bell was the reason that Susan and I were on the cover," Hayes explains. "Plain and simple, Bill is why we were there. It may have been during the head-writing era of Pat Falken Smith when it happened, but it was for the story that Bill wrote. He and Lee and Susan and I all went. He was so proud that night. He was thrilled for *us*."

Chapter 14

"BABY, COME BACK"

There is no way that man would hire me back.

—Clarke Garrison (Dan McVicar) to Margo Lynley (Lauren Koslow) speculating on his chances of working for Eric Forrester (John McCook) again after he jumped ship to go to Spectra Fashions on *B&B*, 1990

There was a myth about Bill Bell, held mostly by people in the soap-opera business who had never worked for him. They'd heard—erroneously—that if you ever quit his employ, he'd never rehire you.

It sounds ominous and perhaps was befitting a man of Bill's stature and influence that he'd have such a policy. Go ahead. Leave the kingdom. But you'll never be allowed back into the castle.

The legend was likely perpetuated by lines of dialogue like the one that opens this chapter. Eric Forrester, in fact, made it clear to a defecting Clarke that his rule was not to hire anyone again who quit his employ. Viewers who saw exchanges like that between Bill's characters sometimes interpreted them as his way of sending a not-so-subtle message to his employees.

But Bill had no such policy. He felt protective of his employees and rehired people many times, not just actors who'd left, but behind-the-scenes personnel, too.

Joanna Johnson, an original cast member of *B&B*, opted not to renew her contract with the show and informed Bill she'd be leaving when it expired. The actress was wildly popular as ingénue Caroline Spencer Forrester, so much so that the show was named *Caroline* in Greece. While Grecian TV execs debated about what they'd call the program after Johnson left, Bill was left to decide whether or not he'd recast the part.

Catherine Hickland, a soap veteran of *Capitol* and *Texas*, was on Bill's short list to take over as Caroline. She'd subbed in *B&B*'s early days for Katherine Kelly Lang, who missed a few performances due to a brief illness. Bill eventually decided that Johnson, like *Y&R*'s Jaime Lyn Bauer, was irreplaceable. He decided to kill the character, but from a nameless disease so that any viewer who had or knew someone afflicted with a similar condition wouldn't lose hope.

On the July 18, 1990, episode of *B&B*, Caroline died as she had lived, beautifully and in Ridge's arms. Bill filled her void with the late beauty's doctor, Taylor Hayes, whose specialty suddenly switched from "dying ingénue disease" to psychiatry, a more marketable field, given the show's cast, which now contained one less ingénue.

"Bill told me he could not recast the part, which was a huge compliment," Johnson says. "I fit into his idea of the Grace Kelly character. He liked that 'good girl.' I was blond, blue-eyed. I was fortunate that he took a real liking to me."

Bill was disappointed when Johnson told him she planned to leave, but he accepted the actress's decision with grace. "He could have said, 'You want to leave? Fine. Good luck. Good-bye. That's it.'" Instead,

Bill asked her to remain on for a few more months to play out Caroline's death, and then he told her that the door would always be open.

"Bill was almost like a father. I didn't think he understood why I wanted to leave, but he was so kind about it." Johnson theorizes her exit prompted Bill to have Ridge choose to be with Caroline. "I don't know that he would have gone that way if I hadn't left," she muses.

The actress recalls Bill and Lee calling her after she departed to see how she was, occasionally asking if she'd be open to returning. "I think they felt, 'Let her go do her own thing and then she'll come back,'" Johnson says. After eighteen months of auditioning and focusing on her screenwriting, the actress took Bill and Lee up on their generous offer. They invited her to their estate in Beverly Hills to discuss the matter further. Soon, Johnson was back on the show as Karen, Caroline's stolen-at-birth twin sister.

"Bill let me go graciously, and he let me come back graciously. Knowing the business as I do now, that's so rare. He understood that when you're young and restless, no pun intended, that you want to go out and find your way. He was very patient."

While Johnson was away, Bill succeeded in weaving Taylor into the show's fabric, perhaps, *too* successfully. Ridge's dance card was filled with Taylor and Brooke. There simply wasn't room on the thirty-minute program for a Ridge-Karen romance.

"I waited a little too long to come back," Johnson reflects. "That was also around the time that Bill handed the reins over to Brad. Brad loved Caroline, too, but he wasn't as big a fan of hers as Bill was." It would have been a leap (but not an impossible one) for Bill to have brought Johnson back as Caroline since she died on camera. His shows are more reality-based than other soaps, but Johnson, in hindsight, theorizes it might have been the better choice.

"The audience loved Caroline," she says. "If I'd come back as her, I would have had more story."

Still, she has no regrets about returning as Caroline's twin or departing the show again in 1994. "I was questioning if I wanted to act. I needed to be hungry and scared. I sold everything and started over."

Johnson has become a successful writer-creator-producer of such TV shows as *Hope & Faith* and the ABC Family series *Make It or Break It*. Bill and Lee's kindness to her has not been forgotten.

"Whenever I'd see Bill in the hallway at CBS, he'd find something nice to say about a scene I'd done," she says. "A lot of writers don't. They think they'll create monsters, but Bill was never afraid to do that. I try to tell actors who work for me now the same thing. I have nothing but wonderful memories of Bill and Lee. I look back and realize what a wonderful experience it was."

Don Diamont, who plays Caroline and Karen's brother, Bill Spencer Jr. on *B&B*, worked for years for Bill over on *Y&R* as Brad Carlton. The character started out as the Abbott groundskeeper and later became a millionaire businessman, seducing several of Genoa City's eligible (and not so eligible) ladies along the way.

Like Johnson, Diamont also wanted to test the waters outside daytime. He left Genoa City in 1996 after fiancée Nikki left Brad at the altar so she could rush to the side of true love Victor, who'd been shot. "Bill came down to the set on my last day and said, 'I can't believe this day has come,'" Diamont recalls. Bill told the actor that *Y&R* would always be there for him.

Diamont learned that Bill was a man of his word after going through personal crises in the late 1980s when both his father and brother passed away.

"Bill was very kind during that time," the actor says. "He brought me up to his office and let me know that if there was anything that he could do, he would. He wasn't just the boss, he was paternal. Bill wasn't a second father. We didn't go to ballgames together, but he reached out to me in a paternal way during the hardest time of my life."

Thanks to Bill, Diamont left *Y&R* with confidence. "I could work with people like George C. Scott, Jack Palance, and Oliver Reed, thanks to the opportunity that Bill had given me," a grateful Diamont acknowledges.

Diamont gifted his boss with an antique fountain pen when he left the show. Bill used the instrument to write to the actor, reiterating that the door was open. Post-*Y&R*, Diamont found acting gigs, but the devoted family man missed the regular schedule that daytime provided.

"I hated being on location," he said. "It was too hard being away from my kids. I called Bill and said, 'I want to come home.' In two weeks, Brad Carlton was coming home from Portofino and I was back on the show."

Alas, characters near and dear to Bill's heart weren't always safe once he was no longer with the show. Brad met a heroic and icy end after saving Nick and Sharon's son, Noah, who'd fallen into a frozen pond. Brad Bell threw his namesake a lifeline shortly thereafter with an offer to portray Bill Spencer Jr. on *B&B*.

"Playing a character named after Bill's own son always meant a lot to me," Diamont says. "I played Brad written by Bill. Now I play Bill, who's written by Brad."

Hunter Tylo also left the Bell camp in 1996. She vacated her role as Taylor after being cast on the nighttime sudser *Melrose Place*. Still, *B&B* invited the exiting actress to pose in the latest cast photo, placing her in the coveted front row where her blue gown could be seen full-length. The gesture was serendipitous. Viewers hadn't seen the last of Taylor.

Melrose producers scrapped their plans to have Tylo move into primetime's most popular apartment complex after learning the actress was pregnant. Aaron Spelling's loss was going to be the Bells' gain. Brad took a page from his father's policy of welcoming stars back home. He re-signed her to the show, put Taylor in a wedding gown, and placed an oversized bouquet in front of her belly to cover any pregnancy bump.

In one of *B&B*'s most shocking twists ever, Ridge, who was set to propose to Brooke at the climax of a Forrester fashion show, changed his mind after mistakenly believing that Brooke had been unfaithful to him with his buddy Grant. Realizing he truly loved Taylor, Ridge popped the question to "Doc" instead. The switcheroo left viewers stunned. Taylor was overjoyed. Brooke was devastated. Stephanie was ecstatic.

"We had always joked on the show about other actors who proudly left the show to become stars, and then nothing ever happened," Tylo recounted in her 2000 memoir, *Making a Miracle*. "They went on to catch the big-time bus and missed it. I felt as though I had caught the big-time bus and had gotten dropped off again. All the same, I was welcomed back and it felt great to be home."

Leaving a show wasn't always the actor's choice. Bill never liked seeing anyone out of work; however, some characters would come to the end of the storyline road, which meant their portrayers were out of a job.

"Bill gave me the opportunity to play twins," says Michael Tylo, Hunter's former husband, who played siblings Blade and Rick on *Y&R* in the early to mid-1990s. "I'll always be grateful to Bill for that. I knew my being written out wasn't a case of being unwanted. My story came to an end. I have no animosity. I've been hired and fired by the best. Bill was a f—ing great writer."

"I hold Bill and Lee in the highest regard," Lauren Koslow, an original *B&B* cast member, said when she exited her role as Margo in 1992. "I have a lot of good memories tied up in the last five years. It's just a case of moving on."

Brad learned from his father that actors and other personnel leaving didn't mean it was forever. In fact, he invited Koslow to reprise Margo for two days in 2002 to help introduce her son, Mark, now a doctor, even though the actress had moved over to *Days* as calculating Kate Roberts. It's highly unusual for competing shows to lend out their actors so Margo's return speaks to the great relationship the Bell and Corday clans still enjoy.

"My father had his team, and if you were on it, you were on it. And if you weren't, you were the competition. But that didn't mean you couldn't return," Brad says. "If you had commitment, talent, desire, and you met with him face to face, he wouldn't hold the fact that you once left against you."

That didn't mean the news of a departing actor was music to Bill's ears. He lost two highly popular stars from *Y&R* in January 1997 when Heather Tom and Michelle Stafford vacated their respective roles of Victoria and Phyllis.

The two fan favorites had front-burner storylines, and *Y&R* wasn't known for losing key players so the news of their imminent exits spread like wildfire. The show's publicity team was ready with statements from Bill when press inquiries were made to see if the rumors were true.

Tom's departure was classified as "temporary."

The actress had visited Bill in his office and said she wanted a break as her contract was winding down. "I told him how grateful I was and what I wanted to do," she recalls. "He told me right then and there in the room that I had a home at *Y&R*."

"Heather just needed a change because I've used her so heavily for so long," Bill said. While he did temporarily recast the role, Tom was back on screen by the end of the year.

"I had no illusion that Victoria would stay off the air forever because she's such an important character to the canvas of the show," Tom says. "But Bill welcomed me back with open arms. I'd heard the rumor about never being able to come back, but I never experienced it."

The show's statement about Stafford indicated that her decision to leave had caught Bill and the show off guard.

"We are surprised and shocked that Michelle Stafford has decided to leave *Y&R* to join a primetime show," Bill said, referring to the actress being cast on Aaron Spelling's *Pacific Palisades*, which aired on Fox. Stafford's choice was understandable. After all, Phyllis did not have the iconic roots that Tom's character had as Victor and Nikki's daughter. The flame-haired villainess's future presence on the canvas was not as guaranteed.

While many of Bill's antagonistic characters (Victor, Leanna, Sheila, and Michael) received reprieves of varying lengths, Bill also never hesitated to bring some bad guys to swift justice. Sociopath David Kimball accidentally killed himself by activating a trash compactor that he was hiding in. Convicted rapist Derek Stuart leapt to his death out of a hotel window rather than face prison time. Was Bill going to do away with Phyllis? He ended up keeping her, but Stafford left anyway.

"There were so many cooks in the kitchen at that time," Stafford reflects. "There were my agents and Aaron Spelling, who was excited to have me on his new show. I don't say this to toot my own horn, but people like to 'steal' people. It's a game."

Stafford later heard that Bill was under the mistaken impression that she had wanted to leave the show. "I care about the Bells, certainly more now because I've spent more time with them," she says. "If I had it to do over again, I would have gone to Bill and talked to him. I owed him that. He was a good man."

Stafford publicly thanked Bill in her emotional acceptance speech at the Daytime Emmys in May when she won the award for Outstanding Supporting Actress in a Drama Series, beating out impressive competition that included costar Victoria Rowell (Dru). Stafford had privately expressed her gratitude to Bill a few months earlier.

"I wrote him a letter and I asked (production assistant) Nora Wade to give it to Bill. She told me that he read it, paused, folded it up, and put it in his pocket."

During Stafford's speech, the camera cut to Bill, who was sitting in the audience. (Bill had also won that night, again for Drama Series Writing team, tying with *All My Children*'s Agnes Nixon.) He appeared to be smiling while Stafford accepted her statue, but he also was somewhat enigmatic, an emotion he'd often ask his actors to play in certain scenes.

"The look on his face was, 'She's not on our show anymore,'" Stafford theorizes. "It was more like that. It was a bummer for him. It was a reminder that [I'd] won an award for what he wrote and now I [couldn't] be there anymore."

While Bill was arguably chilled by Stafford's exit in January, his tone had thawed by the time the Emmys rolled around. "They [both] left on the very best of terms, and they love the show," Bill told *Soap Opera Weekly* in May, referring to Tom and Stafford. "They're not only fine actresses, but fine human beings. Where Michelle is concerned, she made a last-minute decision at a time when we were very deep in negotiations. We felt we had made a deal with her; it was just a matter of a couple of details that had to be worked out, and lo and behold, she joined Spelling.

"I don't know how long that show will last. Perhaps it will last a long time, but possibly it won't, and then who knows?"

"There was no animosity at all," Stafford says. "Bill wanted things his way, and he wasn't digging how it went down. But it was fine. I was still friends with everyone."

A few years later, Bill reconnected with the Emmy winner at a Christmas party at the home of Jerry Birn and Patty Weaver. "Bill told me that he wanted me to come on to *B&B*," Stafford reveals. "He said, 'You need to come back to daytime where you belong.' I said, 'Thanks, Bill!'"

Stafford's successor, Sandra Nelson, filled Phyllis's pumps admirably, earning Bill's praise in the process. He called her to compliment her for work she did during climactic scenes involving Phyllis's desperate ongoing quest to hang on to the family she'd created with her web of lies. Eventually, most of Phyllis's machinations were exposed. She lost custody of her son, Daniel, to ex-husband Danny. Chris represented Danny in the custody case, which caused Phyllis to hate Chris even more. Nelson departed the show in early 1999. Stafford reclaimed the role in summer 2000. She won her second Daytime Emmy, this time for Outstanding Lead Actress, in 2004, and has received numerous nominations.

Bill also rehired writers and consultants. Sherman Magidson, who provided legal expertise to Bill for his courtroom stories, quit *Y&R* to join Sally Sussman Morina's team at *Generations* in the late 1980s.

"Bill called me and said that the show wasn't going to last," Magidson recalls. "He said, 'When it's done, come on by and you'll work for me again. There's a $500 a week increase for you, too.'

"Bill had a very paternalistic feeling toward not only the characters in his shows, but also towards the people he hired and worked with."

It turned out that even Clarke Garrison, who eventually did rejoin Forrester Creations, had feared for naught. "It was a dramatic choice," says Brad of his father writing that Clarke was worried that he'd burned a bridge. "It's more dramatic if you're told you can never come back."

And if there was one thing that Bill knew, it was how to tell a dramatic story.

Chapter 15

MEET THE PRESS

Y&R *is probably the most secretive show when it comes to storyline info.*

—*Soap Opera NOW!*, July 28, 1986

Bill always had a great relationship with the press. He knew from Lee's work as a talk-show host and from his own days in advertising that the media can be a powerful conduit. He invited a few members of the press to his apartment in Chicago to view the premiere of *The Young and the Restless.*

"My stance has always been, gosh, anyone who wants to review it, great," Bill said. "But please never on the basis of one show. It takes a week before an audience or a critic can see what these characters are all about, their interweaving stories and their dimensions. Traditionally, serials are panned because this involvement factor is missing."

Reviews for Bill's shows were often positive and always appreciated. "Bill was extremely polite," recalls Meredith Berlin, former editor-in-chief of *Soap Opera Digest*. "There were some executive producers who I wouldn't say that about. They were much more emotional."

The Superman of storytellers, however, knew that the media could also be kryptonite to his shows. Information that gives away a storyline or key development is called a "spoiler" for a good reason—it can spoil viewers' enjoyment of the show.

If viewers knew who'd win *Survivor* or which lucky lady would be chosen on *The Bachelor*, would those finales garner high ratings? Not likely.

Bill felt that if viewers knew whether or not Nick and Sharon's prematurely born son was going to survive or if Ridge were going to choose Brooke over Taylor, then they'd have less of a reason to tune in.

"I'm opposed to future storylines being printed in advance," Bill told veteran soap journalist Dorothy Vine. "After all, they are our lifeblood. The serial is based on bringing viewers back day after day and having a continuing story. If they know what's going to happen next week, they're going to be less inclined to tune in. It's one thing to tease and another to reveal something more significant."

Bill theorized that less reputable publications weren't above offering money to his employees for advance story points. "I've already warned people in my companies [that] if anyone gives out too much information too far in advance, they'll be fired!"

During most of Bill's career, magazines actually couldn't tip advance storylines because of the publications' production deadlines. Coverage of the Daytime Emmys, which took place in the summer, appeared in fall editions, and pictures from Christmas parties ran in spring issues. Over the years, magazine deadlines shifted, however. Publications started going to press later, and they got out on the newsstands faster than ever. In 1997, eight different periodicals (most weekly) covered the world of soaps.

Bill could have lowered the boom on access and treated the press like an adversary, making it as difficult as possible for publications to acquire any information. Instead, he instructed his publicity team to invite the press to each of his two shows on a weekly basis. Reporters, accompanied by publicists, were given access.

"There was an air of graciousness and welcome that you didn't feel at any of the other L.A. shows," says Roberta Caploe, former West Coast managing editor of *Soap Opera Digest*. "It had the feel of a more smoothly run and well-administered operation. That came from Bill."

Rules about giving away advance storyline were explained and enforced.

"Bill's relationship with the press was respectful," says Rhonda Friedman, *B&B*'s supervising producer. "He had his guidelines. He asked that they be respected, and if they were, he respected you. It was symbiotic."

There weren't a lot of instances in which the press blew storyline, although Brad ripped up a magazine one time when it revealed too far in advance that Ridge was choosing Taylor over Brooke, but the press didn't blow storyline often. On occasion, however, if a storyline were exposed, Bill would issue a terse memo throughout the company that reminded his employees of his policy.

Bill also disliked it immensely when actors complained in the press. "My character would never do that," some would lament on the record. Bill's feeling was that, actually, your character *would* do that—because that's the story direction in which he, the head writer, was taking you.

Keeping mum about where your storyline was going or what your character was going to do next wasn't a lot to ask, given the benefits Bill gave his employees. "To whom a lot is given, a lot is asked," says Linda Susman, a veteran journalist. "Bill gave his employees a great deal. In return, he ran a tight ship. I bring it back to family—if you're having a dispute within your family, it's not cool to take that outside the family. 'What happens in Genoa City stays in Genoa City!'"

Still, some actors occasionally and foolishly aired their grievances about lack of airtime or story direction in the press. Some hoped that by stirring up controversy, they'd maybe get a better storyline or a new love interest. Others saw that they were being written off the show and were just venting on the way out the door.

"It depended on the actor," says Berlin. "When you're in an interview situation, things are going to come up. Some people see it as an opportunity to let loose. That happens when contracts are coming up or when people want to get out of their contracts. If a person is unhappy at work, it's eventually going to come out either in the press or somewhere else. If actors ever said, 'My character's an idiot,' then they either weren't thinking or they just didn't care."

Christian LeBlanc, who originated the role of attorney Michael Baldwin on *Y&R* in 1991, recalls being called to Bill's office after he gave an interview to an international publication that sensationalized a few of his quotes.

"It was one of those stories that had been pumped up just enough," LeBlanc recalls. "I actually don't think I'd even read it." But Bill had and he asked the actor if he thought it was wise to bite the hand that was feeding him.

"I'd been doing press for about ten years at that point and had never had a problem. I got so upset about it that I started having my own little fit. Bill ended up calming *me* down, saying it was okay."

LeBlanc appreciated Bill giving him the opportunity to explain. "I left his office thinking, 'What a nice man.'"

Bill was more interested in a reporter's integrity than he was in a publication's circulation. "Bill was extremely supportive of me before I had a wider venue to publicize his shows," recalls Susman, who was the editor at the subscription-based newsletter *Soap Opera NOW!* prior to joining the staff of the more widely circulated *Soap Opera Weekly*.

"I don't think Bill ever thought that if he did an interview in *Soap Opera NOW!* he'd get more viewership. But Bill always went out on a limb for me. He was just wonderful."

Bill was the kind of man who took the time to take the time. He jotted off a note to *Soap Opera Illustrated*, a short-lived photo-driven publication from the early '90s, after Lauralee and Michael Damian were featured on the cover of *Illustrated*'s premiere issue.

"Hey, I think you've got a winner here, which I'd say no matter who was on the cover," Bill wrote in a note that was printed in a subsequent issue. "I love the concept, the whole presentation. It's fun, a whole new dimension to 'soap' magazines. In short, I'm an instant fan."

Actors were careful not to even inadvertently pass judgment on Bill's characters. "I once made the mistake of saying in front of Bill Bell, 'I think Jack just goes stupid when a particular woman comes in the room,'" Peter Bergman recalls. "What I meant was that he goes weak in the knees because he's so attracted to her. I could not undo what I had said fast enough. Bill loved his characters. He was so invested in them."

Doug Davidson recollects misspeaking in front of his boss, too, when he and the Bells were dining together one night. "I said the neat thing about a continuing drama is that you can reference things that have occurred before," he recalls. "Bill may have thought that I was saying he was repeating story. The more I tried to say that that wasn't what I meant, the more I was digging myself into a hole." Then the actor felt a gentle tapping under the table on his shin with someone's shoe. "It was Lee," Davidson recalls with a smile. "It was her way of saying, 'Stop it. Move on.'"

"Bill was fiercely loyal to the characters and to the story that he was telling," Susman adds. "He expected those with whom he entrusted the telling of that story to be 100 percent behind it. I don't know how he was if they came to him personally and expressed concerns or if actors ever had the guts to do that."

Eileen Davidson told *Soap Opera Digest* in 1992 that she couldn't quite wrap her head around Ashley taking up with Victor Newman since he was still married to Nikki.

"I spoke with Bill Bell and he gave me a different perspective on things," the actress said. "He told me the storyline would have far-reaching ramifications. It wasn't going to be about her just falling in love."

Catching Bill in the right mood could make all the difference. In the early '90s, he wrote a storyline that had Victoria Newman helming the "Brash & Sassy" cosmetics division of Newman Enterprises that would compete against Jabot.

Some actors on the show found the makeup line's name to be a bit of a tongue twister. ("Brush & Sushi," anyone?) Kristoff St. John (Neil) was elected by his fellow cast members to be the one to call Bill with their concern. St. John says: "He got on the phone with me and I said, 'Bill, we were all going over the material and we were wondering about the name 'Brash & Sassy.' Bill said, 'What about it?' I said, 'Well, it's almost comical. It doesn't flow.'"

The actor recalls his boss taking a long pause before stating, "'Kristoff, I'll tell you what—why don't you leave *me* to the writing and I'll leave *you* to the stage?' I said, 'Thank you, Mr. Bell!' and I got off the phone as quickly as possible."

"Kristoff came back to us, and he was as white as Kristoff could get," recollects Heather Tom, St. John's costar and pal. "He'd lost all the color in his face and he said, 'We're saying Brash & Sassy!'"

St. John learned that Bill was firm when it came to the show's writing, but that he was also a generous employer. "Bill made people feel like they were part of his family by allowing them into his house [to] share in Christmas festivities," the actor says, recalling the Bells' annual holiday galas on Sunday afternoons each December.

"We'd all go up the driveway, and Bill and Lee were there to warmly greet you. There would be a big feast and they'd give you a poinsettia on the way out."

Bill and Lee had special reason to celebrate the holidays in 1995; they welcomed their first grandchild, Chasen (Brad and Colleen's firstborn) around the time of their annual holiday bash. When the happy news started circulating among party guests, one genuine well-wisher quipped, "It's a 'Bell heir' (Bel Air) baby!"

There were annual anniversary parties in March at the posh Bel Air Bay Club in Pacific Palisades, too: one for *Y&R* and the other for *B&B*. The guest lists for these dinner and dancing events were a mile long. Bill and Lee would greet each invitee at the entrance and pose for a picture with them.

"Those were always nice events, too," St. John recalls. "I never saw Bill get down and boogie, except for once. He went out there on the dance floor and let everyone know how human he was. When he and Lee would ask about my children, they were genuinely asking."

"Whenever I'd go to L.A. and visit actors, even primetime actors, I noticed that they didn't live exceptionally well, the way you might think that a TV star would live," recalls Berlin. "They'd live in a regular house on a block with neighbors. They were all fine homes, but not what you'd expect. Bill and Lee's home was phenomenal. He lived like an old-time studio head. Part of their roof would retract, and at night you could see the stars. Bill and Lee's house was the only home that I'd been to that belonged to someone who's attached to daytime that was a 'Wow' place."

Berlin's not surprised that Bill and Lee welcomed their employees into their home. "Bill was an owner of his shows," she says. "It wasn't

ABC or Procter & Gamble. Bill was like someone who owned a corporation. He was at the top."

The soap press regularly reported about Bill's shows, and publications competed against each other for coveted covers. Weddings were always a big "get."

The shows were covered to a lesser extent by the mainstream press, including CBS's news and entertainment programs. Bill was puzzled when *CBS This Morning* produced a segment promoting Deidre Hall's return to rival soap *Days of our Lives* in summer 1991.

The NBC sudser briefly jumped to the number-two spot in the ratings soon after Hall's Marlena emerged from the fog. Bill had one question: why was CBS, the network that broadcast *Y&R* and *B&B*, encouraging viewers to switch channels by promoting Hall's return to Salem?

Bill wasn't just puzzled; he was unhappy. It wasn't anything personal against Hall. In fact, pre-*Days*, in 1973 Bill had employed the actress on *Y&R* as Barbara, Brad Eliot's former fiancée, who appeared in the show's premiere. After that role ended, Bill recommended Hall to Betty Corday over at *Days*. "I said I was going to let a girl go and you may want to look at her," Bill recalled. "And the rest is history."

"Everyone tried to be more balanced," recalls a former CBS publicist about the news division doing segments on competing serials. "I understood Bill's reaction. Had we been getting airtime regularly promoting our own shows, it wouldn't have bothered us as much. It wasn't like daytime was getting covered a lot. For CBS to finally do a piece and have it be on an actress from another network stuck in all of our craws."

Y&R often led the pack with Daytime Emmy nominations. But mainstream media usually led with the same angle the day that the noms were announced throughout the '80s and '90s—Is this the year that Susan Lucci, *All My Children*'s Erica, would finally win? The press beat this angle to death every year until 1999 when the fan favorite deservedly won the Daytime Emmy award for Outstanding Lead Actress in a Drama Series after her nineteenth nomination.

Being ignored in the mainstream press wasn't a one-time thing for *Y&R*, the CBS publicist went on to say. "Yes, it's the news division and it's covering what's going on in the world. But if they wanted to talk about how we were being relevant with Bill's social issue storylines, they missed a lot of opportunities. It wasn't always played out the way we liked."

Bill would shut down taping for a week so that the company could attend the Daytime Emmys in New York City. He and Lee went to the theater during the first part of the week to see the latest Broadway shows. On the day before or the morning of the awards, they'd host either a luncheon or a breakfast gathering with the press. It started out as a small reception in their suite at the Park Lane Hotel where a handful of press members from a few publications were invited to drop by and mingle with the Bells and a few actors.

By the early '90s, the gathering evolved to a larger luncheon at Tavern on the Green, and eventually it became an even bigger event with a few hundred guests at the Rainbow Room in New York City.

"That was the signature event that kicked off the Daytime Emmys," recalls Renee Young, former CBS publicity director. "Until you showed up at that party, it wasn't Emmy season.

"Bill and Lee wanted to show the industry that they respected them. They spent money on that event every year. No one took more pride in daytime than Bill. There were many parties on Emmy week, but Bill and Lee's were second only to the Emmys themselves.

Mainstream celebrities from sports and theater came to it. There was only one Rainbow Room and if you weren't there, you missed out."

"That was the big event," Melody Thomas Scott concurs. "People planned what they would wear to the Rainbow Room as carefully as they would what they were going to wear to the Emmys. It was one of the few times we'd be allowed to mingle with journalists at an exclusive event like that. Being there with Bill and Lee was always so special."

In the '90s, the Internet was in its infancy compared to what it is today, but Sony Pictures Television's in-house site, SoapCity.com, produced live reports from the Rainbow Room, which brought fans directly into the event.

Advances in technology have also been the serial drama's enemy, however. Today, actors with accounts on social-networking sites like Twitter and Facebook are encouraged by show producers not to talk about what goes on at the set so that storylines aren't inadvertently tipped.

"Bill would have hated all that Twitter stuff," Susman theorizes. "I think that's why it took him a while to, I wouldn't say 'embrace' the press, but he saw that there wasn't much choice. Given his druthers, I think he would have been happy without it. But he certainly embraced the press as a gentleman and in an honest and responsible way."

Today, Eva Demirjian, director of communications and talent relations for *B&B*, is cautious about storyline teasers and even summary information that's given to the media in advance. "I'll say, 'We shouldn't give this away,' and people here will say to me, 'Oh, you'd be Bill Bell's kind of girl.' I kind of like that."

"Bill never wanted to give anything away," recalls Susan Banks, former CBS director of daytime promotions. "He taught me how to never give any soap secrets away. Never tip the storyline—just tease it. Entice your audience, but don't tell them. Bill was very strict about that.

"When *B&B* launched, it was very important to keep the storylines secret. There was initially very little information to work with. I finally won his confidence and he let me read his scripts. That's when I came up with an idea for *B&B*'s launch called 'You'll Never Forget Your First Time.' I wanted viewers to see this as the beginning of a very long love affair."

"Bill was right," Maria Arena Bell, *Y&R*'s executive producer and head writer says. "When I got here, I was stunned that the previous regime's attitude was, 'Just tell 'em what's coming up. Maybe they'll tune in?' We saw that that wasn't the right approach. We had to go back to the old ways. This is about tuning in tomorrow. You don't want to spoil that. It's delicate. Yes, you want people to be excited, but you can't give story away. We've worked too hard to give it away for nothing."

Chapter 16

THE (SOAP) WORLD ACCORDING TO BILL

Perhaps, soap-opera head writers are born, not made.

—Jean Rouverol, author, *Writing for the Soaps*

"Bill was a genius."

That's the one expression that everyone who was interviewed for this book used in describing Bill Bell. "Genius" is a word that's thrown around a lot, but in Bill's case it was the truth.

People who work in daytime television have said that writing and producing an hour of daily drama is like trying to jump onto a moving locomotive. If that's true, then Bill was the master conductor. He knew when the train was leaving the station, how many passengers were on board, and when it would arrive at its destination.

"It's a very special skill," Michael Brockman, a veteran daytime executive, says of serial writing. "You have to know how to draw where we're going, what this is about, [and] you have to know the end and how you'll get there. But that doesn't mean to be rigid. As you travel the road, you may think of some interesting points to depart to, but you don't lose focus of where you're headed."

Back in the '60s, Ken Corday asked Bill how he managed to plot the show and track the comings and goings of all the different characters on Ken's parents' program *Days of our Lives*.

"Bill told me to imagine a bar with three rolls of toilet paper on it," Corday shares. "Bill said, 'I've unrolled them and written on each sheet the next beat in the story. I rolled them back up and put them back on the bar. On Monday, I'll pull down one sheet from the first roll, two from the second roll, and no sheets from the third one. On Tuesday, I'll pull down another sheet from the first roll, no sheets from the second roll and one from the third.'

"Of course, I know what the last sheet on each roll will be," Bill added.

The young Corday wasn't sure if Bill was pulling his leg or not, but he did know that Bill's talent had saved his parents' legacy. "Writers come to it as their stories unfold," Corday muses. "But Bill's visual of how the stories were peeled out [made it very clear] to me, who, at the time, knew nothing about his genius or the craft."

Bill's example to Corday may have painted an effective image, but there is, of course, far more to Bill's genius than a pen and a few sturdy rolls of Charmin.

"Nobody's better than Bill Bell," said Pat Falken Smith, Bill's successor at *Days*. "When I first went to work for him, I thought his writing was awful. But I soon realized that he played great on-air."

"Bill was a huge believer in the value of human relationships and human experiences," says Kay Alden. "He believed, as I do, that everybody has a story. If you start talking to people, you realize how true that is. Human relationships and encounters and how those feelings are expressed and the people involved with those relationships were the stuff of Bill's stories."

"Bill would say to me, 'Tom, this is about feelings,'" recalls Tom Langan. "'We're writing about people's feelings. Don't ever forget that.'"

Irna Phillips thought Bill was a stronger plotter than he was a dialogue writer, but Bill's shows have had many memorable lines over the years.

"Kind of a drag, isn't it? Stuck in a place like Genoa City," lamented Sally McGuire in *Y&R*'s premiere. "God, I feel so restless."

"So, this is how the other half loves," philosophized Leanna Love to Katherine Chancellor on *Y&R* after witnessing how Jill's machinations ruined her romantic reunion with John Abbott.

"Oh, my Fabio. It's God," *B&B*'s Sally Spectra deadpanned at her bachelorette party when the romance-novel cover hunk made a cameo appearance.

"Your dead baby isn't always uppermost in my mind," Sheila cruelly informed *Y&R*'s Lauren, who was unaware that her baby indeed was alive and well (and in Sheila's clutches!).

There are, of course, thousands of other great examples. Fans appreciate clever dialogue. They remember it and quote it to their fellow soap viewers, but they recall great characters and great stories even more.

"When I came to *Y&R*, it was with experience," says Peter Bergman, who joined the show in 1989 after playing *All My Children*'s Cliff for a decade. "I had an understanding of story. There are story introductions, builds, and peaks. But I could not figure out with Bill where we were in his story—ever. It would seem like we were at a peak, but no, it's kind of plateauing—and now, it's moving over here. That was Bill's magic. He could keep a story at its peak for so long and drain every moment out of it that he could.

"There are times that you have to 'help' stories along in daytime, but never with Bill. You'd ride a Bill Bell story. You'd *ride* it."

"People who don't write for daytime don't understand it," Falken Smith once said. "Writing for daytime is from the gut. It's character and emotion, and that's why Bill Bell's stuff comes alive. And you haven't given the viewers what they think they want, because the moment you do, they turn the knob. When you do that, you've come to the last page of your novel—the lovers are married and now they're going to live happily ever after, or unhappily, together. You can't do that. You've got to keep them apart—you can't marry them off. That's one of the techniques of serial writing and the young writers don't know that. They get desperate and marry everyone off, and they're wrecking all of the shows."

Bill kept his writing team very small and the outlines that would become his scripts very long. They had lots of dialogue in them, too. He learned from Irna that if a head writer makes his or her outline as specific as possible, then it will require less editing after it becomes a script.

"You have to make sure you don't get a script back a week later that is wrong," Bill said. "You'd be out of touch with that script because you'd be six or seven shows beyond that."

Bill wasn't in the habit of sharing his internal documents, but Doug Davidson recalls finding old *Y&R* script outlines in his private-eye character's office filing cabinets. (Set decorators used the documents to fill Paul's files.) "They were essentially scripts," Davidson says of the outlines. "They were word for word, just not yet in script form."

Bill wasn't a fan of technology. He had one of the first VCRs so he could record *Y&R*. Being able to send scripts via overnight mail and fax became godsends, but Bill never embraced the computer age. In the early '90s, one of his writers lost hours of work after her computer crashed. Bill understood. He took a break and walked down the hall from his office at *Y&R* still chuckling over the mishap, sharing with a few people at *B&B*, "I hugged my IBM Selectric and said, 'You *never* do that to me!'"

"I don't think my father would have transitioned to computers," Bill Jr. muses. "His technology and evolution was going from seven-layer carbons to the copying machine. He experienced technology, just not as we're seeing today."

"Bill didn't even like to change his own typewriter cartridges," recalls Christina Knack. "He was just adverse to technology."

Bill also wasn't a fan of comedy in soaps, and he certainly didn't appreciate them being mocked as they were in the 1991 movie *Soapdish*, which starred Sally Field and Whoopi Goldberg. Soap-opera stereotypes in the film included former *Santa Barbara* actor Paul Johannson playing "Bolt" (a dig at *B&B*'s Ridge?). The hunk visited his comatose wife in a hospital wearing a tank top, his arms visibly oiled up.

Additionally, Goldberg's head-writer character, Rose Schwartz, voiced incredulous frustration after being told by producers that she had to write for a character who'd been decapitated. "How am I supposed to write for a guy who doesn't have a head? He doesn't have a head!"

"I could feel my father's body tense up," recalls Brad, who sat next to Bill during the film's premiere. "He was fidgeting. He was, in fact, angry and wanted to leave. He took soap operas very seriously. It's why he was so good. I took the movie for what it was, but he couldn't go there."

However, Bill occasionally wrote a character or two into his shows for comic relief. He created the Spectra gang on *B&B*, remembered fondly for not only Sally Spectra's antics and deadpan reactions by her portrayer, Darlene Conley, but also the banter between Michael Fox's loveable Saul and Schae Harrison's dim-witted Darla.

Bill injected comic relief on *Y&R* when he cast Kate Linder as Katherine's bumbling maid, Esther, in 1982. "I rode a very fine line," says Linder of playing Esther's humor. "Bill said, 'Okay, I like what you're doing, but you're on the edge. Don't go any further.'"

Linder's character initially didn't have a surname. A soap magazine ran a contest in which fans could send in suggestions for one. "Diamond" and "Valentine" made the final cut.

"Bill said to me that I could choose from those two," says Linder, who selected "Valentine." "It made me feel fabulous that he included me in the process."

~

Bill put his faith in his instincts, not focus groups. But he knew how to keep his finger on the pulse of what his audience wanted. He read fan-mail reports that summarized viewer response to storylines and characters. At a taping of *Donahue*, Bill listened attentively to fans who expressed what they did and didn't like about the show. He also attended the annual fan events for both *Y&R* and *B&B*.

"Bill and Lee came to every single event we had for both shows once they moved to Los Angeles, and Lee still does," says Cathy Tomas, fan-club president for the two Bell soaps. "They enjoyed meeting the fans and taking pictures with them. Bill and Lee's example of how to treat the fans is why we continue to have such loyal viewers. Fans who go to other events have told me that no other creators, producers, or writers attend their shows' fan gatherings—at least not with the consistency that Bill and Lee have shown."

~

Bill knew the importance of giving his audience a payoff. In 1989, *B&B* went on location to Long Beach, California, to shoot a week's worth of episodes on the Queen Mary ocean liner.

The ship provided a picturesque setting for the Forrester-Spectra joint charity fashion show. The episodes contained plenty of conflict:

Forrester designer Clarke Garrison was posing as Spectra Fashions artist "Beau Rivage." His secret moonlighting subconsciously led to the creation of duplicate patterns for both company's showstoppers. Also, "Angela Forrester," in reality a disfigured con woman, threatened to expose Thorne as Ridge's shooter.

The highlight of the remote, however, was Ronn Moss's tuxedo-clad Ridge and Joanna Johnson's Caroline in a scene that took place on the deck of the Queen Mary in the moonlight. *B&B* was two and a half years old at this point, but you could count the number of times on one hand that the enigmatic Ridge had ever told either Caroline or Brooke that he loved her.

"Love you," Caroline told Ridge in the premiere episode.

"See you," a noncommittal Ridge replied.

After the remote was completed, producers handed out "Queen Mary Survivor" acrylic coffees mugs as a memento to hardworking cast and crew members, but the real treat was going to the informal viewing party of the QM episodes (prior to them airing on TV) that Bill and Lee hosted in the *B&B* production office.

Everyone gathered to watch the scene on the deck where, after Caroline professed her love for Ridge, he finally uttered the words, "Yes, Caroline, I love you, too." Cue the romantic kiss, and of course, the music.

The fifty or so people who'd assembled for the sneak peek let out a collective sigh.

"That ought to hold the audience for another two years," a voice in the darkened office quipped.

It was Bill. His comment was mischievous, not mean-spirited. He knew that the key to sustaining viewer interest in characters, particularly lovers, was to make the audience wait, wait, and wait some more before giving them this kind of romantic payoff. And he loved knowing that.

"When you spin out a story, it can become a wonderful story, and in daytime you have the time to tell it," Pat Falken Smith said. "Irna Phillips, Agnes Nixon, and Bill Bell are storytellers. And the infinite art is like pulling taffy. There's always one more pull left. Just when you think they're going to snap it off, they give it another yank."

In the shipboard scene, Ridge also promised Caroline (who was briefly leaving town) that he'd "try my damnedest to sort out my feelings. And when you return you will have my answer."

"Note the conditional 'try,'" Bill wryly observed of Ridge's carefully selected words, as if he were offering DVD-style commentary on why he wrote the scene so specifically.

Bill's playful analysis of that episode showed that he knew exactly what he was doing and that he had a genuine connection to his audience's involvement with his shows. Bill had, as Susan Flannery said, "a sly wit."

Bill was a master at the unexpected story twist. He adhered to the philosophy of Spanish playwright Lope de Vega, who once wrote, "Always trick expectancy."

On *Y&R*, Nina's lawyer polled jury members after they found her guilty of trying to kill her devious husband. (Nina's actions were justified; David had planned on murdering both Nina and her toddler son, Phillip, so he could inherit the Chancellor millions.) As jurors were asked to state if this indeed was their verdict, a young panelist shockingly confessed that, in fact, it was not. She'd been pressured into voting for conviction by fellow jurors. The judge then sent the jury back into the deliberation room. Later, a unanimous verdict of innocent was reached!

For months Sheila's stroke-victim mother, Molly, struggled to tell Lauren that "Sheila has your baby." She often got most of the sentence out—except for the word "baby." Lauren still wasn't grasping what

Molly was attempting to reveal as the audience anxiously waited for the day that Molly would finally be able to articulate the whole truth.

That day never came.

"I think the word she's trying to say...is 'baby,'" a gun-toting Sheila stoically announced to Lauren and Molly, whom she had taken hostage. Sheila had grown so sick of Molly's stuttering that she herself confessed the secret!

Not knowing if her husband, Neil, or his half-brother, Malcolm, had fathered her daughter, Lily, Drucilla made the shocking choice to not look at the blood tests that would confirm—or jettison—her worst fear. She'd decided it was better never to know rather than burden her conscience with the truth!

Mamie Johnson poured her heart out to employer John Abbott, professing her deep love for him. She turned to see his reaction, only to discover that John had suffered a stroke. How much—if anything—had he heard Mamie reveal?

Classic *Y&R* moments like these, and scores of others, kept viewers on the edge of their seats, creating lifelong devotion in the process. Bill always knew how to keep his audience wanting more.

"Bill's true gift, aside from having good story, was that [his storylines] always came from character," recalls Lucy Johnson, former CBS senior vice president of daytime, children's programs, and special projects. "He knew how to pace and unfold stories. He saw the twists and turns. It was instinctive. Bill had an innate ability to know when to twist them and when not to," she says

Bill was a master at taking his characters in new directions once a storyline appeared to be "resolved." After *B&B*'s Stephanie manipulated rival Beth Logan out of Los Angeles, she assumed a happy reunion with her semi-estranged husband, Eric, would follow. Eric agreed to remain under Steph's roof, but with the provision that their marriage would be in name only. Bill wrote that Stephanie had won—yet she had not.

Victory was also snatched away from Brad on *Y&R* after he finally escaped from the cage in which his deranged ex-wife, Lisa, imprisoned him. Brad raced to the courthouse to keep true-love Traci from divorcing him, but, upon his arrival, he collapsed from pneumonia and was too late to keep her from finalizing their split. Brad had won his freedom, but Lisa had succeeded in destroying his marriage.

With Bill, the stories always continued.

Bill's tales enlightened audiences about many social issues and different paths of life. While he enjoyed great freedom with the types of stories he was able to tell, Bill found that some topics remained taboo, such as homosexuality and interracial marriage.

"Something like homosexuality you'd never make too explicit," he told the *Chicago Tribune* in 1973. "You're going to turn people off. In *Days*, we suggested that two men might have had a homosexual relationship, but the viewer would have had to have been very perceptive to have gotten it. The men didn't touch; there was nothing overt. Women have very little interest in homosexuality anyway. If you were going to do anything for what is essentially a female audience, lesbianism probably would have more innate interest."

Bill attempted to explore this with the character of Katherine on *Y&R*. He wrote in a 1977 long-term story projection that the character of Joann would go to live with Mrs. Chancellor after her divorce at the urging of Brock, Kay's son.

"We're beginning to see how mutual need and loneliness is manifesting itself in a relationship between these two women that Brock could never anticipate," Bill wrote.

Audiences rejected the story, however, and Bill wrapped it up quickly.

Today, Maria Arena Bell has incorporated gay characters (Phillip, Rafe) onto *Y&R*'s canvas. Bill's exclusion of them was based on the times in which he lived and wrote—not on any personal issues.

"The only people that Bill didn't like working with were people who didn't have talent," says Tom Langan, a former *Y&R* producer. "It didn't matter to him if you were gay, straight, white, black, or Puerto Rican."

Bill lived long enough to see society grow more accepting of interracial romance; the phone lines in the *Y&R* production office lit up when John and Mamie, the Abbott's African American housekeeper, locked lips, but he still got the smooch on the air. A few years later, when Bill wrote Victoria's rebound romance with Neil, the fact that she's white and he's black was barely addressed. Instead, Vicki's lingering feelings for Cole and the emotional devastation of giving birth to his daughter, Eve, who died shortly after delivery, proved to be the couple's undoing.

Bill enlightened viewers on people with disabilities by hiring actress Christopher Templeton, who played Jabot secretary Carol Robbins in the '80s and early '90s. Templeton, who passed away in 2011, contracted polio as a child and used a leg brace, as did her character.

"Carol is not a stereotypical gimp," the actress told *Soap Opera Digest* in 1986. "She's an outspoken, fashionable lady, and Bill Bell is to be applauded. He's the first person to hire and maintain a person with a disability."

Bill reached people on a one-on-one basis with his philosophies, too. Dan McVicar, who debuted as fashion designer Clarke Garrison on *B&B* in 1987, recalls an educational exchange he had with Bill at a party.

"I said, 'Bill, I've gotta go. I have lines to memorize for tomorrow.'" Bill caught the actor's eye and said, "You don't have to—you *get* to," subtly pointing out that employment for an actor was a good thing—not a chore. "I got the message right away," McVicar says. "Bill was exactly right. I got to do the show, and I got to do it for a long time."

A famous soap-opera producer at ABC called one of her writers while he was recovering in the hospital from unexpected surgery.

"Dear, where is your script?" the producer inquired.

The scribe reminded the exec that he'd only recently been operated on and was still recovering.

"Yes, dear. The studio is sending flowers. *Where* is your script?"

Bill, actually, could be equally tough. "Make no mistake," Kay Alden says. "Bill was very demanding. We worked long hours all the time. I worked weekends almost all the time, but Bill did not have that almost obsessive need for control. He welcomed me having a life of my own."

"Writing scripts, blocking out stories, and getting them in on time were the most important things on earth to Bill," recalls Sherman Magidson. "I called Bill the night that I separated from my wife, which was a momentous occasion in my life. I told him that my script would be a day late while I got a new place to live and unpacked. He said, 'It's due here tomorrow morning.'

"Bill wasn't being nasty. It was him translating what Irna Phillips had insisted on and what Bill had come to realize was a necessity. Adhering to a timetable was absolutely necessary if a show was to be successful. My script was there the next morning."

While Irna kept a tight leash on Bill, he gave his writers more geographical freedom. Chicago-based scribe Jack Smith told Bill in the early '80s that he wanted to move to the West Coast.

"Bill said, 'Jack, it's just a question of how we'll make it work,'" Smith recalls. "I moved to L.A., and later Hawaii, and we started doing conference calls."

Hope Harmel Smith had left her job as an associate producer at New York-based *Guiding Light* in fall 1986 to accept a position on *B&B*'s original producing team in Los Angeles. Understandably, she wanted to make the right impression on her new boss. Shortly before relocating to L.A., however, Hope learned that her father needed open-heart surgery.

"I was nervous when I called him about my father," Harmel Smith recalls. "Bill said to me, 'Don't think twice about it. Your place is with your parents, and your job is waiting here for you.'"

Hope realized later it wasn't about her making the right impression on Bill. "He made one on *me*," she says fondly.

"I never had any regrets about being there for my family. And I'll always be grateful to Bill for understanding that. As mythic a figure as he was—and Bill was larger than life—you could still always go to him with the most major or miniscule issue. I never felt like I was wasting his time. He was always approachable."

Jeanne Cooper credits Bill with literally saving her life when she was going through a personal crisis in the mid-'80s that mirrored the dramas belonging to her *Y&R* alter-ego.

"I was going through a horrible divorce and I was drinking," Cooper says. "I'd get stomach spasms. People suggested that I have a brandy to relax. Pretty soon, the brandy was causing the spasms. I couldn't get over my unhappiness over being married to someone who had deceived me. You just think that this is something that happens to other people.

"I came to work drunk a few times," she reveals.

Bill visited Cooper in her dressing room to see how she was coping. Not well, he quickly discovered. Bill contacted her son, Collin Bernsen, so that Cooper would get immediate professional help.

"He told Collin that I had to get into rehab or they couldn't continue with my storyline. Bill said that this was absolutely mandatory that I get help. He and Collin had already contacted St. John's hospital. I thought, 'Thank God, somebody has come to my rescue.'

"Bill understood. I either would have survived, or I would have killed my ex-husband and then been in prison for the rest of my life.

What Bill did was show me that I am the good person that I can be. You can be told that time and time again, but his actions proved it."

Cooper entered rehab and Bill recast Katherine. In fact, "recast" may be too strong a word. Bill hired actress Gisele MacKenzie to come in for a few days. She was there long enough to pack Kay's suitcase and tell Esther that she was leaving town. Bill knew there were some actors that the audience considered irreplaceable and Cooper topped that list.

"Bill said, 'I know one thing. I will never get anyone to play this part. If you're not well, I will write you out. I will not have anyone replace you.'"

Cooper spent a month in rehab and then returned to the show. "Bill and Lee turned my life around. Just knowing them…I didn't have to see him and don't have to see her often to feel the effect that they have on me," Cooper says.

"Bill knew that Jeanne was very valuable to the show," says Langan. "He respected her ability as an actress tremendously. He knew that it was her pain that was causing her to drink. Bill knew that he could have written [the storyline] successfully without her, but he also knew that she cared about the show."

Bill knew the importance of not only keeping familiar faces, but recognizable sets, too. Viewers instantly know they've tuned in to *B&B* when they see Eric's stately decorated office or the off-white sofas and giant mirror over the fireplace in the Forrester mansion. Fans feel the same way about the Newman ranch and the Abbott living room on *Y&R*.

At another CBS soap opera, a temporary producer changed long-standing sets overnight. The replacement ones were spiffier, but the newness was jarring to longtime viewers. The scripts didn't even call for the characters to acknowledge their updated surroundings. Familiar locations were suddenly just gone. Perhaps not coincidentally, the ratings continued to drop and the show was eventually canceled.

Sy Tomashoff, *B&B*'s original production designer, a multiple Daytime Emmy winner who designed sets for *Dark Shadows*, *Ryan's Hope*, and *Capitol*, recalls someone suggesting that the dirty windows at perennial underdog Spectra Fashions be cleaned. "We discussed it with Bill, and he said, 'Don't touch it! It stays the way it is!'

"Bradley is the same way," Tomashoff adds. "Someone in the cast said that their character would have refurnished their set by now. Bradley said, 'Don't touch it! The audience relates to that set and they don't want to see any changes.'"

Much of Bill's success came from the fact that he was left alone by network executives. Their hands-off approach not only created an environment that allowed Bill to nurture *Y&R*, bringing it to the number-one spot, but also gave him the time that he needed to develop and execute *B&B*.

"It wasn't that Bill was left alone," says Eric Braeden. "Bill made them leave him alone. He said, 'You f— with me, I'm out of here!' Running this business by committee is a dreadful mistake on all levels."

"I don't have the pressures of the network that some head writers do because I've been around long enough to know what I'm doing and the network knows that," Bill told Linda Susman in 1987. "I have had no interference from CBS in all the fourteen years I've been here and in the prior six or seven at NBC. When people are confident in you and when you deliver, they're wise enough to leave [you] alone."

Michael Brockman was one of those executives. "The pressures of the business make it very difficult to maintain a sense of stability, which you need for a creative environment," he says. "Writers and producers have to be able to think and to externalize their ideas, to accept and reject what will work and what won't. You have to cocoon them from other forces. That's the job of the executives in charge."

Brockman, Lucy Johnson, and other CBS executives never asked Bill to climax a story to accommodate the ratings sweeps periods in February, May, and November, the time periods used to set advertising rates.

"I don't remember Bill writing to the sweeps," says Brian Frons. "His mentality was, 'We're going to be good all the time.'"

Bill was admired not only by everyone at his own shows, but also by actors and producers at other shows and other networks.

"Everyone at *Y&R* has the greatest respect for who he was and what he did," says Stephen Nichols (ex-Patch, *Days*, and ex-Stefan, *GH*), who debuted as Tucker, Katherine Chancellor's long-lost son in early 2010. "Bill Bell was the rock of the show. In daytime, if there isn't one person who has a very strong vision and sticks to it, then the show eventually goes astray."

"I met Bill, but I never worked for him," says Francesca James, an Emmy-winning actress and executive producer, best known for her roles as twins Kitty and Kelly on *All My Children*. "Bill always had a wonderful reputation. He was remarkably creative and created a wonderful, wonderful family. People like Bill, Aggie [Nixon], and Claire [Labine] are all very diverse but what they have in common is their passion for the medium. They loved the medium."

"Bill was like Agnes Nixon," concurs three-time Emmy-winner Michael E. Knight, who played Tad on *AMC*. "They're master storytellers who don't tell stories by way of focus groups. Bill Bell would say, 'No, this is the story. This is the arc we're doing and we're going to drive the audience crazy and they're going to love it!' I met Bill once at the Daytime Emmys and I was very tongue-tied. But he knew exactly who I was and he was one of the kindest men I'd ever met."

"He was a titan in our business," adds Grant Aleksander, who played Phillip on *Guiding Light*. "I have a great respect for all that he contributed to daytime. Everything I ever saw with shows that were produced by the Bells was that they understand far and away that way, way on top of the mountain is writing good, consistent characters. I always had the feeling that they never stray from the belief in that concept. That's why Bill Bell's shows have done so well. They're still at the top."

"I loved Bill," says Catherine Hickland, who appeared on *Texas*, *Capitol*, and *One Life to Live*. "I had many conversations with Bill over the years. He asked me to fill in for Katherine Kelly Lang for a few days as Brooke after *B&B* first started. I told him I didn't want to because it might rule me out for future roles, but he said it was a huge favor to him. How could I say no?"

"I've worked with some really smart, brilliant people, but I realize now that I was in the company of a true genius when I worked with Bill," says Margot Wain, CBS's director of daytime. "There was nobody like him."

"Bill's stories were like fireworks," Peter Bergman says. "When you're watching his stories and you see something spectacular, you think that has to be the finale, but that wasn't what Bill did. While other shows were gearing up for sweeps, Bill would be doing the most stunning stuff the month before. Bill had his audience in his pocket all the time. In his pocket! I don't think he ever played to sweeps. Just as one of his stories was starting to ebb, another would flow.

"That was," Bergman adds, "Bill's genius."

Chapter 17

FENMORE'S WEST

The baby needs changing.

—Sheila Carter, played by Kimberlin Brown, in TV promos featuring Sheila's move from *Y&R* to *B&B* in 1992

Bill and Lee gave their children many opportunities, but eventually they wanted Bill, Brad, and Lauralee to stand on their own. They couldn't write Brad's scripts for him or go down to the set and play Lauralee's scenes for her.

They treated *B&B* the same way. Bill and Lee gave their half-hour creation all the elements it needed to succeed—compelling story, great-looking actors, lavish sets, and experienced directors—but the one thing they wouldn't give *B&B*, at least in the beginning, was help from its "big sister" *Y&R*.

It would have been tempting to use star wattage like Eric Braeden or Jeanne Cooper. Guest stars from *Y&R* could have shined a spotlight on *B&B* during its first few weeks. It wasn't unprecedented to cross characters over to other shows. *General Hospital*'s Steve Hardy visited *One Life to Live* on ABC. *Guiding Light*'s Mike and Hope Bauer even jumped networks from CBS to spend some time on NBC's *Another World.*

The closest a crossover came in *B&B*'s early years was when *Y&R*'s Jess Walton dropped by Stage 31 to tape a promo spot with Susan Flannery, encouraging *Y&R* viewers to check out *B&B.* As far as Bill was concerned, however, the shows existed in separate universes, which made things less confusing since he'd hired former *Y&R* stars John McCook, Lauren Koslow, and Jim Storm to play roles on *B&B.*

In 1992, Bill realized that he had a situation on *Y&R* where he was going to have to write off the nefarious Sheila, who had committed a host of crimes, including kidnapping Lauren's son, Scotty. She even took the infant to a surgeon to have a birthmark removed to hide his identity.

Knowing Sheila had to either be killed off or imprisoned, Bill came up with a compromise. He realized that Sheila could escape to Los Angeles and become involved with characters on *B&B* who knew nothing about her past.

Bill believed his plan would have maximum impact if no one saw it coming. He needed it to be kept a secret. Kimberlin Brown, who played sociopathic Sheila with chilling perfection, happily entered the conspiracy with her boss.

"I was on set at *Y&R* one day and was told that Bill needed to speak to me," recalls Brown. "It was rare to get a call from Bill so I knew it meant something. He told me that he was either going to have to kill Sheila off or send her to jail."

Bill then floated a third option by the actress. "He said, 'What if she were to escape and go to…Los Angeles?'" Beyond the Fenmore's West reference at the Forresters' Fourth of July party the year before, Bill hadn't tied his two shows together on-air so Brown, understandably, didn't comprehend what Bill was saying.

"Then Bill said, '*Bold and Beautiful* is set in Los Angeles.' He told me Sheila would live and continue her antics in another city and that he'd bring me back and forth between shows. I said, 'Great!' He told me not to whisper a word to anyone or else it wasn't going to work. People asked me what Bill had wanted to talk to me about and I said, 'Oh, he just wanted to give me some direction.'"

Bill said that Brown wasn't the only one initially confused by his words. "I put it that way to most people," Bill said. "And they didn't immediately get it either, but when they did, it was so funny to hear their reactions. Kimberlin was just in heaven. She was as euphoric as I was."

"Bill made me feel like I was a part of the entire process," Brown recalls.

"It was the perfect character to do it with," says Margot Wain. "Sheila couldn't stay on *Y&R* anymore. Her moving to Los Angeles and wrecking havoc on the Forresters was great."

Steps were taken to keep Sheila's move a secret. "We asked Kimberlin to wear a hat when she came to the studio," says Rhonda Friedman, *B&B*'s supervising producer. "We had interns bring Kimberlin her lunch and scripts, which referred to her character as 'Jane.' We did everything we could to protect the secret and we did. It was a brilliant moment for Bill. He was just tickled. He wanted to keep it a secret because it was such a delicious one."

"I didn't say a word," Brown says. "That's one of the reasons the crossover was so successful."

"I was faced with the reality of bringing her back to Genoa City," Bill told *Soap Opera Weekly*. "It was not going to open up much in the way of story because once someone saw her, she'd have been arrested and would have to face [criminal] charges. It seemed a dead end.

"Out of nowhere," Bill added, "I was hit with a thought that just boggled my mind. 'What if she goes to [*B&B*]?'"

Next, Bill presented the idea to Brad and Jack. "Each time I told people my idea, I would become more and more hyper about the story and excited about it."

Bill had to work out some legal issues with Columbia Pictures Television because the studio was partners with Bill and they had a say in how their characters would be used. "Even characters that have been let go," Bill explained. "Because characters do have [continuing] value, but that's all been worked out."

After Sheila supposedly died in a fire on the outskirts of Genoa City, she fled to Los Angeles and applied for a position as a nurse at Forrester Creations. Audiences immediately panicked when Sheila picked up Eric Jr., Brooke and Eric's toddler son, after he'd gotten lost in the hallways of the fashion house.

Bill had placed his characters in jeopardy by having diabolical Sheila infiltrate their lives and only he, and his audiences, knew about it. The character's capacity for violence (she had physically attacked Lauren on more than one occasion and also pumped lead into a defenseless television set) brought *B&B* to dramatic new heights.

"Bill was in a position to take a character from the number-one-rated show in daytime to a show that was still fairly new in terms of soap-opera years and bring [the *Y&R*] audience over, too," Brown says. "Everyone wanted to see what Sheila was going to do next."

Despite promos teasing that "the baby needs changing," the fashion-themed soap hadn't truly needed that many alterations. While Sheila's presence ultimately helped catapult the show to the number-two spot, Bill had fine-tuned *B&B* in its early years. He segued away from the Logans and introduced Sally Spectra, which amped up the show's entertainment value.

"Brooke had taken off, but every time we went to the other Logans it felt as if the energy had dropped," Brad says. "There wasn't the 'pop' we needed out of them. Enter Darlene Conley, who stole the show as Sally Spectra. She was such a fascinating actress to watch."

Producer-director John C. Zak recalls the enthusiasm that Bill had for both the respected actress and her outrageous alter ego. "We saw Bill walk past the frosted glass windows outside the conference room of the production offices one morning," Zak says. "He came in and announced, 'We are getting Darlene Conley to play Sally Spectra. She'll bring something sensational to the show.' The unmitigated glee on Bill's face was something I enjoyed. He was like a little boy with a secret. The character made such a splash in daytime. I don't think anyone's ever been able to top it. That was Darlene, and that was Bill, too."

"Sally was only supposed to be a short-term role," Conley told *Soap Opera Digest*. "She was to come in and steal designs from the Forresters. But I knew right away that the audience was going to love Sally; there hadn't been a woman like this on TV for a long time."

Conley was correct. Sally, with her big hair and even bigger heart, was an instant hit. Her devotion to her daughter, Macy, called to mind classic film heroines of the '40s and '50s played by Joan Crawford and Barbara Stanwyck.

"Hello, Stephanie," became Sally's signature line and opened many a scene between the two matriarchs. With those two words, Conley clearly communicated her character's deep desire to win Stephanie's friendship and approval.

"Bill was huge when it came to subtext," Zak says. "He made sure that the actors were playing it and that it was being conveyed effectively to the audience. 'Subtext' (meaning what characters are truly saying to each other) is a buzzword thrown around in writing classes, but Bill was a master at it. He knew that it matters as much what characters don't say in a scene as what they do say that reveals their true natures. If there's anything I took away from Bill, it's what subtext can do. Why is this character holding back from saying something?"

"Darlene was high energy, unpredictable, everything we needed to contrast the proper and staid Forrester family," Brad says.

While always outlandish and sometimes manipulative, Sally was never violent, as Sheila was. After the naughty nurse was ensconced in the lives of the Forresters, Bill's next step was to bring Lauren over from *Y&R*, a logical move, given that Lauren's position as a department store owner put her on the invitation list for Forrester fashion shows.

The fashion galas became a staple on *B&B* just as the Danny Romolatti rock concerts were at *Y&R*. The extravaganzas had different themes including Felicia's fight for environmental awareness, a salute to Hollywood, and Brooke's fashions for men. But no matter how glitzy the fashion galas became, the real showstopper was whatever Bill and Brad had up their sleeves storywise.

"Bill allowed us to have a lot of input into the theme of the fashion shows," Zak recalls. "Sy Tomashoff and I would come up with concepts and let Bill know what we were thinking." Bill approved their ideas, provided they accommodated his storylines. "When it came to story, there were no 'ifs, ands, or buts.' There was no room for negotiation. You had to dig into his material. If you didn't, you'd hear about it."

And then it was time to move on. "Bill did not die of an ulcer," says Friedman. "He didn't hold things in. If he had an issue with you, he'd tell you and then he'd be done with it."

Bill always incorporated music into his dramatic serials. Jeff serenaded Penny on *ATWT*. *Days*' Doug and Julie sang romantically to each other. Lance, Leslie, and Gina were among Bill's crooners on *Y&R*. The scribe continued his tradition of casting singing actors on *B&B*, and he struck gold with Bobbie Eakes (Macy) and Jeff Tractha (Thorne). The duo played to sold-out audiences around the world.

B&B became the place for guest stars throughout the '90s. Singer

Dionne Warwick (who sang "High upon This Love," a tune used briefly as the show's closing theme), hair stylist Jose Eber, and actors Charlton Heston, Carol Channing, Steve Allen, and Jayne Meadows all played themselves, lending authenticity to the show's Los Angeles locale and the Hollywood-themed fashion show.

Bill, however, wasn't a huge fan of stunt casting. "They titillate the audience," he said of soap-opera guest stars. "It's frosting on the cake, but the story is still the story."

Bill enlisted senior *B&B* and *Y&R* writer Jack Smith to help teach Brad the doctrines of daytime storytelling. Smith later became head writer and coexecutive producer of *Y&R* after Bill retired, but he had hoped that Bill was going to hand him the reins at *B&B*.

"I always assumed that someday I'd be running one of these shows," Smith shares. "I still have a letter that Bill wrote me. He said, 'I'm going to turn *B&B* over to Bradley, and I expect you to help him run the show.' I felt betrayed, deeply disappointed. Whenever I came to Los Angeles from Honolulu, Bill would insist that I stay at the house. I felt like family."

Soon, Smith not only accepted Bill's decision, but he also realized that Bill made the only one possible. "Bill was loyal to everyone, but to his family especially. He wanted his son to write the show. Realizing that, I pitched in and made sure that Brad became the best head writer I could help him to be."

"I can see why Jack felt that way," Lee says about Smith hoping that he'd be put in charge at *B&B*. "He would have been the only other person who Bill would have given *B&B* to, but [Bill] wanted Brad to do it. Bill tested Bradley all the time, in high school, in college, and after college. He'd watch him, wondering if he could do it. Bradley had to prove himself over and over again and he did."

Bill kept a watchful eye on *B&B*, serving as the show's executive story consultant after Brad was made executive producer and head writer. Zak recalls a particularly racy lovemaking scene on *B&B* between married couple Ridge and Taylor, directed by Susan Flannery. In it, Ridge ripped off his wife's negligee straps, lifted her up in the air, and pushed her up against the wall. Soon, Ridge and Taylor were wrapped in the sheets, basking in sweaty afterglow. "What you did to me!" an exhausted Taylor proclaimed to Ridge after a commercial break.

Taylor later theorized that Ridge's passion for her was fueled by his preoccupation with former fiancée Brooke, whom he'd just visited in the hospital. Ridge and Taylor had just made glorious love, but there was still plenty of unresolved tension.

"We didn't have a lot of lead time between when that episode was edited and when it was going to air," recalls Zak. "Brad and I called Bill. He came in, watched it, and said, 'It's fine.' Then he walked out. We got some buzz from the network about it, but Bill appreciated that we showed it to him."

Ultimately, Bill favored romance over passion. He limited the number of scenes like Ridge and Taylor's sexually charged romp. "[They're] more fun to do with the imagination because the viewer will always bring more to it," Bill said.

"It's much better to have it be implied," Brad concurs. "But there are moments when you have to cover your eyes. It *is* a soap opera. Overall, it's more our style to be sexy and romantic, as opposed to being gratuitous."

Meanwhile, Sheila's wicked ways continued. She eventually resorted to criminal behavior to keep her freedom. After seven additional years of blackmail, betrayal, kidnapping, corruption, and a failed suicide attempt, Sheila came to the end of the road. Thanks to Bill's endless imagination and Brown's ability to play a sympathetic but calculating villain, Sheila's reign of terror ran for nearly an entire decade.

"I remember when Kimberlin came on for that little summer storyline for Lauren and Scott," recalled Tracey Bregman. "But she made it last. Bill is wonderful that way. When he sees something and he knows it works, he goes with it. He saw that with Kimberlin and made it happen."

B&B celebrated Brown's run on the set with a farewell cake and photo opportunities in September 1998. Exiting stars smile for the cameras at these events, but the farewells are often emotional roller coasters. Outgoing actors are asked to say something witty, humble, and profound in front of their former coworkers and members of the press just before they head off to the unemployment line. (One veteran performer at ABC Daytime called such gatherings "the champagne kiss-off," though champagne is seldom served.)

Bill and Lee presented Brown with a beautiful watch from Tiffany & Co. Sensing that Brown was very emotional over bringing Sheila to a close, he approached the actress and comforted her with the promise that this was not the last of Sheila. "We will miss you in the interim," he said. "And that's what this will be, an interim."

"That set my heart at ease and made things easier," Brown says. "I believed him. He wasn't the type of man who said something that he didn't mean, which in this business isn't always the case. Some producers tell actors what they want to hear. Bill put his arm around me, and he and Lee thanked me. I got to go home and tell my husband and my family that it wasn't over, it was just a break. Bill, Lee, Brad, and the whole family have been very kind to me and to Sheila."

Sheila returned to *B&B* in 2002 and 2003 to wreak additional havoc. She wounded Brooke and shot Taylor dead in a dramatic slow-motion sequence. Upon returning to *Y&R* in 2005, Sheila learned that Taylor hadn't died after all.

Sheila, in fact, continues to be referred to, even though she herself is now presumed to be dead. "I have an enormous fan base from playing this character that Bill created," Brown says. "They haven't forgotten her."

Brad has continued to focus on *B&B* mainstays, including Stephanie, Eric, Brooke, Ridge, and Taylor, while successfully introducing future generations with Rick and Bridget (Eric and Brooke's children), Steffy and Thomas (Ridge and Taylor's kids), and Hope (Brooke's daughter courtesy of her fling with son-in-law Deacon).

Bill proudly watched as *B&B*, under Brad's creative direction, regularly claimed the number-two spot in the weekly Nielsen ratings. He saw his son earn his first Daytime Emmy nomination for Drama Series Writing Team in 2000. Flannery won Outstanding Lead Actress that year for scenes that contained a dramatic showdown between Stephanie and Brooke at the Forrester's Big Bear cabin. Bill had set up the dynamic between the two rivals, and Brad continues to mine that rich relationship.

Any rivalry that exists between Bill's two shows is far healthier than the one between Stephanie and Brooke. "Doesn't every Number 2 show want to be Number 1?" muses Friedman. "But we've never wanted to see it happen by having *Y&R*'s ratings drop. That would never bring us a feeling of victory. We'd only want to see it by having our ratings go up."

While *Y&R* maintains its dominance in the ratings, *B&B* has beaten the top-rated soap—on the softball field. In games organized by *B&B*'s Cindy Popp, the half-hour soap has triumphed.

Bill and Lee never played favorites with their children, but Bill actually did with his soaps. "I have very special feelings for *Bold* and other creations," Bill told *Soap Opera Magazine* in a 1998 story celebrating *Y&R*'s twenty-fifth anniversary. "But *Y&R* certainly has the biggest place in my heart. I've been through so much with it—the joys, the sorrows, and the euphoria. The positives have far outweighed the negatives. It's a wonderful legacy."

Chapter 18

A "BOLD" MOVE

Without Bill Bell, I don't know what CBS would have become. He has truly been the godfather of our daytime performance, which has won week in and week out for ten years. Without Y&R *and* The Bold and the Beautiful, *I don't know what I would have been able to face in my job. Thank you, Bill, for all that you've meant to me and this network.*

—Les Moonves, president and chief executive officer, CBS Corporation, 1999

I can't think of a more difficult job than being a head writer of a soap opera," says Michael Brockman. "It requires not just creative skill in storytelling, but also great discipline in keeping this template in front of you and in your head. You have to figure out how to plot stories in the most efficient, dramatic, and engaging way."

Bill worked in daytime television for more than forty years. There have been other popular and talented writers, but nobody matched Bill in terms of longevity. And when it came to delivering the ratings, Bill was unparalleled.

Even admired greats at other shows would eventually run out of steam. They'd go through slumps. Fans would still support the show and their favorite characters, but they'd also wish that the writer would go to another soap opera and start anew.

Bill never had to do that. And fans never wanted him to leave *Y&R*. He could always find new stories for Kay, Nikki, Victor, Jack, Jill, and the rest of the citizens living in Genoa City.

And yet, Bill was only a partial partner of *Y&R*, the top-rated daytime drama that's pulled in ratings, viewers, and huge profits for decades.

Columbia Pictures Television (now Sony Pictures Television) and CBS Television, which airs *Y&R* domestically, had reaped huge financial rewards from Bill's genius for many years.

In the late '80s, Bill felt that his dad was long overdue in being given a bigger piece of the pie. He suggested that his father re-address his deal with Columbia Pictures Television insofar as the profit sharing was concerned.

"Billy had a huge impact on negotiating a deal [between Bell Dramatic Serial Company and Columbia] in the late '80s, which made the Bell family a full partner," Maria Arena Bell explains. "It changed Bill from being an employee of Columbia Pictures Television to being an essential owner. It was transformative for the show and enables us to have the integrity that we prize so much today. Bill was the person who suggested to his dad that they could be owners of these shows, produce them, and grow them into a worldwide business."

"My brother said, 'Dad, we're not delivering scripts until we can share in the gross profits,'" recalls Brad. "It came down to the wire where *Y&R* was going to have to stop taping. We had a backlog of scripts under lock and key at the house. [Studio executives] said, 'We'll fire you! You're an employee and we will fire you!'

"My dad was understandably nervous, but my brother dug his heels into the ground. He said, 'Fire him!' Then they just said, 'All right. We'll give you a greater percentage of the gross profits.' From that day forward, *Y&R* became much more profitable for the family."

"It was very tight," one of Bill's long-running *Y&R* producers recalls of the show nearly running out of scripts during this tense time. "Production didn't stop. Scripts had always come in like clockwork. But there came a time when they just were not being delivered."

Gary Lieberthal, the former head of Columbia Pictures Television, recalls that Sony was the lucky one to be in business with Bill Bell. The company wasn't about to endanger its working relationship with the daytime-serial genre's greatest storyteller. And nobody was letting on if there were any residual hard feelings over the family taking a strong stance. In fact, a few years after it was all ironed out, the studio hosted an all-star gala to honor—and roast—Bill at Chasen's restaurant.

"We have a policy at Columbia," Lieberthal quipped at the roast. "We throw a major event for every producer who's been in the business for thirty-five years."

"There are only a few franchises in television," the former studio chief says. "A franchise draws a large predetermined audience not for five or seven years, but for thirty or more. The National Football League is a franchise. *The Tonight Show* is a franchise. The most compelling franchise to add to those two is *The Young and the Restless*. It's been the number-one show in all of daytime for over twenty-two years.

"I would say that I've met two creative geniuses in the television business," Lieberthal continues. "One was Norman Lear (*All in the Family, Maude*), for whom I worked. The other was Bill Bell. Bill was without peer, the thriving creative force of *Y&R* the entire time he was alive. There's no one who compares to Bill Bell. If you ever line up Bill's fans, I'll be in the first ten."

Any renegotiating with Bill that ensured his becoming a greater partner with Sony was "without friction," Lieberthal recalls. However, he remembers a CBS chief chastising him when it came time for Sony to deal with the network. One exec there accused him of single-handedly destroying CBS by bankrupting it in daytime. "That was a real compliment to both *Y&R* and to me," Lieberthal chuckles.

Bill deserved a larger share of *Y&R*'s profits since he was the man ultimately responsible for generating them. "Working with Bill was the easiest thing you could imagine," Lieberthal adds. "You didn't have to worry about production, casting, scripts...Bill ran it all. We were really lucky that we wound up as his partner."

Sony Pictures Television's agreement to renegotiate Bill's position as a greater partner in the profit sharing wouldn't have happened unless the studio acknowledged something that viewers of *Y&R* were already well aware of—Bill Bell was the best storyteller in daytime dramatic serials. He'd been called the "Drama King" many times, but the title speaks to Bill's expertise in storytelling and how he rose to the top of his field, certainly not to his being overly dramatic in his conduct. Bill was easygoing, a kind man with Midwestern values. He had little in common with unapproachable monarchs or autocrats. In fact, he wasn't even comfortable with the term "power."

"I never think of myself or anyone having 'power' per se," he told *Soap Opera Magazine* in 1998 when he was interviewed by the author for a feature on Daytime's Twelve Most Powerful People. "We are in the business of producing television and of telling stories. We all have responsibilities and we collaborate. Some of us are more in the forefront than others, but I've never equated what I have with power. We all have responsibilities and we act accordingly."

Chapter 19

"YOUNG AND RESTLESS" YEARS, PART 3

To set the record straight, anyone out there who is thinking that Bell is thinking of retirement, hear this loud and clear—the best is yet to come!

—Bill Bell in his Lifetime Achievement Award acceptance speech at the 1992 Daytime Emmys

Bill promised the best was yet to come, and given the storylines and characters that he introduced to the show throughout the '90s, he was correct. With Brad accepting more and more responsibility at *B&B*, Bill had more time to devote to *Y&R*.

Now that Chris was enrolled in law school and Nina was on her way to becoming a successful writer, Bill decided it was time to introduce a new young group to the show. He aged Victor and Nikki's son, Nicholas, gave him a rival (Matt Clark), and two girlfriends, Amy and Sharon, the latter of whom became Nick's true love.

Joshua Morrow, who had tried out for the role of Dylan on *B&B*, was hired to play teenager Nicholas. Eddie Cibrian was cast as bad boy Matt. Viewers saw different actresses portray Amy and Sharon before Bill hired, respectively, Julianne Morris and Sharon Case as their definitive portrayers.

"Bill knew how to write love stories," says Case, who earned a Daytime Emmy for Outstanding Supporting Actress in 1999 for her *Y&R* role. "He knew how to make them romantic and meaningful. Nick would carry on about how he felt about Sharon. The words he would say to her were so beautiful. They were mesmerizing. I remember thinking, 'Wow! If any man ever spoke to me that way, it'd be amazing.' Bill knew how to win your heart. He knew how to make his characters speak from their hearts."

Nick and Sharon emerged as the show's new romantic leading duo, just as Snapper and Chris had been in the '70s and Victor and Nikki and Paul and Lauren were in the '80s. Over the next three years, Nick and Sharon endured her rape, Nick's false incarceration for attempting to kill her attacker, and the premature birth of their son Noah (whom Bill named after his sister Mary's grandson and Kay Alden's son).

While they had their share of larger-than-life problems, Nick and Sharon dealt with more down-to-earth woes as well, not the least of which was Nikki's open disdain for her daughter-in-law.

"Bill took everyday events and made them dramatic, as they are in real life," Case says. "Having a baby, getting married—these are *enormous* life events. Bill didn't just rush through them."

Monica Potter, star of NBC's *Parenthood*, was *Y&R*'s first Sharon. "Sometimes Bill would come to me and say that an actor just wasn't handling the material and that we'd have to recast," recalls Jill Newton, then the show's casting director. "I remember the call to Monica. They said, 'You'll be big someday' and they were right.

"Bill said he didn't want anyone else who was 'green,'" adds Newton, but when she spied model Shemar Moore in the pages of

GQ magazine, she saw a strong candidate for the upcoming role of Malcolm, Neil Winters's half-brother.

"I said to Bill, 'I know you didn't want to see anyone else who doesn't have a lot of experience, but this is my job.' Bill had a great sense of humor about it, but he was never so jovial you wouldn't give him your utmost respect."

"Bill Bell took a chance on me," says Moore. "He thought I was a handsome guy and liked that I was hungry. *Y&R* and Bill Bell changed my life."

~

At 4:31 a.m. on January 17, 1994, a 6.7-magnitude earthquake rocked southern California. The epicenter was in Northridge, more than twenty miles from Los Angeles, but the rocking and rolling still left the normally organized *Y&R* production office in disarray.

Erin Stewart, who later became an associate producer at *B&B*, was a *Y&R* intern and had gone to the *Y&R* production office to lend assistance.

"At first, the only other people there were Bill and Jerry Birn, who were working on a story," recalls Stewart, who, along with a production assistant, got the office reorganized. "The great thing was that Bill and Jerry had kept the door wide open during their storyline meeting so we got to listen in on it."

Bill felt that intern duties, which are performed in exchange for school credit, shouldn't include cleaning up after earthquakes—even in California. He instructed coordinating producer Nancy Wiard to have Stewart fill out some tax forms so she could be paid for her efforts.

~

In 1994, *Soap Opera Weekly* launched its inaugural Soap Opera Hall of Fame Awards. Bill, Agnes Nixon, the late Irna Phillips, Douglas

Marland, and Macdonald Carey were the first five inductees. Irna's daughter, Katherine, spoke on behalf of her mother at the ceremony held at Planet Hollywood in New York City. It was also an opportunity for her to reconnect with Bill and Lee. Later, she sent Bill a telegram with a few passages from Irna's unpublished memoir.

"I've not forgotten my promise to let you read Irna's words about you," Katherine said in her telegram. Irna had written: "I knew this young man would carry the torch on and on…there was no pupil as willing and talented. I was a teacher, but this pupil was going to get his PhD on his own…"

"There is more, of course," Katherine added. "'Thank you' aren't the descriptive words I wish to convey for the evening I spent with you; only know you touched me and brought me back to a place and time I deeply miss and treasure. Thanks for being you, Lee and Bill…Katherine."

On October 5, 1994, CBS broadcast a two-hour program, *50 Years of Soaps: An All-Star Celebration*, which featured clips, highlights, and tributes to daytime serials, past and present, from all three networks. The well-researched special reunited favorite couples from past eras, including John McCook and Jaime Lyn Bauer, who steamed up the screen in the '70s on *Y&R*.

Most of the *B&B* cast and crew were shooting Ridge and Brooke's long-awaited wedding in Malibu (the ceremony was invalid, however, because Ridge's "late" wife, Taylor, was actually alive). Still, a few *B&B* players and a large turnout from *Y&R* attended the taping in Hollywood.

The audience was literally a "Who's Who" of soap operas. A select group of notables, including *Days*' Bill and Susan Seaforth Hayes, *GH*'s Jacklyn Zeman, and *GL*'s Kim Zimmer, were invited to speak briefly before introducing a clip of their work. Bill, along with Phillips, Nixon, and Marland, was honored in a segment that paid tribute to soap-opera creators. Bill received a standing ovation and used his air-time to honor Lee, who was by his side, his "partner, both at home and on the job."

Producers selected Bill's breast-cancer tale on *Y&R* with Jennifer Brooks as an example of his socially relevant stories. "We did it for several reasons," Bill said. "There was a need to disseminate information about [breast cancer] as there was before then, and there has been since. The response is always enormous from an audience. They're grateful. You remind them when they need to be reminded."

With the assistance of legal advisor Sherman Magidson, Bill wrote many courtroom dramas. The trials kept Bill's viewers spellbound from opening statements to long after the verdicts were read.

In the mid-'90s, TV audiences were gripped by a real-life case. O.J. Simpson stood trial for murdering his ex-wife Nicole Brown Simpson and her friend Ronald Goldman. The media coverage played havoc with soap-opera fans' viewing habits. While the number of national preemptions that affected Bill's shows was relatively low, (seven in 1994, three in January 1995, and two for the trial and verdict in September 1995), the media circus dealt a blow to daytime-drama viewership. Some markets, including Los Angeles, interrupted regular programming more often than others.

Frank Rich, columnist for the *New York Times*, said that the trial "hijacked our culture."

The case garnered international attention, but David Shaw, a staff writer for the *Los Angeles Times*, wrote, "[T]he trial sent ratings sky-rocketing for CNN, Court TV, and E! Entertainment Television—and sent ratings plummeting for daytime soap operas. There were many weeks during the trial when every one of the nation's fifteen highest-rated programs on basic cable networks were segments of the trial telecast by CNN."

"The Simpson case is like a great trash novel come to life, a mammoth fireworks display of interracial marriage, love, lust, lies, hate, fame, wealth, beauty, obsession, spousal abuse, stalking, brokenhearted children, the bloodiest of bloody knife-slashing homicides, and all the justice that money can buy," wrote the late Dominic Dunne in *Vanity Fair.*

"If somebody sat down to come up with a grand plot outline for a new primetime soap opera and they came up with this story...a studio executive would have said, 'It's too far out, too unbelievable,'" Craig Hume, KTLA-TV's news director said.

"Bill was very sensitive," Christina Knack recalls about her boss's response to the tragedy. "But he didn't understand why the media was giving [Simpson] so much attention and publicity."

The network that wanted ninety minutes of daily drama from Bill appeared not to want any on days that the news division would interrupt the soaps with gavel-to-gavel coverage.

"I wasn't in Los Angeles during the O.J. trial," recalls Magidson. "My guess is that Bill would have objected strongly to World War III's interference with the scheduling of his shows. He felt that entertainment was entertainment, and news was news, and each had its own place on TV and neither should interfere with the other."

Lucy Johnson, CBS Daytime's vice president at the time, recalls *Y&R* being less affected with preemptions than other programs were. "The world would like to blame that trial [for] the demise of soap operas," she says. "But the demise had already started because of lifestyle changes. Computers were becoming more prominent, and cable was always an active competitor. There was a huge social shift in the '90s. It became harder and harder to maintain your audience. Bill, like everyone, struggled with doing that, but he never resorted to gimmicks to get the ratings up."

Instead, Bill continued to tell compelling and socially relevant stories with dynamic, engaging characters.

The exotic, but dangerous Mari Jo Mason arrived on the scene in 1994 to complicate Jack's love life. Mari Jo (aka Marilyn) was a grand villainess, originally cast with David Hasselhoff's then-wife Pamela Bach. The blond, wholesome-looking actress shot an episode or two but was recast with actress Diana Barton, a sophisticated brunette. (Despite the show's publicist punning that "Pamela will be 'Bach,'" another role never materialized for her.) Mari Jo's reign of terror was relatively brief compared to other *Y&R* antagonists, but she managed to cause conflict with Ashley and Blade, break Jack's heart, shoot Victor, and kidnap Christine before being carted away.

Bill created familial drama for the Barber clan, too. He explored the origins of the rivalry between siblings Olivia and Drucilla by revealing that their mother, Lillie Belle, had never wanted a second child. Feeling unloved, illiterate Dru took to the streets. After she got her life together, learned to read, married Neil, and had a daughter, Dru had a dramatic showdown with her mother, snarling at her, "I've survived you!"

Later, Bill delivered another gripping social issue with married Nathan cheating on his wife, Olivia, with HIV-positive Keesha. Bill mixed infidelity, social issues, irony, and drama into a tale of heartbreak, betrayal, and danger when Olivia learned that her husband had been intimate with her patient, Keesha. Tonya Lee Williams (Olivia) and Victoria Rowell (Drucilla) earned Daytime Emmy nominations for their performances in this storyline in 1996. Rowell repeated again in '97 and '98.

"Either you get rid of the 'hoochie mama,'" Drucilla blasted her brother-in-law Nathan, "I mean, *now*, do not see her anymore or else you're going to lose big! You're going to lose your wife, you're going to lose your little boy, and it will be the end of the road for you. I will see to that!"

"Bill knew I added all those 'Dru' lines like 'Cooked my last grit' and 'Smack you into Sunday,'" Rowell says. "But he loved that I put those in and made them authentically 'Drucilla.'"

As he had with Hasselhoff and the short-lived series *Semi-Tough*, Bill worked with Rowell's schedule so the actress could continue to play fan favorite Dru during the day and operate as Dr. Amanda Bentley, a pathologist on the long-running CBS primetime series *Diagnosis Murder*.

"Bill encouraged me to have interests beyond acting," Rowell says. "He gave me carte blanche with the choreography and casting of the dancers in the ballet storyline. He allowed me to oversee the costuming and selection of the music. Bill Bell was seeing me in a different way. I am forever grateful to this man who gave me something a long time ago that resonates with me today. He encouraged me to grow."

Y&R has always been groundbreaking, especially in terms of its sensuality. In the mid-'90s, Bill took a page from *NYPD Blue* and wrote in a few scenes that contained partial male nudity. "Bill thought we should have people on our show who shouldn't be wearing clothes," chuckles Doug Davidson, who was one of the selected stars to push the envelope.

"I was at the gym when Ed Scott called the house. Cindy, my wife, called me and I thought, 'Apparently, I'm working out the wrong muscle!'" recalls Davidson, who shot one semi-nude scene. Don Diamont and also Brent Jasmer, who played hunky Sly on *B&B*, also took part in the brief (or rather "brief-less" experiment).

"And then, that was it," Davidson says. The fad didn't catch on.

CBS rented advertising space on a billboard at the corner of Beverly Boulevard and Fairfax Avenue, which could be seen from the balcony off the *Y&R* studios, in honor of Bill's seventieth birthday in 1997. "That was a terrific time in Bill's life," Nancy Wiard fondly recalls. "Bill was on top of the world. The show had been number one for just under ten years at that point. It was a time of happiness and celebration."

The network was not only grateful to Bill for his enormous success in daytime, but also for writing and producing three *Y&R* primetime episodes that aired in the '90s. Long before the days of hits like *Survivor*, *CSI*, and *Two and a Half Men*, CBS was fighting even harder to stay competitive with the other networks. Bill's nighttime *Y&R* shows served as a lead-in to the Daytime Emmys one year. Another episode was used as counter-programming to the World Series.

Bill had dipped his toes into the primetime waters before with *Our Private World* and *Mad Avenue*, but he had no desire to take *Y&R* into the evening on a regular basis.

"I would just as soon not do that," he said. "It's a way of giving you added exposure, but it's a challenge to come up with that isolated show and yet be able to connect the show leading into and out of that nighttime show. There was no request [from CBS for us] to do that [in 1997], and I was very pleased there wasn't."

"We're not too fond of doing an hour at night," Lee concurred.

Y&R commemorated its twenty-fifth anniversary by preparing a time capsule that was installed on the CBS Television City property. The capsule contains a copy of the show's first script, one from episode # 6359 (which was taped on March 26, 1998), a selection of cast photos, three books dedicated to the show, and a list of the show's fan-club members.

Melody Thomas Scott read a loving testimonial that honored Bill to invited guests at the capsule's dedication.

"Bill, with his amazing imagination, has pushed the meaning of romance into another dimension while goading his audience to want even more. Those of us who have been fortunate enough to be a part of this incredible success marvel at our good luck and our agents rejoice!"

The actress thanked Bill for her many on-screen romances and also for introducing her to her real-life husband, Edward Scott. "The scenes we had produced on videotape all the years prior had prepared us for our real-life romance theater.

"When you read this, twenty-five years from now, I may or may not still be on this show. But if for some reason I'm not around to ask, just know that we all had a hell of a good time, Victor and Nikki are still in love (wherever they may be), and that Bill Bell (fate, destiny, take your pick) taught me to be eternally 'young and restless.'"

Just when you thought all the celebrating had been done, yet another cake would be ordered. *Y&R* began having on-set anniversary celebrations for its actors on an individual basis. Jeanne Cooper was honored first for being on the show for twenty-five years. One for twenty-year veteran Doug Davidson came next.

"Nancy did some research," Bill said at the tribute to the Genoa City private eye, "and tells me that when Doug joined *Y&R* as Paul, it was twenty-two months and 450 episodes before he got a last name, a family, or even a bedroom set!

"Let there be no doubt that Doug paid his dues. He emerged a strong leading man. He has been married to April and Lauren and had a very desperate love with Cassandra, but his ultimate romance has emerged with his marriage to Christine. Doug Davidson is now one of our more lasting stars. He not only has his own dressing room, he even rewrites his own lines—when he gets away with it," Bill chuckled, "which isn't too often."

Davidson thanked not only Bill, but Lee, too, for invaluable advice she'd given him years before. "She said to me, 'Maybe you shouldn't try so hard.' It took me a few years to understand that. Now, I've never been happier."

Six years after Bill received the Lifetime Achievement Award, he readied for retirement. He and Lee decided that he'd announce his stepping down from his daily duties as head writer at their upcoming annual pre-Daytime Emmy press reception in New York City. Bill was deeply content at this time. *Y&R* was—and remains—the top-rated soap opera. *B&B* was an established hit. Most importantly, his and Lee's children were not only a professional success, but all three were married and having (or were about to have) families of their own.

As Bill prepared to step down from a twenty-five-year run of writing stories for *Y&R*, he shared with the author in the pages of *Soap Opera Magazine* that he had one wish, professionally speaking, and that was to relive the entire experience.

"This is the first time I'm saying this to anyone," Bill said. "I'd like to start *Y&R* all over again. I'd like to reshoot it and rewrite part of it. Nancy was nice enough to pull out a tape of the first *Y&R* episode for me. I remember it as being something very, very special. But today we'd do even better work. We have more technology and things are paced differently. The vast majority of our audience never saw those early shows. And the other part might not remember all of them. If

Y&R was a smash hit back in the '70s, then why can't it be again—this time for a whole new generation?"

Chapter 20

AFTER THE RAINBOW ROOM

After all these years, we now need some time together, time to take a deep breath or two and reaffirm a love that was never, ever in question.

—Bill to Lee and their guests in his retirement speech given at the Rainbow Room in New York City, May 14, 1998

Bill's storylines played out over years and, in some cases, like the ongoing Katherine-Jill dynamic on *Y&R*, decades. The time that he and Lee had together once he retired was cut cruelly short.

After Bill turned over the writing reins to Kay Alden, he and Lee were able to travel more freely. It was rare that they got away on vacation while Bill was writing and producing up to ninety minutes of daily drama. Now, they could do so without having to pack Bill's typewriter. They went to China and, when *B&B* went on remote, to Italy where they could enjoy their creation's enormous international success. There was also more time to spend with the grandchildren. Brad and Colleen's oldest child, Chasen, was two and a half when Bill stepped down, a perfect age for doting grandparents.

Not surprisingly, though, Bill didn't embrace retirement easily. He continued to read scripts, give notes, and watch both *Y&R* and *B&B* daily.

"Bill always would keep in touch with Kay," Lee recalls. "When he retired, we tried to figure out where his office would be. He gave up his big office at *Y&R* and then came down to mine for a while at *B&B*. He'd go down to the studio and watch the shows being taped. He had a good time doing that."

Bill sat down with veteran journalist Alan Carter, who was working for the Academy of Television Arts & Sciences, on July 15, 1998, to recall his career. He recounted everything from his days of writing advertising copy at McCann Erickson to creating *B&B*.

There continued to be cake celebrations at the studio. March was always a particularly sugar-filled month as it was not only the anniversaries of his two shows, but also Bill's birthday (March 6).

"In the beginning, there were the Brooks and the Fosters," Bill would say at set-side gatherings, fondly recalling the original families that he and Lee created to launch *Y&R*.

In fall 1999, at the Academy of Television Arts & Sciences in North Hollywood, TV newsman Harry Smith hosted a tribute to Bill, which was produced by Nancy Wiard and David Michaels. Hundreds of past and present company members from Bill's programs turned out for another well-deserved honor to the Drama King. Around this time, an Al Hirschfeld drawing of Bill was commissioned. The artwork incorporated Bill's trademark red Flair pen.

That night, Bill sat onstage and was interviewed by Smith. He answered questions about his career and legendary shows. Bill cut loose with an impersonation of one of his iconic characters. "Julia! Julia!" Bill barked, recalling Victor Newman's first scene. The audience roared with laughter at Bill's spot-on rendition of Genoa City's mustached mogul.

Bill's last major interview was with journalist David Johnson in

2000, who spoke to him for *Soap Opera Weekly*'s "Soap Opera's 25 Most Intriguing People" list.

"I can't tell you the nights, the weeks, and the months when I only got two hours' sleep," Bill recalled to Johnson in explaining what it was like writing serials. "The demands were enormous, the rewards were fabulous. I'm not talking financial rewards. I'm talking about the creative rewards—the fulfillment of your characters, your stories."

In many ways, Bill was in charge of not two, but three soap operas simultaneously during most of his career. He not only steered the course of *Y&R* and *B&B* (or *Days* and *Y&R*), but he also helmed the backstage "soap operas" that went on at the studio.

"Everybody wanted to be as valuable as they could be to Bill," says Wiard. "He was 'Daddy' to a whole lot of people. As all good parents do, you don't ever let another child know how much you love the other one. Each one feels that he or she is important, special, and that his or her contributions are tremendous. Bill loved all his 'children.'

"He adored Kay Alden," Wiard continues. "She brought something very special to his role as a head writer that no one else did. Ed Scott would have slayed dragons and done heroic things for Bill."

Bill had long ago left *Days* behind, but he shared a mini-reunion with two of his leading ladies from that show one day in 2003 at CBS. *B&B* wanted to bring Tracey Bregman back over from *Y&R* so that she could help Jacqueline "Jackie" Payne (Lesley-Anne Down), a buyer for Fenmore's department store, settle into Taylor's old beach house. But Lauren was appearing in continuous episodes on *Y&R*, so a quick trip to Los Angeles would have been logistically improbable. *B&B* reached out to Susan Seaforth Hayes instead, inviting her to reprise Joanna (Lauren's mom) on *Y&R*'s sister soap to act in the scene with Down.

"It was wonderful," Seaforth Hayes recalls. "I came on for that one episode, and Bill, Lee, and Susan Flannery (Stephanie and formerly Laura on *Days*) were there to greet me. Bill was always there for my first days on his sets."

Time magazine has described Alzheimer's as a "degenerative brain condition that is not content to kill its victims without first snuffing out their essence." Signs of Bill having the illness began showing slowly.

Bill and Lee got together one night to play cards with their longtime friends, Wally and Barbara Phillips. (Wally, no relation to Irna, was a popular radio personality in Chicago. He also passed away from Alzheimer's disease in 2008.)

"Barbara picked up on it very quickly," Lee recalls. "Bill was always very good at cards. Barbara told me later she thought that Bill had Alzheimer's. I said, 'No. No, he doesn't.' But, later, I knew she was right."

Bill and Lee had always embraced challenges and battled adversities together—dealing with Irna's eccentricities, raising the children, Brad being hit by the car, fighting NBC to get Bill's stories on the air, cocreating *Y&R* and *B&B*, and relocating from Chicago to Los Angeles.

But the Alzheimer's robbed Bill of his memories, forcing Lee to face this devastating challenge without her husband. Family and close friends rallied to support them.

Bill's sister, Mary, and Lee's brother Russ visited from the Midwest. Bill and Maria, Brad and Colleen, and Lauralee and Scott all lived nearby and provided much needed emotional and physical support.

Bill's caretaker, Tony O'Brien, accompanied him everywhere.

Medical advisors presented Lee with the option of moving Bill to a facility to lessen her burden, but she wouldn't hear of it. "I wouldn't let him go to a home," she says. "He had his room at the house."

Brad recalls his mother being there for Bill in his final years with dignity, grace, and love. "She totally rose to the occasion," he praises. "He was her complete reason for living, from morning till night, to take care of him, to make him smile, to be there emotionally and in every way. She's tackled many challenges in her life, but this was her greatest one and she did it beautifully."

"She was really there for him," Colleen concurs. "They had a beautiful love story. Their children were the center of their universe."

"Lee's a saint," says Mary.

Bill took his plate and stepped away from the dinner table at Thanksgiving one year to catch a breather from his family's lively conversation. His grandson, Chasen, then eight, picked up his plate and followed Bill into the living room. Colleen recalls: "He said, 'Hi, Grandpa. Mind if I take a seat?' There was silence. Chasen said, 'I'll take that as a yes!' The two of them sat there together. It was a lovely moment between them."

Joanna Johnson saw Bill and Lee in the row behind her at the Daytime Emmys in New York a few years before he passed away. "Lee whispered to Bill, 'It's Joanna,'" the actress recalls. "He said, 'Joanna! It's so great to see you!' A little bit later, I turned around again and he said, 'Joanna! It's so great to see you!' Lee gave me a look as if to say, 'This is how it is now.' I thought, 'That's a nice marriage. She loves him. She wasn't impatient. She just loves him.'"

"I was visiting Bill and Lee, and one night I saw a light go on," Mary recalls. "I got up and saw Bill. I got to spend time with him. He looked at me and said, 'Honey, it's so hard not to remember the people you love.' I knew he was having a clear moment then and it was so frustrating for him."

"It was very sad," Jerry Birn recalled. "Our families used to have

Christmas Eve parties together. I remember the last one. For about a minute, maybe two, he was as lucid as hell. Suddenly, out of nowhere, he was Bill again. It was almost like he was saying good-bye."

"It was hard for Brad," Colleen recalls. "One time, he whispered in his dad's ear, 'I know this is hard for you. We're here for you and we love you. It's going to be okay.'"

"It was a difficult, difficult time," says Scott, Lauralee's husband. "The saddest thing was taking Bill's car keys away from him because we knew we were taking away his autonomy.

"It was painful to witness, seeing him deteriorate. There were a few times when we'd be at the hospital with him and we had to brace ourselves. Was this it? [Would] it get worse?"

Lee, Bill, Brad, Lauralee, Maria, Colleen, Scott, and Tony were with Bill in his room at the UCLA medical center on April 29, 2005, when he passed away from Alzheimer's disease. They were there to take care of him the way that he had taken care of them—and so many others—for so many years.

"We all sat with him, held his hand, kissed him, told him we loved him," Scott recalls. "The sun that came through his window had been on his face all afternoon. Bill was searching for us with his eyes. He was still there with us, but at the same time he wasn't."

"I got there just as the light was shafting through the window onto him," Brad recalls. "He was being kept alive with a ventilator. They held him for me. We had a moment. He looked me right in the eye, as clear as day. He said he was proud of me and squeezed my hand. Then, he passed away."

Hundreds of people from *Days*, *Y&R*, *B&B*, CBS, and Sony Pictures Television joined family and close friends at Bill's funeral the following week. Actors, producers, directors, production personnel, crew members, office staff, and network executives came to pay their respects. Some photographers, without their cameras, and a few reporters, minus their recorders, also attended. Jerry Birn, Eric Braeden, Brad, and Colleen each spoke at the service. The burial was private. After the service, the family hosted a reception at the Beverly Hills Hotel on Sunset Boulevard where Bill and Lee had written the bible to *Y&R* and where show anniversaries had been celebrated.

"What I saw that day was how revered Bill was," shares David Hasselhoff. "It was like Merv Griffin's funeral. We'd lost a legend. Nobody was there for publicity. Everyone was there to say, 'I'm sorry' and to pay their respects to Bill and to Lee and their children."

The annual Daytime Emmys was held less than three weeks later on May 20 in New York City. Susan Flannery introduced an on-air tribute to her friend and *Days* and *B&B* boss.

"The death of William Bell is not just a loss of a great writer and producer," she said. "But it portends the passing of a great era as well. Storyteller, poet, dreamer—Bill was all of these. He was a dream catcher, a weaver of tales like poets of old. He enlightened, educated, and he entertained millions in our global village. His talent was a gift; his vision, unique. Like Dickens, his roles [teemed] with life, packed with emotion, outsized characters, and a sly wit. Such a storyteller shall not pass this way again."

Later, Braeden and Aretha Franklin, a longtime *Y&R* fan, were set to announce the final award of the evening, Outstanding Drama Series. Braeden took a moment before opening the envelope to go off script and pay tribute to Bill.

"God Bless Eric Braeden," he misspoke, quickly correcting himself, "I mean, 'God Bless Bill Bell!'

"It was the biggest embarrassment in my public career," Braeden told *Soaps In Depth* magazine about saying his own name, not Bill's. "I still can't believe it. I had this overwhelming thought to thank Bill

Bell, who was such a powerful presence in this business for [more than] forty years." The actor spoke to the Bell family immediately after the show. "They understood that my intentions were very good ones."

"Poor Eric," Maria recalls. "It was a total slip of the tongue. We knew what he meant." Were there similarities between the two men? "Completely," she says, "and with John Abbott, too. Bill and Jerry Douglas, who played John, looked similar. There were various sides of Bill's personality in those characters. He wasn't one or the other. It was both. Bill was archetypical in that way."

Winsor Harmon (Thorne, *B&B*) read a tribute written by his TV brother Ronn Moss at the non-televised Creative Arts Daytime Emmy ceremony in Los Angeles earlier in the week.

"Bill would see us in the hallway and subconsciously refer to us by our character names. We all got used to it because that's how he saw us. That's how he lived with us every day. Bill was the best there is. Daytime will never see the likes of this legend again."

Daytime drama is not a genre known for its strong male characters, but Bill wrote some of the best ones in the business so appropriately, *Y&R* swept the actor categories at the Emmys that night. Gold went to Greg Rikaart (Kevin), David Lago (ex-Raul), and Christian Jules LeBlanc (Michael). Both Rikaart and LeBlanc paid tribute to Bill in their acceptance speeches. "Bill's legacy and his contribution to daytime [are] why I have a job," acknowledges Rikaart. "It was important for me to honor him and his family."

CBS, the Bells, Sony, and Procter & Gamble Productions hosted a party at the Waldorf Astoria hotel following the ceremony.

"That was the hardest night," Maria recollects. "We all sat in a row together and the tribute to Bill was just heartbreaking. Lee, Bill, and I walked into the hotel. We turned to each other and said, 'Let's just leave.' We couldn't handle it. We wanted to go in and celebrate the victories, but it was just too much."

~

After Bill retired, dramas unfolded at the studio—and not just on screen. *Y&R* had had a mere four main producers (John Conboy, Patricia Wenig, Wes Kenney, and Edward Scott) during Bill's twenty-five years as the show's head writer. Bill maintaining consistency was a key factor in the show's success. There was always greater turnover at other shows and it affected what viewers saw on screen. Fans tend to tune out if a show's creative direction changes drastically.

Once Bill was no longer there to protect his personnel, to insist that they remain, *Y&R* became like a lot of the other shows. The revolving door at the Genoa City Athletic Club might as well have been positioned two stories up in the show's production office. Changes in front of and behind the camera didn't occur overnight, but they were still happening.

The actors playing supporting characters Lynne, Gina, Mary, Miguel, Mamie, and Doris began appearing less or were written off the show entirely. Granted, not all of these players were victims of budget cutbacks; some retired or moved on to other professions. Still, Bill knew the importance of these key characters. Audiences see Paul Williams as an even richer character when they know his lovelorn secretary Lynne (who was played by Laura Bryan Birn, Jerry Birn's daughter) is pining away for him in the private eye's reception area.

"Bill protected all of us," says veteran cast member Doug Davidson, Paul's portrayer. "He was like a giant oak and we were allowed to flourish under his branches. We didn't realize what it was like outside of that protection. He did things for us that we were unaware of."

When Bill wrote the show, Sharon Case (Sharon) recalls, "Characters had someone they could go to and talk about how they felt. Sharon always had her mom to speak to. That helped bring out who the characters were."

"There was a mad battle for the scepter," observed one long-running Emmy-winning cast member regarding the backstage climate following Bill's retirement. "It was Shakespearean. I had a front-row seat and it was fascinating to watch."

"If they'd turned the cameras the other way, we would have gotten a 6.0 rating and a 30 share," says one former writer.

"In Bill, I had a boss who cared," says another actor. "As time went on and Bill had to step down, the caring left with him. Now with a corporate-run show, you don't get that feeling, not at all."

"It was a very strange period of uncertainty," one Emmy-winning actress recalls, speaking of the time after Bill stepped down and veteran executive producer Edward Scott left the show, too. "We were a ship without a captain."

Bill fought against interference from network and studio executives throughout his career. Irna Phillips referred to them as "temporary people making permanent decisions."

When Bill was in charge at *Y&R*, he refused to allow a studio executive to be on-site in the show's production office, keeping an eye on the studio's interests. That changed after Bill stepped down.

Jack Smith, who'd left *Y&R* in 2001 to focus fully on *B&B*, returned to Genoa City the following April to assist Alden with head-writing duties.

"Jack was very good for the show," says Case. "He had worked with Bill for so long. He wrote Cassie's death. Every writer who's come on since then has kept that as a big part of who Nick and Sharon are."

Veteran producer Nancy Wiard, who oversaw all levels of production, acted as the show's point person for contract renewals, and also organized the show's Daytime Emmy submissions, exited in 2003. Other long-running personnel in casting, publicity, and other departments started leaving *Y&R*, too.

Producer David Shaughnessy was made executive producer in

2002. He left at the end of 2003. Edward Scott, who had left in 2001, returned as supervising producer.

Why all the change? One reason was that Bill's heirs at the studio were expected to bring in the same ratings that he did, but they weren't given the same autonomy that Bill had earned.

"The work didn't necessarily flow from Bill's successors," one network executive reflects. "People were clearly trying to redefine their roles and that backfired on them. It wasn't necessarily good when people left the show, but it was felt that they 'had' to."

Brad took advantage of his father's key personnel being on the market. He offered spots on his writing team to Kay Alden, Jack Smith, and Jerry Birn, who passed away in late 2009. Alden has become Brad's cohead writer. In 2010, Brad brought Edward Scott on to *B&B* as a producer, following Scott's tenure as coexecutive producer at *Days*, during which time he'd helped that show earn a Daytime Emmy nomination for Outstanding Drama Series.

"Kay and Jack both had great runs at *Y&R*," Brad says. "They wrote fascinating stories, but they had that incredible challenge, too, in being the head writers of *Y&R* who came after my father. He was a full all-encompassing presence and such a unique talent.

"I have great respect for Kay, Jack, and Ed. I know what they're able to do from when they worked under my dad. I never thought I'd see the day when they'd become available, but they're all great talents and were trained by the best."

Alden opted to remain in Chicago when she succeeded Bill as head writer in 1998. Just as Bill and Lee had done, Alden chose to stay in the heartland of America where she and her husband, Vern Nelson, brought up their three children.

"Bill and Lee both valued the opportunity to raise their family in the Midwest," Alden says. "Bill never pressured me to move to Los Angeles. I am eternally grateful to him because of that. Would it have made a difference had I chosen to move? Probably. It would have meant getting more involved with the production, but that's not the choice I made and I don't regret it."

"Kay's the one who's really good at fleshing story out and writing scenes between characters," says Scott. "She brought another level to Bill's writing. She could fulfill what he wanted to see."

Bill's inner circle, whom he had so proudly introduced that night at Chasen's in Beverly Hills back in 1992 and on many other occasions, had all been phased out from *Y&R* by the end of 2006.

CBS Daytime vice president Lucy Johnson, who had a hands-off approach with Bill, left the network in early 2003. Her successor, Barbara Bloom, a former director of daytime at ABC, exited the network in January 2011.

In fall 2005, Lynn Marie Latham joined *Y&R* as a creative consultant. Latham is a successful, award-winning writer known for her tenures on primetime serials including fan favorite *Knots Landing* and the critically acclaimed *Homefront*. Her daytime credit experience was head writing the ABC Daytime soap opera *Port Charles*. Latham was the first show-runner in charge of *Y&R* who hadn't apprenticed under Bill. As one would expect, the situation was fraught with political minefields. Latham was expected to honor the show's past and take it into the future but without the full autonomy that Bill had.

Under Latham, veterans remained in the forefront. Stories took on an arguably more plot-driven, quicker pace. Her tales earned Kristoff St. John his second Daytime Emmy for playing Neil and brought overdue gold to Outstanding Lead Actress winner Jeanne Cooper, who gave one of the most entertaining acceptance speeches in television history.

Changes were made. Characters no longer talked at length on how they felt about something or why they reacted to an event the way they did—at least not in the character-driven, introspective way that Bill, and also Kay and Jack, had written the show.

Flashbacks continued to be used effectively (a "video" of Nikki's stripper days surfaced when she ran against Jack for a state senate seat). New characters were kept to a minimum and effectively tied to existing players. Tammy Lauren joined in the recurring role as Maggie, a lady cop who helped rejuvenate Paul, who'd been in romantic limbo since Christine's departure.

Characters from the past returned—April, Hope—but they were now being played by different actors. Bill preferred originals, but actors weren't always available. The past was being used to mine current stories like Malcolm finally being revealed as Lily's dad. Shemar Moore expressed an interest in returning to the show during his hiatus from *Criminal Minds* so that he could help bring closure to that storyline. It never transpired; scheduling conflicts were given as the reason.

Katherine confessed to Jill that she had switched Jill's son Phillip with another infant so Jill wouldn't raise the Chancellor heir, which resulted in Daniel Goddard (*Beastmaster*) being added to the cast as appealing leading man Cane Ashby, Jill's "real" son. Kay's recollection, however, was later revealed to be a false memory.

The most jarring story twist was arguably the revelation that Brad Carlton was, in reality, George Kaplan, whose father and sister had been murdered by Nazis and that George took the name of his late friend Brad Carlton as his own.

The Abbott clan took the biggest hit when family patriarch John Abbott was killed off (his portrayer Jerry Douglas joined the show in 1982) and Eileen Davidson (Ashley) found her contract was not renewed.

The Abbott house, a mainstay of *Y&R* for more than twenty years, had become "Jack's place."

Bill had killed off parental figures, too, including Bill Foster and Jennifer Brooks. Still, the loss of John Abbott was devastating to longtime viewers. Perhaps, given Bill's resemblance to Douglas, it was a reminder that Bill was no longer there, too.

"It gave us great story—for two weeks," said one actor of John's death.

Some critics slammed Latham's tenure because the quickened pace was a diversion from the way that Bill unfolded his sagas. But the show maintained its position as daytime's top soap. Latham won *Y&R* its seventh Daytime Emmy for Outstanding Drama Series in 2007.

Latham opted to join her fellow writers on the picket line during the 2007–08 Writers Guild of America strike. Her last *Y&R* show aired on December 25, 2007.

WGA strikes can be devastating to continuing drama since substitute writers, who may not know the show, can make characters quickly seem unrecognizable. Bill made every effort to anticipate work stoppages and write ahead so that characters would stay the course until a new contract for writers could be settled. Maria Arena Bell stepped up to the plate during the last strike. She and writer Josh Griffith sacrificed certain benefits related to their WGA memberships and went "financial core" status, which enabled them to write for the show during the strike.

Maria became sole head writer in March 2008. She and Paul Rauch became coexecutive producers six months later. Maria became executive producer in late 2010. Rauch exited the show the following April. During a Paley Center for Media tribute to *Y&R* in the spring of 2008, which honored the show's thirty-fifth anniversary, actors praised Maria for forfeiting her position in the guild to keep *Y&R* going.

"My challenges are more complex in some ways than when Bill was in charge," Maria says. Bill had full creative control of the program. "He did what he wanted."

Bill's passing was marked by tributes in the soap-opera magazines and also mainstream publications, including *USA TODAY* and *TV Guide* magazine.

"The world of daytime has lost its lion king," wrote Michael Logan in *TV Guide*. "[Bill's] slow, hypnotic storytelling was rooted in romance and family, but Bell also embraced controversy with landmark plots about AIDS, incest, date rape, euthanasia, and homelessness."

Logan praised Bill as a "tough and supremely confident showman who paid no mind to focus-group research and tolerated no interference from the CBS 'suits.' In the exchange for that autocracy, he gave the network two wildly popular cash cows—*Y&R* and *B&B*."

"He was the greatest, the most successful storyteller and producer in television," Brad says. "He's remembered for his one-of-a-kind drama and his legendary characters. He was well-liked and respected, a man who was admired."

"Bill set a gold standard that *Y&R* wasn't just a place to work, but it was a family," Eileen Davidson told the author for Australia's *Daytime TV* in 2005. "It hit me that he was truly gone when I saw that picture of him in the funeral program. I saw his eyes, so clear, and they had that spark to them."

"Bill loved life," says Katherine Kelly Lang, *B&B*'s Brooke. "He was always very positive, very nurturing, as well. He was such a family man. He loved his family. He lived for them. He always had that charming smile and a glint in his eye that I'll never forget."

"Bill was an incredible man," adds Jess Walton. "He combined loving his work and his family. He had a great storyline."

Chapter 21

CLIFFHANGER

My children are treated exactly like any other employee would be. I'm not always going to be around, and they'll have to stand on their own two feet.

—Bill Bell to Roberta Caploe in
Soap Opera Digest, 1991

A blank sheet of paper rests in Bill's IBM Selectric typewriter in his study. His next story will never be written, but his family continues his legacy of dramatic storytelling.

Bill feared that the genre was headed for some rough times when he made his retirement speech at the Rainbow Room in 1998. "I have a deep conviction about the state of the serial today, although it does not apply to all of them," Bill stated. "But it relates to the need to create stories that an audience can relate to, stories that deal with real people that have real problems and real relationships, God willing, that can impact positively on the lives of our viewers. Enough said."

Legendary television executive Fred Silverman, who ran CBS

Daytime in the '60s when Bill was partnered with Irna Phillips, fears that Bill's words fell on deaf ears. Since Bill stepped down as head writer in 1998, a staggering eight network soap operas, including veteran serials *Another World*, *Guiding Light*, *As the World Turns*, *All My Children*, and *One Life to Live*, have all been canceled. *AMC* and *OLTL* were licensed to continue online by a company called Prospect Park soon after being canceled. Sadly, Prospect Park announced on November 23, 2011, that it was suspending its efforts to continue the two ABC soaps on the Web.

The industry was now left with four broadcast soap operas—two of which were created by Bill and Lee.

Is Silverman surprised that Bill's two shows are the last ones standing? "No. They are head and shoulders above the others. When I joined CBS Daytime, P&G Productions was the major outfit. You had people running it who really knew the form, like Bob Short, Ed Trach, and Paul Rauch. They were really professionals and had the respect of the writers. They lost that and, ultimately, lost talent like Bill Bell."

Fortunately, Bill passed along the lessons he learned from Irna to Bradley, Maria, Kay Alden, and Jack Smith.

"The Bells have been doing this for a long time," says Nina Tassler, entertainment president for CBS. "They are the consummate professionals and great storytellers. They're smart about writing storylines for the characters that the audience loves."

Knowing he wouldn't always be here was one of the reasons that Bill was such a stern taskmaster with Brad. "He edited my scripts, which I didn't think were that bad in the beginning," Brad recalls. "Sometimes there were more red marks on the page from his Flair pen than there was white on it. He wanted to teach me so he took the extra time to help me. He expected us to be as consumed by the business as he was. Lauralee became a great actress, and Bill has succeeded on the business end. We've all carried our own weight."

Bill's untimely passing has left both the ultimate cliffhanger for his audience and the ultimate challenge for everyone working in daytime serials today—how can the remaining shows survive?

"We have two hundred competitors, not to mention this thing called the Internet," Brad says. "It's never going to be like it was, but there is a future for soaps."

In summer 2011, *Y&R* launched a real-life Jabot Cosmetics product line to generate additional revenue. "It pays homage to Bill and his original idea for Jabot," says Tracey Bregman (Lauren), who acts as the product line's spokesperson.

"The cosmetics line is brilliant," adds Tassler. "They're trying to stay ahead of the curve and what the audience is responding to."

"Putting the show first is key," says Bill Jr., regarding the genre's survival. "That's where the debilitating aspect of interference can become clearly a negative. Things have changed. The advertiser-supported model is enormously damaged. The direction for the future is a new business model."

Bill's absence has left an immeasurable void. "My father was a lightning rod in terms of enthusiasm and passion," Bill says. "He's definitely missed. There will be challenging times ahead."

"We may never see the likes of Bill Bell again because no one will ever be given the kind of creative control that Bill had," offers Peter Bergman. "Networks will never allow that kind of freedom."

If Bill were writing serials in today's world, he wouldn't have compromised his style despite the constant slashing of budgets. "He'd still be writing the same show," Bergman theorizes. "He seemed to believe that if [it wasn't] about family, power, glamour, sex, or money, it wasn't worth having on the show."

Y&R received a three-year renewal in 2010. As executive producer and head writer, Maria communicates regularly with CBS and Sony Pictures Television to go over her long-term stories.

"Sometimes it feels like defending your thesis every week," she says. "But I've found a way to work with both sides. I have actually won the support of the network, but it took time and effort to gain its trust."

Five years after his father passed away, Brad explored the devastating disease that claimed Bill's life by afflicting *B&B*'s Beth Logan with Alzheimer's.

"That was a story I wanted to touch on because of his passing and the impact it had on all of us," Brad says. Once the major beats were played, Brad had Beth die by accidental drowning after she fell into the Forrester pool. Her passing was the catalyst that ended Donna and Eric's May-December marriage and led to yet another reunion between Eric and Stephanie.

"To draw out Beth dying would have been a sad, depressing march till the end," Brad says. "It's not something entertaining. We touched on the informative aspects of it and saw a family come together."

B&B's Brooke, essentially a good character, continues to do bad things, including accidentally having sex with her daughter's boyfriend, which incurred the wrath of her nemesis Stephanie. The two women have an occasional truce, but, fortunately, it never lasts for very long.

Maria continues to mine *Y&R*'s rich history. She undid the controversial (but well-executed) storyline that revealed Kay was Jill's mother by making Jill's true birth father the late Neil Fenmore, Lauren's dad.

Y&R's 2010 Christmas show was a stand-alone episode that featured Victor Newman examining his life à la Charles Dickens's *A Christmas Carol*. The ghosts of Christmas Past (Hope), Christmas Present (Sabrina), and Christmas Yet to Come (Colleen) each paid haunting visits to Victor, who'd become an emotional Ebenezer Scrooge to Nikki and his children. He woke up the next morning no longer wanting to control his loved ones' lives. (Fortunately, Victor's revelation, like the truces between Brooke and Stephanie, didn't last.)

"I've been worried since Bill's passing," Eric Braeden says. "I'm not worried now. Maria really understands it. She has Bill's sensibility."

The wedding of a reluctant Billy Abbott to ambitious Chloe was among the shows submitted that earned *Y&R* the 2010 Writers Guild of America award for daytime writing.

"My father would be unhappy about a lot of changes in the business with it being so bottom-line oriented," Bill says. "But he'd be very happy with the way *Y&R* is going now. He'd be very proud of Maria."

"My style is shaped from my relationship with Bill and having studied under him," Maria says. "If I'm continuing his legacy, that would be the greatest accolade I could have."

Maria earned an Emmy in 2011 for Outstanding Writing, Drama Series. "Bill Bell is the whole reason I'm in this business," she said. "I was really his protégée, and he spent a ton of time with me. I got to see through his eyes what great storytelling was. I hope that I've picked up something from that experience. I know it certainly changed me."

Lauralee reprised Christine for short arcs in 2010 and 2011. "I felt it was important for me to come back for my dad," Lauralee says. "He was always so happy when he knew I was a part of the show. It was great seeing so many cast and crew members. It made me feel very good and close to him.

"Knowing that Brad and Maria are doing so well on each show, having Mom still in the office, me on stage, and Billy overseeing it all would have to make my sweet dad proud. I give him a big smile each time I walk into CBS and see the portrait of my parents in the hallway."

Brad took home the Daytime Emmy in 2010 for Drama Series Writing for two episodes that featured the death of Stephanie's mother Ann (Betty White). Those same shows also won Brad his second consecutive statuette for Outstanding Drama Series.

Like his father, Brad was inclusive of the people who got him to the winner's podium. "We had great scenes that starred Susan Flannery, Betty White, and Alley Mills that were just off the charts," Brad said in his acceptance speech. He also thanked his producers, directors, and writers by name.

"And there's one other writer who's with me with every word I ever write, and that's my father, Bill Bell."

Brad continues to carry on his parents' legacy of combining entertainment and social awareness. On October 28 and 29, 2010, *B&B*'s episodes featured Stephanie going to the Union Rescue Mission and to Gladys Park, the heart of Skid Row, in Los Angeles, to talk to homeless individuals, hoping to shed light on their plight.

"So many people are just a paycheck away from homelessness or living in a shelter," Brad told Michael Logan of TVGuide.com. "Our entire production company has been changed by this experience. Hopefully, so has our audience. To be a great country we need to take care of these people."

Brad won his third consecutive Emmy for Outstanding Drama Series on June 19, 2011, at the *38th Annual Daytime Emmy Awards* in Las Vegas for the homeless-themed episodes.

"My dad would be incredibly proud," Brad said in the pressroom.

"I was hoping to win one of these when he was still alive, but I know he's here and is very proud of this accomplishment, not only what we've done here on stage, but also the accomplishment of [the whole family]. He was such a great family man, and this evening would have been one for the record books for him."

Lee has returned to her broadcasting roots, appearing in promotional Web videos for *B&B* created by show producer Casey Kasprzyk. "My mom is funny," Brad says. "She'll do anything for the show. This creation is part of her family."

On June 11, 2010, Lee was honored at "A Salute to Chicago Television," sponsored by Nielsen and the Museum of Broadcast Communications. The gala was held at the Chicago Hilton's Normandie Lounge and Grand Ballroom. Scores of past and present TV personalities and museum supporters from the Windy City were on hand for the event. Lee, along with beloved film critic Roger Ebert and Illinois governor Pat Quinn, received one of the evening's few standing ovations.

"Lee talked about things on her show that women talked about in the 1950s and also things that they did not talk about," praises Bruce DuMont, the museum's president. "She is a winner of numerous awards and is, without question, the First Lady of Chicago Television."

On September 21, 2010, the International Alliance of Theatrical Stage Employees, Local 33, presented Lee with an honorary lifetime membership in recognition of her decades-long contribution to the union and the livelihood of its members who have worked on *Y&R* and *B&B*.

Lee has said many times that her greatest successes are not the accolades that she has received as a broadcaster, documentarian, and soap-opera cocreator, but rather her dual roles as Bill's wife and mother of Bill, Bradley, and Lauralee.

"I'm quite clear that Bill believed he owed his success to his partnership with Lee," says Susan Seaforth Hayes. "Who knows where ideas for a writer come from? Those little geniuses that whisper into your ear and make stories and scenes just tumble out onto your keyboard and into scripts of gold. Maybe it was because the person beside Bill was not belittling, but was instead enthusiastic about his every achievement? I would not be a bit surprised if that fountain of work came out of a perfect love.

"Bill Bell was one human being in a million who had the grace to share his success and say that it came out of his marriage to Lee. How great was that?"

SELECTED BIBLIOGRAPHY

Books

Corday, Ken. *The Days of our Lives: The Untold Story of One Family's Dream and the True History of* Days of our Lives. Naperville, IL: Sourcebooks, 2010.

Gilbert, Annie. *All My Afternoons*. New York: A&W Visual Library, 1979.

Irwin, Barbara and Mary Cassata. *Special Silver Anniversary Collector's Edition,* The Young and the Restless. Los Angeles, CA: General Publishing Group, 1996.

LaGuardia, Robert. *From Ma Perkins to Mary Hartman, the Illustrated History of Soap Operas*. New York: Ballantine, 1977.

________. *Soap World*. New York: Priam Books, 1983.

________. *The Wonderful World of TV Soap Operas*. New York: Ballantine, 1977.

McNeil, Alex. *Total Television: A Comprehensive Guide to Programming from 1948 to the Present*. New York: Penguin, 1996.

O'Neil, Thomas. *The Emmys*. New York: Perigee Books, 1998.

Rogers, Lynne. *The Love of Their Lives*. New York: Dell Publishing Co., 1979.

Rouverol, Jean. *Writing for Daytime Drama*. Stoneham, MA: Butterworth-Heinemann, 1992.

_________. *Writing for the Soaps*. Cincinnati, OH: Writers Digest Books, 1984.

Schemering, Christopher. *The Soap Opera Encyclopedia*. New York: Ballantine Books, 1988.

Simon, Ron, Robert J. Thompson, et al. *Worlds without End: The Art and History of the Soap Opera*. New York: Harry N. Abrams, 1997.

Tylo, Hunter. *Making a Miracle*. New York: Pocket Books, 2000.

Vine, Dorothy. *As the Wonderful World of Daytime Soap Operas Turns*. LaVergne, TN: Xlibris, 2009.

Articles

Browning, Norma Lee. "He's Wed to a Celebrity." *Chicago Tribune*, August 27, 1958.

Caploe, Roberta. "Life With Father." *Soap Opera Digest*, June 22, 1993.

Daniels, Mary. "Lee Phillip Is a Success in Any Rating." *Chicago Tribune*, April 4, 1976.

Kahwaty, Donna Hoke. "*The Young and the Restless*, Steady as a Rock." *Soap Opera Digest*, January 21, 1992.

Maloney, Michael. "*Beautiful* Won't Eschew Issues." *Variety*, March 22, 2007.

_________. "Bell Family into Soap Opera Business." *Variety*, March 22, 2007.

_________. "Candid Cooper." TVGuide.com, February 15, 2000.

———. "King of Soap." *Daytime TV* (Australia), Daytime Emmys Special, 2005.

———. "Soaps' 12 Most Powerful People: For Whom the Bell Tolls." *Soap Opera Magazine*, June 1998.

McGarry, Mark. "Chasing Emmy—With 20 Nominations, Will *Y&R* Be the Bell of the Ball?" *Soap Opera Weekly*, May 27, 1997.

"Sex and Suffering in the Afternoon." *Time* magazine, January 12, 1976.

Susman, Linda. "Bill Bell Doesn't Skirt the Issue: He Predicts *B&B* Can Sew Up Its Audience in Just One Week." *Soap Opera NOW!* March 9, 1987.

Terry, Clifford. "Just Plain Bill." *Chicago Tribune*, October 14, 1973.

Zwick-Weiss, Hildee. "We Are Number One." *Soap Opera Digest*, February 18, 1992.

Journals

White, Les. "Imperial Soap Opera." *Common Review*, Spring 2005.

Video

Bell, William J. Interview with Alan Carter. Archive of American Television: A Program of the Television Academy Foundation. Beverly Hills, July 15, 1998.

The 8th Annual Soap Opera Awards. NBC. January 10, 1992.

The 13th Annual Daytime Emmy Awards. NBC. July 17, 1986.

The 19th Annual Daytime Emmy Awards. NBC. June 23, 1992.

"The Young and the Restless." E! True Hollywood Story. Narrator: Kieran Mulroney. May 20, 2001.

ACKNOWLEDGMENTS AND NOTES

I am extremely honored to have been chosen by Lee Phillip Bell to write this biography and history of her husband, Bill Bell, as well as Lee and their family. Lee's patience, belief, and trust mean more to me than words could possibly convey. I am forever grateful to her.

I have immense gratitude as well to Bill Bell, who chose to follow his passion in life. His love of family and storytelling, and his commitment to the serial genre have provided hundreds of people with lifetime employment and continue to bring awareness of important social issues and enjoyment to millions of viewers. I'm grateful to Bill and Lee for graciously supporting my career move in 1991 from *B&B*'s production office to becoming a member of the fourth estate, too. Writing this book has brought everything full circle.

I also want to thank Bill and Maria, Bradley and Colleen, and Lauralee and Scott.

I'm especially grateful to Brad and Maria for taking time out of their hectic schedules running *B&B* and *Y&R*, respectively, to speak with me; to Bill, who, despite not liking interviews, is actually quite good at giving them; to Lauralee, who returns emails faster than anyone I know, for her warmth, support, and confidence; to Scott for his candor; and to Colleen for sharing many memories and welcoming me into her and Brad's home.

I also want to thank the people who championed this book and helped make it a reality. Peter Lynch, editorial manager, Sourcebooks, for his support and terrific editing. Also, Dominique Raccah, publisher, Sourcebooks.

Thanks to Russ Phillip (Lee's brother) and Mary Bell Neuenschwander (Bill's sister) for sharing their personal stories of Lee and Bill.

The late Jerry Birn for sharing memories of his and Bill's days in advertising, their soap opera reunion, and their friendship, which spanned more than fifty years.

Kay Alden for her support, kindness, and willingness to share her memories of Bill and of her career as cohead writer and Bill's successor as head writer at *Y&R*.

Dawn Owens, editor-in-chief of *Soaps In Depth* magazine, for her support and thoughtfulness.

Deborah Obad, my agent, for her unparalleled belief, tenacity, and sense of humor.

Thanks and immense gratitude to Greg Meng, *Days of our Lives'* coexecutive producer, executive in charge of production, and senior vice president at Corday Productions for his support, encouragement, and friendship.

Eva Basler Demirjian, director of communications and talent relations for *The Bold and the Beautiful*, for her tireless support and devotion in making this book a reality.

Thanks to David Hasselhoff for his time, and for sharing his memories and providing the foreword.

Bill and Susan Seaforth Hayes for their support and for sharing their unique memories and details of their professional and personal relationship with Bill and Lee.

Thanks to Sherman and Gail Magidson for their insights into Bill's life and career, and their great hospitality in Chicago, which included inspiring visits to Irna's and Bill and Lee's former residences on North Astor Street and East Lake Shore Drive, as well as their own personal tour of Chicago. *B&B*'s Ron Weaver, senior producer, for overseeing this project. *B&B*'s Rhonda Friedman, supervising producer, for reading the manuscript and support. *Y&R*'s Josh O'Connell, associate producer, for providing research material including a copy of the treatment for *Another World* and Bill's 1977 story projections for *Y&R*.

Elise Bromberg, executive director for publicity, *Y&R*, for coordinating interviews.

Alan Carter for support and his interview with Bill Bell for the Academy of Television Arts & Sciences' Archive of American Television series.

Al Schwartz and Bruce DuMont for recalling stories of Lee's time as Chicago's First Lady of Television at WBBM-TV.

Thomas Phillips, Paul Rauch, Don Hastings, and Fred Silverman for sharing their memories of Bill and also of the late, great Irna Phillips, Bill's mentor and legendary soap-opera creator.

Actors who worked for Bill on more than one show and were therefore able to give greater insights into him including Susan Flannery, John McCook, and Kimberlin Brown.

Thanks to Ken Corday, Denise Alexander, and Suzanne Rogers for sharing their memories and insights into Bill's time at and enormous contributions to *Days of our Lives*.

Thanks to past and present network executives Nina Tassler, Brian Frons, Michael Brockman, Lucy Johnson, and Lin Bolen for their memories of working with Bill and insights into daytime television.

Special thanks to Margot Wain, CBS director of daytime, for sharing her extensive experiences of working with Bill and Lee. Also, thanks to Susan Banks, executive vice president of marketing and creative services for TV One and former CBS director of daytime promotion, for sharing her memories.

Jeanne Cooper, Edward J. Scott, Peter Bergman, Eric Braeden, Jess Walton, Kristoff St. John, Tricia Cast, Heather Tom, Michelle Stafford, Victoria Rowell, Tom Langan, Tracey Bregman, Brenda Dickson, Beth Maitland, Sharon Case, Doug Davidson, Christian LeBlanc, Greg Rikaart, Don Diamont, Christina Knack, Jack Smith, Michael Tylo, Nancy Wiard, Sally Sussman Morina, Joshua Morrow, and Thom Bierdz for providing additional insights into Bill and *Y&R*.

Also from *Y&R*: Eva Archie, Matthew J. Olsen, Erin Yeomans, Sarah Smith, Laura Walsh, Jacquie Dore, and Julie Mitchell.

And past and present personnel from *B&B*: Joanna Johnson, Lauren Koslow, Katherine Kelly Lang, Daniel McVicar, Ronn Moss, Hope Harmel Smith, Hunter Tylo, John C. Zak, Sy Tomashoff, and Cindy Popp.

Also at *B&B*: Rich Ginger, Erica Ginger, Rachel Herman, Casey Kasprzyk, Mark Pinicotti, Jennifer Tartaro, Cathy Tomas, Ann Willmott, and Cherol Derrick.

Publicists including the terrific Jennifer Mulhall at *B&B*, as well as Cindy Marshall, Meredith Tiger, Cristin Callahan, Andrea McKinnon, Sheri Goldberg, Kyley H. Jona, Laura Gallagher, Jori Peterson, Mitchell Messinger, Lauri L. Hogan, Judy Katz, Howie Simon, Charles Sherman, Frank Tobin, and Brenda Feldman.

Thanks to actors, authors, journalists, and historians who offered their insights into Bill, the Bell family, and the soap-opera world, including Grant Aleksander, Meredith Berlin, Martha Byrne, John Kelly Genovese, Catherine Hickland, Francesca James, David Johnson, Michael E. Knight, Robert LaGuardia, Michael Logan, Mark McGarry, Stephen Nichols, Tom O'Neil, Maureen Russell, Linda Susman, and the late Christopher Schemering.

Past editors for employment, including Garrett Foster, Ben Mitchell,

Debra Birnbaum, Maggie Furlong, Steve LeGrice, Stuart Levine, Jon Weisman, Cynthia Wang, Antoinette Coulton, Lynn Leahey, Richard Spencer, Delaina Dixon, Laura Raposa and Gayle Fee, Mark Perigard, Carole Glines, Michaela George, and Vesna Petropolous.

Thanks for encouragement and support to Dianne Butler, Amy Astley, Leona Barad, Bill Benson, Mariellen Bergman, Diane Brounstein, Andrew Criscuolo, Ron Davis, Thomas DeLorenzo, Dr. Gregory Dumanian, Bobbie Eakes, Dean Georgio, Bill Graff, Michael Herbertson, Catalin Jercan, Jennifer Johns, Sharon Lee Jones, Kathie Gunn, Tom Lind, Julie McElwain, Laura Passero, Lou Perrotta, Todd Powers, Maeve Quinlan, Jonathan Reiner, Rosemary Rossi, Dave Rupel, Libby Slate, Elvera Roussel, Jean Rouverol, Hillary B. Smith, Erin Stewart, Toni Veltri, and the late Lilyan Chauvin.

The security department at CBS Television City, especially Antonio Wagner and Anthony Jones Jr.

Also, Loida and Jean-Yves Mazire, Elvina Paiz and Sally Villareal, Tony and Brenda O'Brien, Christine Lai Johnson, Gina Chappa, Ross Fuentes, Missy Sandora, and Linda Grand.

I'd also like to thank for their assistance Eileen Fulton, Chip Capelli, Shemar Moore, Judy Katz, and Robyn Anne Nelson.

Special thanks to Maitland Ward, Terry Baxter, Sally McDonald, Deborah Ginger, Lauri Moorman, Sean Kanan, Michael Bruno, and also "the two most powerful women in daytime."

Finally, thanks and appreciation to my family: my mother, Mary Lou Maloney, for her love and support; Larry, Anne, and L.J. (especially for their hospitality in Chicago); and David, Lisa, Amelia, and Brian; as well as Bob and Jane, Meg and Mike, Jane, Emma and Teddy, Maureen and Chris, Rob and Christel, and Katie and Kevin. Also, my late father, Lawrence Maloney, and my aunt Patricia Twohig.

Interviews for *The Young and Restless Life of William J. Bell* were conducted between April 2009 and February 2012. Other resources for this book included articles and information from issues of *Soaps In Depth*, *Soap Opera Magazine*, *Soap Opera Digest*, *Soap Opera NOW!*, *Soap Opera Weekly*, *Daytime TV* (Australia), *Soap Opera Update*, and Q&As that appeared on TVGuide.com.

Also, broadcasts of *The Daytime Emmys* and *The Soap Opera Awards* provided valuable information.

ABOUT THE AUTHORS

Michael Maloney is a contributing editor at *Soaps In Depth* magazine.

He began his TV career as a page at CBS Television City and worked for two years on the production staff of *The Bold and the Beautiful.* He is the former West Coast editor of *Soap Opera Digest* and has also been on staff at *Soap Opera Magazine*, *Soap Opera Update*, *In Touch*, and *Inside TV.*

In addition, he has written and reported about soap operas and television for *Variety*, AOL TV, TVGuide.com, the *Boston Herald*, *Television Week*, *People Magazine Celebrates All My Children*, *TV Guide Canada*, and Australia's *Soap World* and *Daytime TV.* A graduate of Boston University's College of Communication, Michael is a member of the Television Critics Association.

He appeared in the film *Charlie's Angels* and in the CBS Daytime promotion campaign "Soap Central."

He lives in Los Angeles.

Lee Phillip Bell is known to millions of TV viewers as a soap-opera creator, coexecutive producer, television talk-show host, and documentarian.

She was married to William J. Bell for fifty years. She was a pioneer in broadcasting and hosted talk shows (*The Lee Phillip Show* and others) and documentaries at WBBM-TV in Chicago from 1952 to 1986. She's won seventeen regional Emmys, Golden Mike awards, a Daytime Emmy for Outstanding Drama Series as cocreator of *The Young and the Restless* in 1975, and the Daytime Emmy's Lifetime Achievement Award in 2007.

Together, Lee and Bill cocreated *The Young and the Restless* and *The Bold and the Beautiful.* They have three children, William James Bell, Bradley Phillip Bell, and Lauralee Kristen Bell Martin; and eight grandchildren, Liam and Sabrina Bell; Chasen, Caroline, Charlotte, and Oliver Bell; and Christian and Samantha Martin.

Lee lives in Beverly Hills.